WRITING IN A NEW LANGUAGE

AN INTRODUCTION TO ACADEMIC WRITING

Scott Robert Reed | Brenda Tuberville

FOUNTAINHEAD
PRESS

Our green initiatives include:

Electronic Products

We deliver products in non-paper form whenever possible. This includes pdf downloadables, flash drives, & CDs.

X Electronic Samples

We use Xample, a new electronic sampling system. Instructor samples are sent via a personalized web page that links to pdf downloads.

FSC Certified Printers

All of our printers are certified by the Forest Service Council which promotes environmentally and socially responsible management of the world's forests. This program allows consumer groups, individual consumers, and businesses to work together hand-in-hand to promote responsible use of the world's forests as a renewable and sustainable resource.

Recycled Paper

Most of our products are printed on a minimum of 30% post-consumer waste recycled paper.

Support of Green Causes

When we do print, we donate a portion of our revenue to green causes. Listed below are a few of the organizations that have received donations from Fountainhead Press. We welcome your feedback and suggestions for contributions, as we are always searching for worthy initiatives.

Rainforest 2 Reef

Environmental Working Group

Cover and interior photography: Mark Howsen, Kenneth Reed, and Scott Reed
Cover and interior designer: Doris Bruey

Books may be purchased for educational purposes. For information, please call or write:
1-800-586-0330
Fountainhead Press
Southlake, TX 76092
Web site: www.fountainheadpress.com
E-mail: customerservice@fountainheadpress.com

First Edition
ISBN: 978-1-59871-456-2
Printed in the United States of America

TABLE OF CONTENTS

FOREWORD

We write thousands of things in our lifetimes: e-mails, letters, messages, grocery lists, things that vary in importance and length. The act of writing is not new; what *is* new—especially for you—is the world of academic writing, a world that requires certain things of us as writers and of what we write. In many ways, this new world challenges us to think—and to write—in ways that may be frustrating at first since it is "new."

During your college career, you will be called on to write different things for various audiences. Many students look on this as a challenge they cannot meet; others struggle to adapt to this new way of writing and of thinking. Make no mistake: academic writing requires you to challenge yourself not only in the way you express yourself but also in the way you think—about the world, about your classes, and about yourself. If you ignore that challenge, your college career will, most likely, be a difficult one; however, if you determine that you are going to meet and perhaps even exceed that challenge, you will become more proficient and successful as a writer.

This book is the result of years of teaching students just like you to be more successful writers, the result of endless nights of frustration wondering how to get these very important concepts across to our students, and the result of our unfaltering belief that, by better understanding these basics, our students will be just as prepared—if not *more* so—for academic writing than any other student.

Ours has become a society on the move, constantly going, constantly letting others know where we are and what we are doing. Many people are even discovering other countries, exotic places that once only lived in the imagination or in a book or magazine photo. All of this travel, however,  poses a particularly messy (and potentially embarrassing) problem. If all you know is English, how can you expect to communicate with the people in the country to which you are traveling?

In some respects, many college students approach this new adventure in their lives—college classes—as though they are the kind of tourists who give the larger group a bad name: they refuse or simply neglect to learn the language spoken in this new country, and thus their experience is much more frustrating (not to mention costly and dangerous) than it would have been if they had learned the language.

Academic writing is a formal level of discourse that allows you the writer to communicate with your peers in such a way that your message will be taken seriously by your audience and you will be taken seriously as a scholar and a professional. Learning to communicate through academic writing is like learning that foreign language. As a student, you have travelled to this place that, perhaps, in the past only existed in dreams and the pages of books and magazines. You are standing on "foreign" territory where people speak and think and *write* differently. How can you hope to communicate with these people?

> "Good writing establishes a clear point of departure that turns the reader's attention in a particular direction, sustains reading in that direction through a series of connected passages, and leads to a real destination."
> *Keith Hjortshoj, The Transition to College Writing*

By becoming more familiar with this new "language," academic discourse, you soon will find yourself better able to communicate and more likely to be taken seriously by the people who inhabit this "land." Like any other foreign language, academic discourse has its own rules; like any other foreign language, you learn it only through practice; and like any other foreign language, knowing how to communicate with it will broaden your horizons and your potential for success.

At this point, you are in this class to learn the basics—to begin your experience with this new language. The first few attempts will not be perfect, but you will find that, with each new experience with this new language, you will feel your confidence grow. You are not alone on this journey; you have instructors, classmates, and tutors who are more accustomed to the language than you who can help you through the frustrating times.

Academic discourse (or, as it is sometimes called, "college writing") is only one tool you will need to make your experience in this new territory a meaningful one. *Reading* this new language is also a skill that requires practice in order to become good at it. You are going to encounter ideas and people and ways of seeing the world that may seem odd at first. To deny yourself, on the other hand, this important facet of your college experience just because you do not want to read this "new language"

is to diminish the value of your college education. Yes, it will be challenging and frustrating at first; however, the more you do it, the better you will get at it.

Like any other skill, like learning any foreign language, learning to write in this new language takes practice to get better. The ability to write well—especially in academic language—is something that takes work, and you *will* work hard in honing your academic writing skills. However, the time spent in practicing will pay great dividends in your other classes and in other aspects of your life as well. Knowing how to write well, to communicate clearly and effectively, is a skill that all employers look for in their employees; if you can write well, then you will have an advantage over those prospective employees who cannot. This is because knowing how to write well involves so many other skills that will benefit you: knowing how to read and think critically, knowing how to approach a problem and come up with a workable solution or approach to that problem, knowing how to organize your thoughts in a logical fashion so that you will be taken seriously by those working or studying with you.

DEBUNKING WRITING MYTHS

Writing well involves a process, a series of steps that you must go through in order to produce the best possible writing that you can. Chapter 1 will address that process; however, before we embark on that journey, some myths about writing should be addressed:

- The writing process is not "mysterious." The ability to write is not something that you are "born with," nor is it something that people possess as a "gift" but is something that comes about after hours and hours of hard work.
- Writing is *never* "perfect." Despite all those hours of hard work, you may still find things about your writing to correct or make better; you can only make it as good as it can be on the day that your assignment is due. In other words, **writing is never *done*, just *due*."**

- Some of the things you were told about writing in other classes or in high school may, in fact, be wrong or inappropriate for academic writing. Be willing to challenge what you know about writing as well as willing to challenge yourself to be better with every writing opportunity.

- No "one correct way" to write exists. Good writers are flexible. You may find in your college writing experience that no two instructors will ask for the same format, or you may find that different disciplines have different rules for academic writing. You have to be flexible and make your writing adapt to any situation.

- Getting better in writing depends on getting input from someone who can see your writing objectively. Often writers, regardless of their experience or skill level, get too "invested" in what they have written and cannot objectively judge its effectiveness; after all the hours of hard work they put into their writing, they cannot (or choose not to) see where the weak spots or mistakes are. In those cases, we all need someone—a writing tutor—to look over what we have written who can ask us questions that can help us clarify what we have said and show us where improvements can be made.

- As you make progress in your writing, you may discover that other problem areas arise that were not problems before. Yes, your sentence structure problems are getting fewer and fewer in number; however, suddenly you discover issues with organization, or suddenly you see commas where they never used to be. This is *normal*; because you are concentrating so much on getting better in one area, your concentration on other aspects may allow other problems to surface. As you challenge yourself and move from one skill level to the next, you may encounter some "resistance." If you have ever worked out or trained for something over a period of time, you know that, at first, the new level is difficult; however, with practice, it becomes easier and easier—until the time comes to reach for that next level, and the process begins anew. The same is true with writing, so do not get discouraged if (to use sports terminology) you "hit the wall."

- Being in a basic writing class does *not* mean that you cannot be a good writer. Being in a basic writing class simply means that you are being given the opportunity to solidify your writing fundaments. With a stronger foundation in the basics of academic writing, you will improve your chances of being successful in other classes where writing is involved.

All of us have had to battle one or more of these myths about writing and about ourselves as writers, so do not let your frustration keep you from putting everything you have into this journey. Writing—and becoming a writer—is a process that often takes time, but this will be time well spent if you use it wisely to hone your writing skills and become more adept at communicating at an academic level.

THE TEXTBOOK, UNIT BY UNIT AND CHAPTER BY CHAPTER

In order to help you succeed as an academic writer, this textbook takes a two pronged approach: Unit I of the book focuses on paragraph and essay structure while Unit II is a handbook that you can and will refer to frequently for guidance with sentence structure, grammar errors, diction, and punctuation.

Unit I—An Approach to Academic Writing

The first unit of the text breaks down the writing process, paragraph and essay structure, and the rhetorical patterns you will be focusing on in composition courses. The chapters for this unit are arranged in the following manner:

Chapter 1: The Writing Process

This chapter starts your journey by looking into the writing process itself, moving you from gathering rough ideas to polishing a finished product.

Chapter 2: Moving from Sentences to Paragraphs:

Chapter 2 looks at paragraphs—a group of related sentences that forms the basis of academic essay—and their essential elements, such as topic sentences, supporting details, and concluding sentences.

Chapter 3: Moving From Paragraphs to Essays

This chapter examines the essay, the basic format for all academic writing, and how it builds on the foundation of solid paragraph structure covered in Chapter 2.

Chapter 4: Rhetorical Patterns

An introduction to composition, this chapter briefly describes the rhetorical patterns used in academic writing, the building blocks that all writers have at their disposal when putting together an academic essay.

Unit II—What You Want to Know but Are Afraid to Ask

After Chapter 4, you will find Unit II, which details basic sentence structure and helps you target the most common grammar, diction, and punctuation errors that composition students commit. The chapters for this unit break down in this way:

Chapter 1: Parts of Speech and Sentence Structure

In this chapter, you will learn about the parts of speech and their relationships to one another as well as basic sentence structure.

Chapter 2: Grammar, Diction, and Sentence-Level Errors

Chapter 2 covers the most common grammar and usage errors, how to recognize them and avoid them in your own writing.

Chapter 3: Choosing the Best Words to Communicate Your Meaning Effectively

Chapter 3 explains the meaning of diction in formal academic writing and how to avoid these kinds of errors.

Chapter 4: Punctuation and Capitalization

In this chapter, you will read about how to use commas correctly, what a semi-colon actually does, and how to make a dash. This chapter should provide you with the basic rules of punctuation that you need for your own writing.

Chapter 5: MLA Format and Grading

Hopefully this chapter will demystify the grading process and explain how to format a formal academic paper according to MLA.

Having a good understanding of these building blocks is vital for any college writer, and these chapters will show you how these blocks interact with the others to make your writing stronger and more effective.

SOME THINGS TO KNOW BEFORE WE GET STARTED

Before we get started on this journey, you may be wondering how you can chart your progress—in other words, how to get better as a writer. Here are some things you can do to enhance your chances of improvement:

1. ***Write***: This particular piece of advice may seem painfully obvious, but many students forget that the best way to improve as a writer is to write. In an age when "writing" has become synonymous with texting, tweeting, and e-mail correspondence, many students do not get a lot of practice actually writing in full sentences, full paragraphs, and full essays. Like any other skill that you acquire, writing takes practice; as most athletes, artists, musicians, and chefs will tell you, measurable progress comes through utilizing that skill over and over again. To become a better writer, you must apply what you have learned in actual writing situations.

2. ***Read:*** We are surrounded constantly by things that demand our attention, and we are often so overwhelmed that we gravitate to those things that do not require much effort. Unfortunately, reading is seen by many students

as something that requires too *much* effort, so they either do not read or simply let the words pass before their eyes without engaging the thought processes required to read and comprehend a text as fully as possible. In college, you will be required to read a lot, perhaps more than you ever have in your life up to this point; this exposure to texts (and textbooks) has a sometimes surprising effect: the more you read, the better you will write. Reading a wide variety of texts will give you exposure to different writing styles as well as different perspectives on certain subjects, so you should take advantage of every opportunity you have to enhance not only your reading skill but also your writing skill.

3. ***Be patient***: The goal of this course is to *start* you on your way toward becoming a good writer—not to make the entire journey with you. Becoming a good writer is not something that happens overnight or even over the course of a semester; most writers will tell you that writing well is a never-ending process that takes a great deal of patience. You may be very tempted to get frustrated and discouraged if you do not see immediate improvement or if you feel that your progress has tapered off, but do not let these feelings stop you. Your writing will improve throughout your academic career; these are just your first steps, so be patient with yourself and your instructor.

> ## We are what we repeatedly do. Excellence, then, is not an act, but a habit.
> *--Aristotle*

LEARNING THIS "NEW LANGUAGE": WHAT WRITERS NEED TO KNOW

If writing were a mathematical formula, then plugging in the right words would result in a "right answer" every time. Unfortunately, what writers soon realize is that, as in math, certain variables exist that, as a student writer, they need to be aware of, such as the following:

> **FOUR CONSIDERATIONS FOR EVERY ASSIGNMENT:**
> 1. **Purpose**
> 2. **Topic**
> 3. **Voice**
> 4. **Audience**

In short, knowing *who* you are writing to (your ***audience***) and *why* you are writing (your ***purpose***) will affect *what* you say (your ***topic***) and *how* you say it (your ***voice***). We will be discussing topics in future chapters—how to pick a topic if one is not assigned to you, how to generate ideas regarding that topic, how to prioritize those ideas, and how to form those ideas into sentences for a paragraph or paragraphs for an essay. This section takes you on the next step in that journey: finding a purpose, a voice, and an audience.

Finding a Purpose: Why Are You Writing?

In many academic writing situations, your purpose, on a general level, will involve writing assignments or tests for which you will receive a grade. Imbedded within those assignments and tests are more specific purposes. On a general level, most writing can be classified as one of three major purposes:

- to INFORM: to pass on information
- to PERSUADE: to get your reader to agree with you or to at least consider your stand on an issue or topic
- to ENTERTAIN: to tell a story or describe an object or event in a creative way that involves the reader's senses.

Occasions may arise when two or more of these purposes will overlap; however, most writing situations will ask you to focus primarily on one of these.

In these situations, you may be able to find clues as to what purpose you are being asked to address in the actual assignment. For example, if the assignment contains the words *take a stand*, you are being asked to persuade; on the other hand, if the assignment contains the words *explain* or *illustrate*, you will want to write an essay that informs. Reading the assignment or test question carefully will help you determine your purpose for writing.

These different categories of essays and rhetorical pattern choices will be explained more fully in Chapter 4.

Voice and Audience: How You Say It and Who Will Read It

In every-day conversation, we have several clues at our disposal to determine exactly what someone means. Voice inflection (tone of voice) or body language can take a seemingly positive statement like "I like this class" and make it into something completely different. However, in writing, these audible or physical clues are not available to us; instead, we must rely on *how* something is said to determine its true meaning.

A writer's **voice**, then, is affected by his or her word choices, and these word choices must conform to the standards of academic writing if the writer is responding to an assignment for a college class. These rules may differ from professor to professor and from discipline to discipline, and a good writer always becomes familiar with what each professor expects and what specific rules apply to writing assignments. However, overall, these rules and expectations include certain "no-no's," things that mark writing as not academic, such as:

- **No contractions**. We use them all the time in conversation – words like *isn't, can't, wouldn't,* and even derivatives like *shoulda, coulda,* and *gonna*, and so on - but they are too informal to be considered good academic writing.

- **No slang, jargon, clichés, or "textspeak."**

  o **Slang** is the verbal shorthand we sometimes use in spoken conversation. Examples of slang might be "this is not his first rodeo" (unless, of course, you are writing about someone competing in his or her first rodeo) or "She cleaned his clock" (not particularly useful unless you are writing about someone whose job it is literally to clean clocks).

  o **Jargon** is a very specific kind of slang that is used primarily by members of a certain profession or discipline to refer to things within that profession or discipline. For example, referring to medications as "meds" may make sense only if you are writing to a nursing audience or to people in the medical field; otherwise, you would do well to use the full word, "medications."

  o **Clichés** are those words or phrases that, with the passage of time and over-use, have come to mean nothing. Phrases like "laugh my head off" or "adding insult to injury" may have, at one time, meant something quite specific, but because they have been so over-used, they now actually add very little to your writing.

  o **"Textspeak"** is the shorthand used in texting, tweeting, emailing, and other computerized communication. "Textspeak" is extremely inappropriate in academic writing, and using texting acronyms ("b4" for "before," "LOL" for "laughing out loud," etc.) or texting shorthand ("r" for "are" or "u" for "you") or emoticons ("J" and the like) can mark your writing as immature and not on the same level of effort required for academic writing.

- **No use of second person ("you")** – Technically, this is called "direct address to the audience" and is allowable in very limited instances in academic writing. For example, if you are writing a process essay about how to build a model airplane from balsa wood, you might employ second person pronouns to address directly your instructions to your reader; however, in those situations, you might better choose to use the "command" mode where the "you" is unstated but implied. In almost all other instances, use of second person is dangerous for two reasons: (1) it becomes annoying or "preachy" to say "You should do this" or "you must know that"; (2) it can lead the writer to make bold, generalized statements that he or she cannot support, like "as you all know" or "as you are aware."

By observing these restrictions, you will be making a very important step in your awareness of your *voice* and how your word choices can either negatively or positively impact your reader.

Point of View and Verb Tenses: Keep It Consistent

Voice and word choices also include matters such as **point of view** and **consistent verb tense.** When it comes to point of view in writing, a writer has three choices:

First Person		Second Person	Third Person	
Singular	Plural	Singular & Plural	Singular	Plural
I, Me, My,	We, Our, Ours,	You, Your, Yours	He, She, It	They
Mine	Us		His, Hers, Its	Theirs
			Him, Her, It	Their

In writing, point of view must be consistent and is determined by the point of view used in the topic sentence of the paragraph. For example, if the first sentence of a paragraph reads "Breaking my leg was the most painful experience of my life," pronouns such as "my" let you know immediately that the rest of this paragraph must be told from a first-person point of view. To do otherwise is to cause a shift in point of view, which can be distracting and confusing for your reader.

Look at the following paragraph for an example:

> Breaking my leg was the most painful experience of my life. It happened on a family ski trip to Vail, Colorado, last winter. I was being very careful, but before you know it, he could not avoid this bump in the course. At first they did not know if your leg was broken, but when I tried to stand up, it became obvious that something was wrong.

The shifting in point of view from first person to second person to third person and back again makes the meaning of the paragraph and the message of the paragraph hard to follow. Being consistent in your point of view as you write will make *your* message much less confusing. With a consistent point of view, the previous paragraph would read as follows:

> Breaking my leg was the most painful experience of my life. It happened on a family ski trip to Vail, Colorado, last winter. I was being very careful, but before *I knew* it, I could not avoid this bump in the course. At first they did not know if *my* leg was broken, but when I tried to stand up, it became obvious that something was wrong.

In this revised paragraph, the consistent point of view makes the writer's message clear and the story easier to follow. Good writers are always aware as they write that their word choices – including point of view – will ultimately affect how the audience will perceive them.

Verb Tense Consistency

Another aspect of word choice is consistent verb tense. Like point of view, the verb tense of the paragraph is determined by the first or topic sentence. Before we discuss the problems that come with shifts in verb tense, a review of verb tenses will help you see why these shifts can be difficult for a reader to navigate.

Verb tenses are generally classified as **past, present,** and **future**. Past tense verbs tell what has happened. Present tense verbs relate current events, and future tense verbs reveal what will happen. In writing, the goal is to keep the verb tense consistent with the story being told. Like shifts in point of view, shifts in verb tense are very distracting and confusing for a reader. Take a look at the following paragraph:

> I decided to come to college at literally the last minute. I am facing a job that I hate and the prospect of never getting a promotion, and I will never get ahead without a college degree. Therefore, I came to campus during my lunch break, filled out the application, and here I am.

In this paragraph, the writer takes the reader on a roller-coaster ride of verb tenses – from the past to the present to the future and back again – and makes the story very difficult to follow.

Like point of view, the verb tense that a paragraph must conform to is determined in the first or topic sentence. In the above paragraph, the writer begins her story in the past—'I *decided* to come to college'—and, therefore, every other verb in the paragraph must be past tense forms of these verbs:

> I decided to come to college at literally the last minute. **I was** facing a job that **I hated, and I was facing** the prospect of never getting a promotion and never getting ahead without a college degree. Therefore, I came to campus during my lunch break, filled out the application, and **was accepted**.

With consistency in verb tenses, this student's story is much easier to follow and understand. Consistency in verb tense and point of view makes writing clearer for both the writer and the reader, the audience.

Another major consideration for any writer is who will be reading what he writes—the *audience*. In some instances, the audience for your writing will be dictated by the assignment ("write a process essay for a group of third graders"); in other instances, you will be responsible for determining who your audience will be. Regardless of whether your audience is given to you or decided by you, your ultimate audience will be the instructor who will be grading your writing (even in some cases where the assignment gives you an audience). This makes your word choices and all the decisions you make about your writing and as you write much more important; how well you make these decisions and integrate them into your writing will signal to your instructor how serious you are about being taken seriously as a student writer.

Let us look at an example – the example mentioned above regarding a process essay intended for a group of third graders - to see how word choices can be affected by your audience. If your assignment is to write a process essay on how to assemble a bologna and cheese sandwich for a class of third graders, you have to choose words that third graders will understand, and you will want to break the process down into very simple steps, defining certain terms as necessary. How would *you* describe this process to a third grader? Now, imagine that your assignment is to describe that same process to a group of 19-21 year-olds in your speech class. How might your word choices change? How would you describe this process to your new audience?

Successful communication, in speaking but especially in writing, depends on matching your word choices to your audience. Good writers think through these choices very carefully before they begin to write. You will find that the more you practice this skill, the better you will get in making the best choices.

> *Just remember:*
> *Knowing who you are writing to–your*
> *audience–and why you are writing–*
> *your purpose–will determine*
> *what you say—your topic—and how*
> *you say it.*

LINTON WEEKS—"THE NO-BOOK REPORT: SKIM IT AND WEEP"

Jeremy Spreitzer probably wouldn't read this story if it weren't about him. He's an aliterate – someone who can read, but chooses not to.

A graduate student in public affairs at Park University in Kansas City, Mo., Spreitzer, 25, gleans most of his news from TV. He skims required texts, draws themes from dust jackets and, when he absolutely, positively has to read something, reaches for the audiobook.

"I am fairly lazy when it comes to certain tasks," says Spreitzer, a long-distance runner who hopes to compete in the 2004 Olympics. "Reading is one of them."

As he grows older, Spreitzer finds he has less time to read. And less inclination. In fact, he says, if he weren't in school, he probably wouldn't read at all.

He's not alone. According to the survey firm NDP Group—which tracked the everyday habits of thousands of people through the 1990s—this country is reading printed versions of books, magazines, and newspapers less and less. In 1991, more than half of all Americans read a half-hour or more every day. By 1999, that had dropped to 45 percent.

A 1999 Gallup Poll found that only 7 percent of Americans were voracious readers, reading more than a book a week, while some 59 percent said they had read fewer than 10 books in the previous year. Though book clubs seem popular now, only 6 percent of those who read belong to one. The number of people who don't read at all, the poll concluded, has been rising for the past 20 years.

The reports on changes in reading cut to the quick of American culture. We pride ourselves on being a largely literate First World country while at the same time we rush to build a visually powerful environment in which reading is not required.

The results are inevitable. Aliteracy is all around. Just ask:

- Internet developers. At the Terry Lycos portal design lab in Waltham, Mass., researcher William Albert has noticed that the human guinea pigs in his focus groups are too impatient to read much. When people look up information on the Internet today, Albert explains, they are "basically scanning. There's very little actual comprehension that's going on." People, Albert adds, prefer to get info in short bursts, with bullets, rather than in large blocks of text.
- Transportation gurus. Chandra Clayton, who oversees the design of road signs and signals for the Virginia Department of Transportation, says, "Symbols can quickly give you a message that might take too long to read in text." The department is using logos and symbols more and more. When it comes to highway safety and getting lifesaving information quickly, she adds, "a picture is worth a thousand words."
- Packaging designers. "People don't take the time to read anything," explains Jim Peters, editor of Brand Packaging magazine. "Marketers and

packagers are giving them colors and shapes as way of communicating." For effective marketing, Peters says, "researchers tell us that the hierarchy is colors, shapes, icons, and, dead last, words."

Some of this shift away from words – and toward images – can be attributed to our ever-growing multilingual population. But for many people, reading is passé or impractical or, like, so totally unnecessary in this day and age.

To Jim Trelease, author of "The Read-Aloud Handbook," this trend away from the written word is more than worrisome. It's wicked. It's tearing apart our culture. People who have stopped reading, he says, "base their future decisions on what they used to know."

"If you don't read much, you really don't know much," he says. "You're dangerous."

Losing a Heritage

"The man who does not read good books has no advantage over the man who cannot read them." – Mark Twain

One thing you can say for illiteracy: it can be identified, nailed down. And combated. Scores of programs such as the Greater Washington Literacy Council and the International Reading Association are geared toward fighting readinglessness in the home, the school, and the workplace.

Aliteracy, on the other hand, is like an invisible liquid, seeping through our culture, nigh impossible to pinpoint or defend against. It's the kid who spends hours and hours with video games instead of books, who knows Sim Cities better than *A Tale of Two Cities.*

It's the thousands of business people who subscribe to executive book summaries – for example, Soundview's easy-to-swallow eight-page pamphlets that take simply written management books such as *Secrets of Question-Based Selling* by Thomas A. Freese and make them even simpler.

It's the parent who pops the crummy movie of *Stuart Little* into a machine for his kid instead of reading E. B. White's marvelous novel aloud. Or the teacher who assigns the made-for-TV movie "Gettysburg" instead of the book it was based on, *The Killer Angels* by Michael Shaara.

There may be untold collateral damage in a society that can read but doesn't. "So much of our culture is embedded in literature," says Philip A. Thompsen, professor of communications at West Chester University in West Chester, Pennsylvania. Thompsen has been watching the rise of aliteracy in the classroom for 20 years, and "students today are less capable of getting full value from textbooks than they were 10 years ago."

He adds that these aliterate students are "missing out on our culture heritage."

That literature-based past included a reverence for reading, a celebration of the works and a worshipful awe of those who wrote.

To draw you a picture: Where we once deified the lifestyles of writers such as Ernest Hemingway and F. Scott Fitzgerald, we now fantasize about rock-n-roll goods, movie starlets, or NBA super-studs (e.g. MTV's "Cribs"). The notion of writer-as-culture-hero is dead and gone. Comedic monologuists such as Jay Leno or David Letterman have more sex appeal than serious fiction writers. The grail quest for the Great American Novel has ended; it *was* a myth after all.

Where we once drew our mass-cult references from books ("He's a veritable Simon Legree"), we now allude to visual works—a Seinfeld episode (not that there's anything *wrong* with that ...) or "The Silence of the Lambs" (the movie, not the book). A recent story in *Salon* speaks of "learning to read a movie."

Where we once believed that a well-read populace leads to a healthy democracy, many people now rely on whole TV broadcast operations built around politics and elections. Quick; name a Wolf Blitzer book.

Non-readers abound. Ask "Politically Incorrect" talk show host Bill Maher, who once boasted in print that he hadn't read a book in years. Or Noel Gallagher of the rock band Oasis, who has been quoted as saying he's *never* read a book. You can walk through whole neighborhoods of houses in the country that do not contain books or magazines—unless you count catalogues.

American historian Daniel Boorstin saw this coming. In 1984, while Boorstin was serving as librarian of Congress, the library issued a landmark report: "Books in Our Future." Citing recent statistics that only about half of all Americans read regularly every year, he referred to the "twin menaces" of illiteracy and aliteracy.

"In the United States today," Boorstin wrote, "aliteracy is widespread."

Several of the articles in the report alluded to the growing number of non-readers. In one essay, "The Computer and the Book," Edmund D. Pellegrino, a former president of Catholic University who is now a bioethicist at Georgetown University, observed: "The computer is simply the most effective, efficient, and attractive form for transmittal of processed information. Added to the other non-book devices like films, tapes, television, and the popular media, the computer accelerates the atrophy of the intellectual skills acquired for personally reading the books from which the information is extracted."

Reading for Bliss

Kylene Beers has talked about the evils of aliteracy for so long and so loud, she's losing her voice. Today, she's in the lecture hall of Oakton High School bending the ears of 100 or so middle school teachers.

If someone graduates from high school and is aliterate, Beers believes, that person will probably never become a habitual reader.

One of the few academics who have written about the phenomenon, Beers, a professor of reading at the University of Houston, says there are two types of reading: efferent and aesthetic.

Efferent, which comes from the Latin word *efferre* (meaning to carry away), is purposeful reading, the kind students are taught day after day in schools. Efferent readers connect cognitively with the words and plan to take something useful from it – such as answers for a test.

Aesthetic is reading for the sheer bliss of it, as when you dive deep into Dostoevski or get lost in Louisa May Alcott. Aesthetic readers connect emotionally to the story. Beers believes that more students must be shows the marvels of reading for pleasure.

On this late afternoon, she is mapping out strategies for teachers who hope to engage reluctant middle school readers. Teaching grammar and parts of speech, such as dangling participles, is the kiss of death, she says. "You don't want to talk about dangling anythings with middle-schoolers," she says in her Texas drawl. And the room laughs.

Aliteracy, she continues, is no laughing matter. Using an overhead projector, she explains that alliterate people just don't get it. Unlike accomplished readers, alliterates don't understand that sometimes you have to read efferently and sometimes you have to read aesthetically; that even the best readers occasionally read the same paragraph over and over to understand it and that to be a good reader you have to visualize the text.

To engage non-reading students – and adults – she proposes reading strategies, such as turning a chapter of a hard book into a dramatic production or relating tough words to easier words.

She writes the word "tepid" on the acetate sheet. Then she asks the audience to supply other words that describe water temperature. "Hot," someone calls out. "Freezing," somebody else says. Others suggest: cold, warm, and boiling. Beers arranges the words in a linear fashion, from the coldest word, "freezing," to the hottest, "boiling." "Tepid" falls in the middle of the list. This method, she says, will help reluctant readers to connect the words they don't know to words they do know. "Aliterates," she tells the teachers, "don't see relationships."

Apparently, teachers don't always see the relationships either. Jim Trelease is concerned that teachers do not read. The aliteracy rate among teachers, he says, is about the same, 50 percent, as among the general public.

There is some good news on the reading front, according to Trelease and others. The Harry Potter series has turned on a lot of young readers, and megabookstores, such as Barnes & Noble and Borders, are acrawl with people.

But there is plenty of bad news, too. Lots of aliterates, according to Trelease, say they just don't have the time to read anymore. "The time argument is the biggest hoax of all," he says. According to time studies, we have more leisure time than ever. "If people didn't have time, the malls would be empty, cable companies would be broke, video stores would go out of business. It's not a time problem, it's a value problem. You have 50 percent in the country who don't value reading."

Like Beers, Trelease believes that youngsters should be encouraged to read aesthetically. Reading aloud to children, according to Trelease and other reading specialists, is the single best way to ensure that someone will become a lifelong reader.

"Even Daniel Boorstin wasn't born wanting to read," Trelease says. "Michael Jordan wasn't born wanting to play basketball. The desire has to be planted."

Surfing Through Grad School

Trelease and Beers and others are scrambling for ways to engage aliterates. For all kinds of reasons. "What aliteracy does is breed illiteracy," Beers explains. "If you go through school having learned to read and then you leave school not wanting to read, chances are you won't put your own children into a reading environment."

"What you have to do is play hardball," says Trelease. He suggests running public awareness campaigns on TV. "That's where the aliterates are."

"Aliteracy may be a significant problem today," says Philip Thompsen. "But on the other hand, a narrow view of literacy – one that defines literacy as the ability to read verbal texts – may be a significant problem as well."

Many of the messages that we have to interpret in day-to-day life, Thompsen says, "use multiple communication media. I think it is important to realize that as our society becomes more accustomed to using multimedia messages, we must also expand our thinking about what it means to be 'literate.'"

Olympic hopefully Jeremy Spreitzer plans to become a teacher and maybe go into politics someday. For now, he's just trying to get through graduate school.

He watches a lot of television. "I'm a major surfer," he says. He watches the History Channel, A&E, Turner Classic Movies, and all of the news stations.

"I'm required to do a lot of reading," he says. "But I do a minimum of what I need to do."

But how do you get through grad school without reading? Spreitzer is asked.

He gives an example. One of his required texts is the recently published *Bowling Alone: The Collapse and Revival of American Community* by Robert Putnam. In the book, Putnam argues, among other things, that television has fragmented our society.

Spreitzer thumbed through the book, dipped into a few chapters and spent a while "skipping around" here and there.

He feels, however, that he understands Putnam and Putnam's theories as well as if he had read the book.

How is that? he is asked.

Putnam, he explains, has been on TV a lot. "He's on the news all the time," Spreitzer says. "On MSNBC and other places. Those interviews with him are more invaluable than anything else."

Weeks, Linton. "The No-Book Report: Skim It and Weep." *The Washington Post* 14 May 2001. C1. Rpt. in *Making Sense: A Real-World Rhetorical Reader.* 2d ed. New York:Bedford, 2005. 522-7. Print.

Discussion Questions for "The No-Book Report: Skim It and Weep"

1. How does Weeks define "aliteracy"? What is the difference between aliteracy and illiteracy? According to that definition, are *you* aliterate, and how did you get that way? If you do not consider yourself aliterate, what habits do you maintain to remain a comprehensive reader?

2. To what does the writer (and his sources) attribute America's growing problem with aliteracy? Do you agree or disagree?

3. How effective is Weeks' use of this "personal example" as a hook? How does Weeks, then, help you as a reader transition from this hook to his thesis? What exactly *is* his thesis, and where do you find it?

4. One of Weeks' sources, Jim Trelease, states that "the aliteracy rate among teachers ... is about the same, 50 percent, as among the general public." Do you find anything shocking or alarming about this? Think about some of the teachers you've had in the past; would you classify them as literate or aliterate, and why?

5.   Referring back to the introduction, define critical thinking, and explain why you believe you are or are not a critical thinker. How important is critical thinking to becoming a well-rounded individual and competent writer? What role does reading play in helping a student become a critical thinker?

UNIT 1

WRITING PARAGRAPHS AND ESSAYS
IN A NEW LANGUAGE

THE WRITING PROCESS—A PARABLE

You are sitting at your desk as the full moon looks over your shoulder. You read the writing assignment and begin to realize that you should have started your work on it much sooner in order to produce the level of work expected by a university. The clock on the wall ticks away the minutes until the  sun rises and your paper is due. You notice that your desk lamp is emanating more heat than usual, and the cyclopic computer screen sneers back at you unblinking. You muster your courage and squelch your frustration and begin typing just to fill the word count requirement and get something done.

The beams of morning's first light pierce your eyelids, and you raise your head from your desk, wipe the drool from your mouth with your sleeve, and print your paper. You are too delirious to be concerned as you pass your paper up the row to the instructor. A sinking feeling creeps into your chest as you walk out of English toward your history class, but you sufficiently suppress it. After all, your writing method served you well in high school. You always made passing grades on your essays about the gestation period of the great white shark and the necessity of balancing the pH in a freshwater aquarium. Reviewing the essay in your mind as you head back home, you reassure yourself by recalling the "little darlings" of your work, the phrases and sentences you thought were especially clever.

You forget about the work you turned in as the week passes, and Saturday and Sunday manage to wipe your memory completely. Back in English class Monday morning, the fear again rises over you like a shadow as the instructor returns the essays to his students, frowning at some and quietly praising others. He looms over your desk and drops your essay as if it were garbage. You look down and gasp as you see the essay bloodied with red ink and the prominent failing grade etched across the top like an epitaph. This is the moment you realize that you must do better. You must put in the time and get the help you need to become a successful college level writer. You must break your writing into stages and spend weeks on a single work.

Fortunately, writers have developed, over time, a strategy that has, if not simplified the often arduous task of writing, made the approach more manageable. The writing process can and should be broken down into stages. Most writers would agree that these stages include the following:

STAGES of WRITING PROCESS

1. **Prewriting**
2. **Organizing**
3. **Drafting**
4. **Revising**
5. **Editing**
6. **Reviewing with Peers**
7. **Workshop**
8. **More Revising and Editing**

As this list implies, a piece of writing is never finished—it is simply due. The writing process gives you a plan from which you can build a timeline and accomplish your goals.

PREWRITING—GETTING IDEAS ON PAPER

Prewriting is the process of simply getting your ideas onto paper. This stage is often neglected by students facing deadlines but is an essential first step in producing a complete and organized work. The methods used for accomplishing this vary; you should practice each and choose those that work best for you. Prewriting will help ensure that your final product is specific and well supported. It removes the worries over sentence structure, punctuation, and organization.

Where to Start—Be Honest

Students often find that one of the most difficult stages of the writing process is simply beginning. Instructors do not always assign a specific topic, so coming up with one can be daunting. Even when a topic is assigned, the number of directions a writer can take with a topic is limitless. Of all the possible topics or directions available, focusing on just one may seem impossible, but when the fledgling writer sits down to consider what interests her, the number of possibilities quickly dwindles. The list shrinks even more when the author thinks about what she has experience with or knowledge of. The struggle can diminish still further once the student decides to write about something she has some knowledge of but would like to learn even more about.

Prewriting, however, does not necessarily involve research; it can be as simple or complex as looking around, even at yourself, and resolving to be open and honest about what you find. This practice of introspection can be challenging, even painful, but is ultimately rewarding. Prewriting is the first step in the process of self-discovery.

Where Ideas Come From—Look Around

One of the most common and simplest forms of prewriting involves simply paying attention to the world around you. Every day, each of us is bombarded with so much information that we have learned to tune it out or passively file it away in our subconscious. A simple conversation between you and a friend, professor, classmate, or family member can conjure ideas and information that may be interesting in a paragraph or essay. Reading a magazine or newspaper article, short story, or novel provides the opportunity for you not only to become engrossed in other worlds, but these sources also allow you to learn more about yourself—your opinions, your feelings, and your imagination. Searching the internet can expose you to countless points of view and fascinating facts. A simple walk down the street or from one class to another can reveal people, places, and things that arouse your curiosity and perhaps eventually your reader's interest. Observing yourself in your environment is not only a method of prewriting; it is also the essence of critical thinking and self-awareness.

Stages of Prewriting—for Topic, Direction, and Support

Prewriting is accomplished in stages that focus on three aspects of your writing. Whichever method of prewriting you adopt, you should complete it in the following steps:

1. Usually you will begin by hunting for a **topic**, which is your subject or what you are writing about.

2. Next you will start a new prewrite centered on a **direction**, your attitude toward your subject or what you are writing about.

3. Finally you will prewrite again to gather **support**, the details that reinforce your topic and direction and make your writing interesting.

Types of Prewriting—Disciplines for Thought

Although giving more attention to your conversations, your reading, and the world around you may be an excellent first step in producing a written work, you still lack one essential ingredient in the writing process: getting something on paper. Forcing yourself to sit down and stare at a blank document on your word processor sometimes has the effect of erasing your own thoughts, so when you have an assignment, take notes as you go about your day. When you have some rough notes and are facing the infamous blank document, you still may not see how to translate these notes into something useable. This is an instance when other more disciplined forms of prewriting may be useful. These forms of prewriting include the following:

TYPES of PREWRITING
1. **Freewriting**
2. **Questioning**
3. **Brainstorming**
4. **Keeping a Journal**
5. **Talking**
6. **Observing the Media**

Freewriting—A Force of Will

Freewriting is a form of prewriting that attempts to form complete sentences but ignores any problems with grammar and organization. The rules for freewriting are simple.

1. Set a given amount of time to write, say ten to fifteen minutes.

2. Do not stop writing during that time.

3. Avoid concerns about grammar or making sense or anything else.

Once you have completed your first attempt at freewriting, review it. You may be surprised to find that some good ideas popped up once you stopped worrying about the requirements of the assignment. Do not get discouraged if you begin with absent-minded statements like the ones below:

> so I'm supposed to write something because my teacher told me to and she told me to try freewriting but I don't know what to talk about but Im gonna try this anyway. Yesterday at dennys I talked to my sister about freewriting and she saisd she likd to brainstorm but we haven't talked about that in class yet and som I am just sitting here waiting for the fiftenn minutes to runt out….

Something happens as you force yourself to continue writing. Information of value begins to appear as you engage more fully into what you are doing. Your freewriting gathers substance, and you focus on a topic of interest. Look at how the prewriting below has evolved and see if you agree.

> …I had this assignment in psych the other day where I was supposed to write something about what I thought ethics and weird but I saw this guy panhandling on the corner off outside of campus I felt like I should help him but I was in a hurry to get my assignment in and be on time to class. That made me think about the hypocrisy by which I live my life. Turns out the bum was actually someone planted by my professor to see what students would do…

At first glance, this material may seem worthless, but a closer look may reveal some good potential topics for a writing assignment. The hesitant writer begins to ask herself questions about her first attempt at freewriting. If the event was staged, what does it say about the ethics of psychologists who get their results from deceiving their students? What does it say about someone who ignores those in need? Obviously, many observations and ideas can arise that you may otherwise dismiss or never catch without freewriting. Sifting through your prewriting can help you discover genuine topics of interest.

Encouraged, the author begins freewriting to find a clear direction. After another ten minutes of freewriting, she realizes she is most angry about the hypocrisy of a professor teaching ethics who advances his work by deceiving his own students. She then starts to freewrite to gather the support, the specific details of the event relevant to her topic and direction. She is completing the first step in the writing process.

Exercise 1

Choose from one of the general topics below, and freewrite for three sessions of ten minutes. First, freewrite for a more specific topic. Second, freewrite to find a clear direction for your more specific topic. Freewrite a third time to gather support for your topic and direction.

long lines   a day at the park

when your computer fails   your first impression of college

1. **(freewrite for specific topic)**

_____

_____

_____

_____

_____

_____

_____

_____

_____

_____

2. **(freewrite for direction)**

_____

_____

_____

_____

_____

_____

_____

_____

3. **(freewrite for support)**

_____

_____

_____

_____

_____

_____

_____

_____

Questioning—Socratic Method of Discovery

Another form of prewriting that may be inspired by your freewriting, **questioning**, involves w hat the name suggests, sparking your curiosity about a given topic by asking who, what, where, why, and how about it. The questioning method of prewriting is similar to the process journalists work through routinely to put together a story.

For example, a student who works for the school newspaper is assigned the topic of describing a comfortable place to study. Though initially dismayed by her own potential lack of interest in her story, she may discover that questioning can reveal untapped information about a seemingly fruitless topic. She begins to ask herself questions about her topic.

Who? Who wants to know about this topic? Who might be interested in the information she gathers? She realizes that, obviously, other college students would be inquisitive about what tips she might have that could improve their own place of study and habits. High school students also might want to learn more about the

type of setting and discipline needed to become a successful scholar. By identifying her audience, she has also begun to realize her direction, which, in this case, is instructive.

What? What makes a student both comfortable and productive? She begins a conversation with her readers about the equipment, such as computers and printers, necessary to be productive. She also focuses on conditions like silence and amenities like cozy chairs, desks, and even couches. This reporter might suggest to her newly identified audience that the choice of where to study comfortably is not as obvious as it seems.

Where? Where can all the conditions and amenities necessary for productive and comfortable study be found? A bedroom, complete with all its creature comforts, may seem ideal for this activity, but students may want to avoid places where they typically relax or sleep. For one thing, studying in a bedroom might only reinforce their natural urge to doze, and in the end, they accomplish nothing. Perhaps even worse, lying in bed may turn their important place of rest into an area that is no longer conducive to sleep. By associating their bedroom with study, scholars may find themselves staring at the ceiling at three in the morning, mentally chewing their homework rather than getting their coveted eight hours. The question then becomes where *exactly* should a student study? Mastering vast amounts of complex material might be better done in a quiet setting like a bedroom, but this ideal place should be one students associate already with this kind of work. Where to study might then be a library where it is quiet, and needed resources such as books, desks, computers, and professionals ready to assist them are all provided. The answer to the question "where?" might also be a study hall or a coffee shop where classmates can form a study group.

Why? The answer to where the typical undergraduate or high school student should study might be even more fully answered by simply asking why he is studying in the first place. Is he preparing for an exam, writing an essay, completing a math assignment, or reading chapters from a textbook? The answer to these questions may not only determine where he studies but also how he completes his task.

How? How will the pupil know which environment will be the most conducive to the completion of his goals? The answers to the previous questions can help the intrepid reporter advise her readers on how to find an environment that will meet a student's particular needs. If the student is studying for a test, maybe he should meet some classmates at the coffee shop. If he has to write a paper, maybe he should go to the library or a writing lab.

As with freewriting, the reporter sifts through her first prewrite, taking notes along the way, to discover potential topic and direction. The example below reveals what the reporter's questioning might look like and the responses they may elicit:

- Question: Who is the audience?
- Answer: high school and college students

Potential direction—to give advice

- Question: What does a student need to be comfortable and productive?
- Answer: computers, printers, books, comfortable seats, etc.

- Question: Where can all of these things be found and still keep the student productive and comfortable?
- Answer: a library or coffee shop, etc.

Potential Topics—

1. *What you need to study*

2. *Where these things can be found*

- Question: Why does the student need to study in the first place?
- Answer: He has a test, reading or essay to do.

3. *How to determine what you need to study and where to find it*

- Question: How will he know which is the best place to work?
- Answer: It depends on what he is preparing for or completing.

This investigative prewriting, questioning, often raises more questions and more points to consider. Simply carrying on an internal dialogue about your topic may produce a wealth of information that will enlighten both you and your potential readers. However, like the reporter, you must narrow your topic, focus on a clear direction, and gather detailed support by completing all three steps of prewriting: setting a given amount of time, not stopping during that time, and ignoring grammar and structural errors.

Exercise 2

Choosing a different topic than the one you used in your freewriting, use questioning to narrow a topic, find a direction, and gather support.

long lines   when your computer fails

a day at the park   your first impression of college

1. **(question for specific topic)**

_____

_____

_____

_____

_____

_____

_____

_____

2. **(question for direction)**

_____

_____

_____

_____

_____

_____

_____

_____

3. **(question for support)**

_____

_____

_____

_____

_____

_____

_____

_____

_____

Brainstorming—Bringing the Monster to Life

Many students will already be familiar with the form of prewriting known as brainstorming. In many ways, it possesses the advantages of both freewriting and questioning. As with the former methods, brainstorming can be used to help you discover a topic, direction, and support. Unlike freewriting, however, you can temporarily abandon the need to complete even a sentence, and unlike questioning, you can ignore all semblance of structure and simply jot down words and phrases that come to you. **Brainstorming** is the act of making a list of topics, directions, and supporting details.

Consider that you have been given a writing assignment, either a paragraph or essay, with specific length, format, grammar, and diction requirements, but your instructor was kind or cruel enough to give you no topic at all. Of the possibilities roaming your mind, the ones that make it to the page are probably those that are of most interest to you. As with freewriting and questioning, limit your time when brainstorming to control the flood of ideas that pour onto the paper. Begin brainstorming for topics, and then review this list to find your best potential topic. Next, brainstorm for direction, and once you have that narrowed down, brainstorm for supporting details. You should now have three detailed lists from which to begin your next step in the writing process. Consider a student who is assigned a paragraph but given no topic. In the examples below, he brainstorms for topic, direction, and support:

history research	cyber friends	online gaming
censorship	online shopping	addiction
loss of privacy	viruses	predators

At first these topics seem to have no clear relationship with one another. Perhaps, the brainstorming experiment merely revealed the writer's concerns over some history homework as he stares at a blank screen; nevertheless, once patience prevails, the links between topics become clearer.

Many of the topics appear to be tied together by their effect of the web on culture. Still, such a vast topic could never be adequately covered in a paragraph or even an essay. Therefore, the now less frustrated student selects a specific topic provided in the brainstorm: cyber friends. Now he can brainstorm for direction:

isolates from real people	creates new avenue for
promotes anonymity	predators
encourages text messaging	allows bullies into homes can
spelling and acronyms	meet people from around the
	world

Our now encouraged essayist has discovered his own attitude toward cyber friends and can single out the one he prefers to write about. He chooses to write about what he does not like about cyber friends: he is isolated from real people. Now he can gather support for his topic and direction.

Exercise 3

Choose a third topic from the list below and brainstorm for specific topic, direction, and support. After completing this exercise, review the methods of prewriting you used in the previous exercises and think about which you liked best or whether a combination of methods suits your needs.

long lines   a day at the park

when your computer fails   your first impression of college

1. **(brainstorm for specific topic)**

_____

_____

_____

_____

_____

_____

_____

_____

_____

2. **(brainstorm for direction)**

_____

_____

_____

_____

_____

_____

_____

_____

_____

3. **(brainstorm for support)**

_____

_____

_____

_____

_____

_____

_____

_____

_____

Keeping a Journal—Building a Library of Prewriting

Even in these hurried times, many people stop to reflect on their thoughts and activities on a daily or weekly basis. These observations are recorded in a personal **journal**, diary, or a blog. Some journals are based on a theme such as romantic interests, research, or even progress in a sport or class. Others are more general, based on interests and concern s. Those who do keep journals often have an advantage over others. The topics, directions, and support they need for more formal writing are already gathered. They also have better insight into themselves through the very process of keeping a journal. A journal requires more discipline and time than many of us consider we have, but the effort can bring its own personal, academic, and professional rewards.

A journal requires you to set rules for yourself. First, you should decide how often you will make an entry and stick to your schedule. Second, you should set a loose theme for your journal to maintain some focus. Third, date your journal entries to measure your progress. Finally, you should be willing to break your rules when prudent; the important thing is to enjoy the practice. Before you know it, keeping a journal will become a habit, and you will gain in invaluable source for your writing and personal growth. The example below exemplifies a typical journal entry for a college student:

August 11, 2010
①I missed the first class of my college career. I was already nervous as I wandered among the big building with the imposing columns. When I went into one of them and sat down in the back of the class, I felt some relief, but when the professor welcomed us to Zoology 101, I knew with horror I was in the wrong place, probably not even in the right building. I felt like a moron, so I just sat there pretending I was supposed to be in there. Nobody seemed to have their books yet, so I just snuck glances around the room—looking at the clock, all the students already taking notes, and the exit which seemed to laugh at me②He kept going on about phylums and speices and mitochondria and some other junk while I felt a a cold sweat drip down my armpits. God, I still had thirty minutes to go. I looked around and noticed some guy throw stuff in his backpack. Acting as bored as he was, I collected my things and avoided all eye-contact, focusing on the smirking exit. I heard a pause in the professors voice but kept moving. Once out the door, I quickend my pace, and wandered into the bright sunlight. Campus was empty because everyone else seemed to know what they were doing. I wound up dropping the class I was suppose to be in to avoid any further humiliation. Jeez, that was the first and worst day so far.

Notice that the author did not overly concern herself with grammar and sentence structure, especially as she immersed herself in the content of her entry. Much like freewriting, the focus is on content.

Talking—Just to Hear Yourself Think

Something we do every day without a thought of its purpose is **talking**, engaging in conversation with others. When you do it for the purpose of prewriting, you can get feedback from others that will help you find your topic, direction, and support for a given writing assignment. Imagine a conversation you and your classmates have shared with a friend a hundred times, but this time you are talking with purpose. The example below shows Ashley talking with her friend in search of a specific topic.

Ashley: I have to write a paragraph on what I like or don't like about writing.
Friend: That sounds hard. Are you supposed to write about both your likes and dislikes or one or the other?
Ashley: You have to choose.
Friend: Which way are you going?
Ashley: Of course, I am going to go with what I don't like. That will be much easier.
Friend: It's always easier to be negative, but what good is that?
Ashley: I figure if I can talk about the negative stuff I can figure out why I don't like writing.
Friend: Writing makes you think.
Ashley: Yes, and it has a lot of rules. Why do we have to have those?
Friend: Isn't that so others can understand what you are thinking?
Ashley: I guess so. I should probably write this down.

Notice that talking is much like questioning, except in this instance the dialogue is external. See if you can find the basic questions or the other forms of prewriting in this conversation.

The Media—Our Common Bond

The media is any form of mass communication—the internet, television, radio, music, literature, and periodicals. You can think of these as the sources of a national, even international, conversation we are all having. From the media, you can find an infinite inspiration for topics. The difficult thing about the media is knowing whom to listen to.

WARNING: The media provide information from other people's writing, regardless of whether written or spoken. You should never use someone else's words and ideas without giving full credit to your source. This is considered plagiarism (see Chapter 2: Moving from Sentences to Paragraphs.)

PREWRITING—A RECAP

Although prewriting is but a small step toward completing a viable essay or even paragraph, it is an essential one. Prewriting is the process of discovering ideas and the relationships between them. It is also a crucial step toward producing specific details that make your writing interesting and useful. The following items mark the first steps in the writing process:

1. **Prewriting**, getting ideas on paper, begins with your own observations and experiences.

2. Prewriting involves three steps:

   a. Searching for **topic**, your subject or what you are writing about.

   b. Finding **direction**, your opinion of your subject.

   c. Gathering **support**, the details that reinforce your topic and direction.

3. You can get started writing in several ways:

   a. **Freewriting** is the act of writing for ten to fifteen minutes without stopping or worrying about grammar.

   b. **Questioning** asks the who, what, when, where, why, and how about a rough topic.

   c. **Brainstorming** allows you to list your ideas.

   d. **Keeping a journal**, starting and maintaining a habit of informal writing about aspects of your life, provides you with a wealth of potential ideas.

   e. **Talking** with others can give you feedback on your work and inspire ideas.

   f. Borrowing from the **media**, the source of the world's conversation, is something that you can tap into.

ORGANIZATION—PUTTING YOUR THOUGHTS IN ORDER

Prewriting for topic, direction, and support helps you begin get your ideas on paper, but practicing some simple organization techniques can help you discover the full extent of the relationships between these ideas and even flesh them out. **Organization** is the order in which you discuss your topic, direction, and support through a prescribed form, such as a paragraph or essay, that emphasizes your purpose. Paragraphs and essays can be organized in two ways: clustering and outlining. **Clustering** is usually the precursor to the more formal outline, and it can also be an aid to prewriting. This bridge between prewriting and organizing maps your writing by circling ideas on paper and connecting them with lines to show their relationships to one another. Like a skeleton, **outlining** lists your ideas in order of importance and establishes the framework of a paragraph or essay. Organization is the final step in the writing process before drafting.

Clustering—Getting Ideas into Groups

The most basic type of organization, known as clustering, does what its name implies—puts together your ideas in a way that allows you to see the links between them. As you will discover, the stages of the writing process often have blurred borders. Clustering, which can be used for prewriting and organization, is a prime example of this gray area. This form of mapping your writing can help you both prewrite *and* organize for topic, direction, and support.

Clustering for a Topic—Finding the Common Link

Look at the brainstorm for a topic used earlier in the chapter put in cluster form. See if you can figure out what the topics all have in common:

When the brainstorm appears merely as a list, the common link between the ideas is not always clear, yet when put in a cluster, the writer can easily see that the topics fit into one category—aspects of the internet. The writer has found his general interest but knows that a paragraph or essay cannot adequately cover such a broad topic. He starts a new cluster centered around cyber friends, but this time she is looking for direction.

When clustering his brainstorm for direction, the author notices that some directions seem to be closely related while some have no link to the others at all. He also realizes that most of his ideas are not as closely related to cyber friends as they are to what he considers the negative aspects of social network services. Since most of his clusters for direction seem to be discussing the negative aspects of social network services, he decides that will be his primary direction. From this point, he can begin a third cluster for support with a more specific topic and direction in mind.

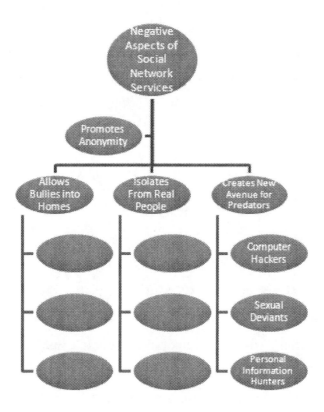

Notice that, as a result of his clustering, the author has also been organizing his writing. He even finds more support through this process and knows that he can categorize entire groups of subtopics. Most surprisingly, he finds he can move to a new more specific central topic if needed or develop what he thought was only going to be a paragraph into an essay. The writer is surprised to find, in fact, that he has come up with a topic in which he is much more interested, and he knows he will have to do some more prewriting on this new topic. After more clustering, the student is ready to organize his work more formally so that he can begin drafting: he is ready make an outline.

NOTE: Writing is not a linear movement, but a zig-zag back and forth, from beginning to end. The steps of the writing process are not rigid procedures but guidelines that overlap to enable the process of discovery.

Exercise 4

Choose from one of the prompts below, and on a separate sheet of paper, prewrite and organize using clusters for specific topic, direction, and support. Notice how the process draws out and orders the relationships between your ideas.

text messages	staying up late
driving	bicycling

The Outline—Making a List and Checking It Twice

An outline takes the cluster one step further by not only organizing the central idea and its subtopics by their relationships but also determining what order these topics will be presented in a paragraph or essay format. Just as the cluster is a blend of prewriting and organization, the outline is a mix of organization and **drafting**, putting your writing in sentence form. Since academic writing is organized around paragraphs and essays, definitions of these forms of writing and some of their parts should make the outline easier to understand. More detailed explanations of paragraphs and essays will be discussed in chapters 2 and 3.

Paragraph Outline—Ordering the Parts

A **paragraph** is a block of writing of seven to thirteen sentences that focuses on a limited subject. An outline for a paragraph includes a rough **topic sentence**, the first sentence in a paragraph that explains what the paragraph is about, and all supporting points for that topic sentence. An outline for a paragraph that you have been prewriting and clustering looks like the template below:

PARAGRAPH OUTLINE TEMPLATE

I. **Topic Sentence**

    a. **Support 1**

    b. **Support 2**

    c. **Support 3**

In the p   ken his topic, negative aspects of socia   e familiar with.

    I.   T   vices such as Facebook

      a   o connect friends, they

      se   between these friends.

      a.   acronyms and shorter

      b.

      c.

NOTE: *precursor to drafting does no*   *se forms of writing. At these st*   *u have at the time. In the following ch*   *complete structure of paragraphs and e*

Essay Outline—

A basic **es**   n a broader but still specific subject.   **tement,** the central idea around whic   **body paragraphs,** the paragraphs in   esis statement; and supporting points for the body paragraphs. An outline for an essay looks like the following example:

ESSAY OUTLINE TEMPLATE

  I.   **Thesis Statement**

  II.   **Topic Sentence 1**

      a. **Support 1**

      b. **Support 2**

      c. **Support 3**

  III.   **Topic Sentence 2**

      a. **Support 1**

      b. **Support 2**

      c. **Support 3**

  IV.   **Topic Sentence 3**

      a. **Support 1**

      b. **Support 2**

      c. **Support 3**

The outline is especially useful for longer pieces of writing, such as essays, in which the writer is more likely to stray or fumble for examples. If the author working on his cyber friends paragraph needs to expand his topic for an essay, he might construct something like the outline below:

Working Title: Spider's Web

I. Thesis Statement: Despite the revolutionary advances society has made through the internet, this technology has also spawned negative side effects on culture such as loss of privacy, personal isolation, and abuse.

II. Topic Sentence 1: The World Wide Web has brought the world closer together but at the sacrifice or personal privacy.

    a. Support 1: personal records

    b. Support 2: search engines

    c. Support 3: messenger sites

II. Topic Sentence 2: The internet has isolated people from actual face to face contact.
    a.   Support 1: too convenient
    b.   Support 2: socially inept surfers
    c.   Support 3: loss of personal identity
IV. Topic Sentence 3: As with all things humanity interacts with, the internet is abused.
    a.   Support 1: degradation of the English language
    b.   Support 2: addiction

    c.   Support 3: bullying and predators

ORGANIZING—A RECAP

Organization is officially the second stage in the writing process but can also include prewriting and drafting. The following characteristics of organization should help the writer order his thoughts and help him prepare a rough draft:

1. **Clustering** is the act of laying your ideas out on paper, circling them, and connecting them with lines to draw out their relationships. Clustering often inspires new ideas and topics and could, therefore, also be considered an advanced form of prewriting.

2. **Outlining** is the process of putting your thoughts in the order they will appear in your writing and organizing them into rough paragraph or essay form. Outlining requires complete sentences for the topic sentence of a paragraph and the thesis statement and topic sentences of an essay.

Exercise 5

Using the information you gathered from Exercise 4, construct an outline for a paragraph. Write a complete sentence for the topic sentence and list your supporting details in the order you think they should appear.

_____

_____

_____

_____

_____

_____

_____

_____

_____

DRAFTING—PUTTING YOUR ORGANIZED THOUGHTS IN SENTENCE FORM

Once the framework of a paragraph or essay is established through an outline, you can finally begin drafting. **Drafting** is the act of putting your ideas in sentence form and organizing your sentences into paragraphs or essays. When writing a first draft, you should not be as concerned with sentence structure, grammar, or punctuation as completing a rough draft of your entire paragraph or essay. If you get stuck on one part, move to the next section and go back to it later. Your primary focus should be on the topic sentence and support if you are writing a paragraph and a thesis statement, topic sentences, and support if you are writing an essay. The important thing is to keep writing and remain open to any details not discovered in your prewriting and organizing that drafting may inspire.

Notice the example draft below has mistakes and much refinement is still necessary, but the basic form of our student's paragraph is now on paper. He is ready to move to the next step in the writing process, revision.

Although social networking services such as Facebook and MySpace are revolutionary in their ability to connect friends and familuy, they seem to reduce the depth of conversation shared between these friends. When they speak to one another through an instant message or an email the conversations are usually short and limited to immediate plans or silly jokes. The form of communication, itself, encourages abbreviated spelling and discussions of only two or three exchanges. Sitting at a computer or staring at a cell phone is a poor substitute for a face to face conversation, and there is no guarantee that the person you think you are talking to is really on the other end or whether your talk is private or bweing viewed by entire groups of people you don't necessarily want knowing your business.

Exercise 6

Turn the outline you created in Exercise 5 into a complete draft of a paragraph. Remember to focus on completing the work with an adequate topic sentence and support rather than being concerned with grammar and structural errors.

_____

_____

_____

_____

_____

_____

_____

_____

_____

_____

REVISION—SEEING DOUBLE

Revision, reviewing your work to make it clear, logical, and well supported, is probably the stage in writing in which most of the work is done. As often occurs in the earlier steps in the process, revision may reveal the need to do some more prewriting, organizing, and drafting. Remember, each step in the writing process builds on the others and incorporates them.

Revising for Unity and Development—Maintain and Support One Idea

The first time you sit down to look at a draft with the aim of revising, focus on one or two aspects of the work that you want to improve. Many writers direct their attention to the topic sentence and support of a paragraph for their first revision. Again, ignore issues with grammar, punctuation, and spelling for the time being. After all, major revisions often add and remove entire sentences and sections, so fixing any misspelled words or throwing in a few commas may, in the end, be a waste of time at this stage.

When the author of the cyber friends paragraph reviews his first draft, he notices that he lacks much needed supporting details. He attempts to add these crucial details, but then he observes that although he has items of **major support**, details that extend the meaning of the topic sentence, he has virtually no **minor support**, or examples, for them. Writing without adequate support indicates a lack of **development**. For each item of major support he includes, he also needs parallel minor supporting details. In other words, each of his examples should include at least two sentences: one for major support and one for minor support.

As the author reviews his first revision (shown below), he also notices that some sentences seem to have nothing to do with his topic or direction. Therefore, he has a problem with unity. **Unity** means that all support directly relates to the topic sentence of a paragraph. In the case of an essay, all body paragraphs directly relate to the thesis statement, and the supporting details of each body paragraph directly relate the respective topic sentence.

Look at the author's first revision below and find the issues with unity and lack of development. Which sentences do not relate to the topic sentence, and which areas could use further development?

> Although instant messages are revolutionary in their ability to connect friends and familuy, they seem to reduce the depth of conversation shared between these friends. When they speak to one another through one of these forms of communication, the conversations are short and self-serving. I hate it when my cell phone dies in the middle of a text message conversation. The form of communication, itself, encourages abbrevieated spelling and discussions of only two or three exchanges. My brother texted me the other day. He expected me to know why my mother was angry and seemed to be removing himself from all culpability for a situation between us that resulted in a ruined rug. All meaning in the message was implicit, and it was meaningless to anyone else. Sitting at a computer or staring at a cell phone is a poor substitute for a face to face conversation. Had my brother actually sat down and discussed possible solutions to the problem, I might have avoided punishment and a strong desire for revenge against Mark. My only option through the text was to reply sarcastically. There is no guarantee that the person you think you are talking to is really on the other end or whether your talk is private or bweing viewed by entire groups of people you don't necessarily want knowing your business. "Be home by three o'clock p.m., young man!" was the response I shortly received. I could tell by the syntax and spelling that my brother's phone was now in the hands of one of my parents. My parents are not to be trifled with.

Revising for Coherence—Making Sense

Revising for unity and development can greatly improve a piece of writing, but more revision is obviously necessary before the writer of the cyber friends paragraph can hope for a decent grade. In the example below, you should note that the topic sentence is much more focused, and specific examples, including both major and minor supporting details, have been included for additional support and interest. Nevertheless, the writing still lacks **coherence**, the logical progression of one idea to another for readability. By focusing on coherence, our writer concentrates on four other aspects that will make his writing more clear and establish a rhythm:

FOUR ASPECTS OF COHERENCE

1. **Transitions**—words or phrases that link ideas. Without transitions, the paragraph is essentially a list.

2. **Sentence Variety**—changing the patterns of sentences to make writing interesting and flow smoothly.

3. **Repetition of key words and phrases**—duplicating words and phrases such as those that represent the main idea to emphasize a point.

4. **Concluding sentence**—a final sentence in a paragraph that brings a sense of closure to the writer's thoughts and reiterates the paragraph's or essay's purpose. The concluding sentence must restate the topic sentence or thesis statement in a new and interesting way that gives the reader a second perspective on the central idea. An essay will have its own conclusion as well; the details of an essay's conclusion are discussed in Chapter 3.

 NOTE: Simple transition words and phrases usually include subordinating words and prepositions. Students often try to use coordinating conjunctions (for, and, nor, but, or yet, so) as transitions, but these words are ineffective for this purpose. Do not use them as transitions.

Consider the changes the writer has made that improve unity and development in his second revision below, but look for weaknesses in coherence.

Instant messages seem to reduce the depth of conversation shared between them and sometimes cause confusion and problems. When members of a household "text" one another, the conversations are usually short and self-serving. When the form of communication, itself, encourages abbrevieated spelling and discussions of only two or three exchanges, you must consider your own interests first. My brother texted me the other day with this message: "LMAO, moms mad btw." He expected me to know why my mother was angry and seemed to remove himself from all culpability for a situation between us that resulted in a ruined rug. All meaning in the message was implicit and meaningless to anyone else but loaded with danger for me. The frustration I felt at being reduced to discussing this grave situation through IM made me intensely aware that staring at a cell phone is a poor substitute for a face to face conversation. I angrily considered that had my brother actually sat down with me and discussed possible solutions to the problem, I might have avoided punishment and a strong desire for revenge against Mark. My only option was to reply sarcastically, "Thx a lot." I then quickly learned there is no guarantee that the person you think you are talking to is really on the other end or even that your discussion is private or bweing viewed by entire groups of people you don't necessarily want knowing your business. "Be home by three o'clock p.m., young lady!" was the response I shortly received. I could tell by the syntax and spelling that my brother's phone was now in the hands of one of my parents. Many problems can be avoided by simply sitting down with someone in person, or at least, picking up the phone and doing a little old fashioned speaking.

REVISION—A RECAP

The majority of the work that goes into writing is in the process of revising. Revising gives you a second and third look at your work with an eye out major weaknesses. The characteristics below mark a well-revised paragraph or essay, preparing the way for editing:

1. A **unified** work ensures all support directly relates to the topic sentence or thesis statement and the topic sentence or thesis statement adequately summarizes the support provided.

2. A **developed** work provides adequate support, details reinforce the topic sentence or thesis statement.

3. A **coherent** work guarantees the writing makes senses through the logical and clear progression of ideas. Coherence is provided in four ways:

a. Transitions are words and phrases that link ideas between sentences.

b. Sentence variety is changing the pattern of sentences to establish a rhythm and make the writing flow smoothly.

c. Key words and phrases are repeated to emphasize ideas.

d. A **concluding sentence** gives closure to the writer's thoughts by restating the topic sentence or thesis statement in a new way.

Exercise 7

Revise the draft of the paragraph you drafted for Exercise 6 twice in the spaces provided below. For your first revision, focus on unity and development. For your second revision, concentrate on eliminating issues with coherence.

(unity and development)

_____

_____

_____

_____

_____

_____

_____

_____

_____

(coherence)

_____

_____

_____

_____

_____

_____

_____

_____

_____

_____

EDITING—SWEATING THE SMALL STUFF

Although a second revision makes the paragraph flow much more smoothly and provides definite closure, sentence structure and punctuation must still be improved for greater clarity. However, at this stage, the lines begin to blur between revision and editing. In what many consider the final stage of writing, **editing**, all issues of grammar, punctuation, and paragraph or essay structure are handled to be sure the writing is as clear and meaningful as possible.

Our writer is now doing all he can do on his own to prepare the paragraph for an audience. A good writer takes his reader by the hand and carefully leads him to the main point through a series of smaller points and entertaining examples. Although the paragraph below is well supported and is structurally sound, it still contains errors in grammar and punctuation. See if you can find and correct these errors.

Instant messages are revolutionary in their ability to connect friends and family; however, they seem to reduce the depth of conversation shared between them and sometimes cause confusion and problems. When members of a household "text" one another, the conversations are usually short and self-serving. After all, when the form of communication, itself, encourages abbrevieated spelling and discussions of only two or three exchanges, you must consider your own interests first. For example, my brother texted me the other day with this message: "LMAO, moms mad btw." From this broken phrase, he expected me to know why my mother was angry and seemed to remove himself from all culpability for a situation between us that resulted in a ruined rug. All meaning in the message was implicit and meaningless to anyone else but loaded with danger for me. The frustration I felt at being reduced to discussing this grave situation through IM made me intensely aware that staring at a cell phone is a poor substitute for a face to face conversation. At that moment I angrily considered that had my brother actually sat down with me and discussed possible solutions to the problem, I might have avoided punishment and a strong desire for revenge against Mark. Instead, my only option was to reply sarcastically, "Thx a lot." I then quickly learned there is no guarantee that the person you think you are talking to is really on the other end or even that your discussion is private or bweing viewed by entire groups of people you don't necessarily want knowing your business. "Be home by three o'clock p.m., young lady!" was the response I shortly received. I could tell by the syntax and spelling that my brother's phone was now in the hands of one of my parents. In the end, many problems can be avoided by simply sitting down with someone in person, or at least, picking up the phone and doing a little old fashioned speaking.

Finally, the once frustrated and overwhelmed student has taken some vague ideas he discovered in his prewriting and transformed them into a unified, coherent, developed, and entertaining paragraph. Although still far from perfect, his writing effectively communicates his ideas and is ready for a second pair of eyes to review. The example below is his final draft before peer review. Notice that even during the editing process, he still includes changes that make his writing more concise and clear.

> The revolution in technology has reduced the depth of conversation I share with my family and sometimes leads to negative consequences and confusion. When the individuals of my household "text" one another, we usually only engage in short and self-serving announcements. After all, when the form of communication, itself, encourages abbreviated spelling and discussions of only two or three exchanges, we must all consider our own interests first. For example, my brother, Mark, texted me the other day with this message: "LMAO, moms mad btw." From this broken phrase, he expected me to know why my mother was angry and seemed to remove himself from all responsibility for a situation between us that resulted in a ruined rug. All meaning in the message was implicit and meaningless to anyone else—but loaded with danger for me. The frustration I felt at being reduced to discussing this grave situation through an instant message made me intensely aware that staring at a cell phone is a poor substitute for a face to face conversation. At that moment, I realized my brother was avoiding sitting down with me and discussing possible solutions to the problem in order to save himself. If Mark had been more loyal, I might have avoided punishment and never formed the strong desire for revenge against him. For the time being, my only option was to reply sarcastically, "Thx a lot." With a new message, I quickly learned he was no longer the one at the other end of the conversation. "Be home by three o'clock p.m., young lady!" was the response I received. I could tell by the syntax and spelling that my brother's phone was now in the hands of one of my parents. I was doomed! In the end, many problems can be avoided by simply sitting down with someone in person, or at least, picking up the phone and doing a little old fashioned speaking.

Exercise 8

Edit and type the paragraph you have revised to make any improvements needed in grammar, punctuation, and formatting. Have it ready for class on the date given to you by your instructor.

PEER REVIEW—SUBMITTING YOUR WORK TO CONSTRUCTIVE CRITICISM

Getting someone else to review your work is essential. Regardless of whether or not this person is an expert in writing, he will know what sentences makes sense and what sentences do not, which ideas are clear and which are not, and what is fun and educational to read and what is tedious and without value. Being inside your own world of ideas and words can be so engrossing that a second perspective is necessary to be sure this world is clearly revealed on paper.

Many basic writing, composition, and upper level English courses schedule routine **peer reviews**. Under the instructor's guidance, students exchange their treasured documents and submit them to scrutiny. This can sometimes be a painful process, for having someone criticize something you worked so hard on is an apparently dismissive and cruel act on your teacher's part. Remember, though, that the point of a peer review is to help you improve your work. You, in turn, are also tasked with a serious responsibility—helping your peers succeed in the course through constructive criticism that enables them to go back to the stages of writing and refine their work.

 NOTE: Many students do not feel worthy to inspect another's work. After all, they too are just learning. Your instructor is aware of this fact and should establish clear guidelines and tips for you to consider. Use these tips to help you become useful in a peer review:

1. *Before reviewing someone's work, for example, carefully analyze the original assignment and any questions or points that the teacher gives you for the peer review.*

2. *Do not try to correct someone else's work; that is not your job. Instead, it can often make a bad situation worse. Remember that a peer review is a discussion of the work.*

3. *Review the work in stages much as you move through the writing process.*

   a. *A paragraph: Determine whether the topic sentence adequately summarizes the paragraph.*

      An essay: Be sure the thesis statement adequately summarizes the essays and previews its main points.

   b. *A paragraph: Review the support to see whether it all relates to the topic sentence.*

      An essay: Review all body paragraphs to be certain they relate to the thesis statement and their respective topic sentences.

   c. *A paragraph: Look at the support and ask yourself whether enough detail, both major and minor, has made it into the paragraph.*

      An essay: Be sure all body paragraphs are adequately and equally supported. Also, be certain to include the necessary details for a strong introduction and conclusion (see chapter 3).

d. *Examine the work for issues with coherence.*

e. *Identify issues with grammar, punctuation, and diction. Even if you are not sure what exactly the problem is, circle it and discuss any potential signs of trouble you see with the author.*

Exercise 9

Exchange the paragraph you edited for Exercise 8 with another student in your class. Under your instructor's guidance and using the guidelines provided above, review your classmate's paragraph. Be sure to ask questions and avoid correcting what you perceive as errors; instead, circle questionable areas and discuss the work with whoever is reviewing your work. Once the peer review is complete, make any new changes you feel are necessary.

Working with Writing Tutors and Instructors—Successful Writers

Once you have had your paper reviewed by a peer, you may be required or encouraged to take it to a tutor or even your instructor. **Tutors** are students who have already passed the class you are now taking, are familiar with your instructor's methods, and can give a more educated opinion of the quality of your work. This does not mean they are experts. They cannot give your writing the thorough examination an instructor can, but they can be invaluable to you during any stage of the writing process. They are providing a service you are already paying for through your tuition, so take advantage of the opportunity. When you do schedule an appointment in a writing lab, come prepared:

1. Bring at least a completed rough draft, your assignment, and your text book.

2. Do not sit idly back and wait for them to fix your writing. Tutors are not editors; they are facilitators of the learning process. Together, with active participation from both parties, you can find your weaknesses and improve your writing.

3. No matter who reviews the work with you, however, understand that the writing is your responsibility alone.

4. Keep in mind that three or four tutors may be all the department has on hand to support hundreds of students. Schedule an appointment with them early on when given an assignment, and be prepared to make follow-up appointments for more help.

Your instructor can be your greatest ally in writing a successful paper. All college level instructors keep weekly office hours, and you will find most of them eager to help you improve. In lieu of scheduled peer reviews, many instructors hold workshops. **Workshops** are class periods that are set aside solely for the purpose of letting you work on your paragraph or essay under your teacher's guidance. As with tutor sessions, come prepared with a draft of your essay and specific questions about your work.

Exercise 10

Bring the paragraph you have polished following the peer review to a Basic Writing tutor. Come prepared with at least one specific question about your work and acquire documentation that verifies your appointment and the areas of your writing that were discussed. Make any changes to your paragraph you feel are needed as a result of your session and prepare a final draft to be collected and graded by your instructor.

THE WRITING PROCESS—CONCLUSIONS

For many college students, especially freshmen, writing is a mysterious and often frustrating chore. Hopefully, this chapter has broken it into more digestible parts that can be tackled one at a time. That being said, you will often find yourself doing some prewriting in the organization stage or drafting in the stages of revision and editing. You may even find yourself lacking concrete ideas or support after submitting to a peer review and find yourself going back to the start. One essential key to good writing is giving yourself time. Consider all the writing and rewriting that went into the brief paragraph the basic writer used in this chapter's examples. What would be the result without struggling through the writing process and giving himself the time to do it? You too need time to circle through the stages and let the work come out and become something of which you can be proud.

Writing is an essential process in critical thinking. It can allow you to tap into hidden inner resources and elucidate your thoughts. Give yourself the time you need to bring your ideas to light. Use the tools given to you in this class to become a critical thinker and, therefore, a better writer. Writing is a general requirement of this university and those across the country for a reason. Although the primary focus of many students is to get a degree to get a good job, universities demand that students become at least competent writers, historians, scientists, and mathematicians so that they become informed, balanced contributors to society.

ROGER ROSENBLATT—"I AM WRITING BLINDLY"

Besides the newsworthy revelation of Lieut. Captain Dimitri Kolesnikov's dying message to his wife recovered from the husk of the sunken submarine *Kursk*—that 23 of the 118 crewmen had survived in an isolated chamber for a while, in contradiction to claims by Russian officials that all had perished within minutes of the accident—there was the matter of writing the message in the first place.

In the first place, in the last place, that is what we people do—write messages to one another. We are a narrative species. We exist by storytelling—by relating our situations – and the test of our evolution may lie in getting the story right.

What Kolesnikov did in deciding to describe his position and entrapment, others have also done – in states of repose or terror. When a JAL airliner went down in 1985, passengers used the long minutes of its terrible, spiraling descent to write letters to loved ones. When the last occupants of the Warsaw Ghetto had finally seen their families and companions die of disease or starvation, or be carried off in trucks to extermination camps, and there could be no doubt of their own fate, still they took scraps of paper on which they wrote poems, thoughts, fragments of lives, rolled them into tight scrolls, and slipped them into the crevices of the ghetto walls.

Why did they bother? With no countervailing news from the outside world, they assumed the Nazis had inherited the earth; that if anyone discovered their writings, it would be their killers, who would snicker and toss them away. They wrote because, like Kolesnikov, they had to. The impulse was in them, like a biological fact.

So enduring is this storytelling need that it shapes nearly every human endeavor. Businesses depend on the stories told of past failures and successes and on the myth of the mission of the company. In medicine, doctors increasingly rely on a patient's narrative of the progress of an ailment, which is inevitably more nuanced and useful than the data of machines. In law, the same thing. Every court case is a competition of tales told by the prosecutor and defense attorney; the jury picks the one it likes best.

All these activities derive from essential places in us. Psychologist Jerome Bruner said children acquire language in order to tell the stories that are already in them. We do our learning through storytelling processes. The man who arrives at our door is thought to be a salesman because his predecessor was a salesman. When the patternmaking faculties fail, the brain breaks down. Schizophrenics suffer from a loss of story.

The deep proof of our need to spill, and keep on spilling, lies in reflex, often in desperate circumstances. A number of years ago, Jean-Dominique Bauby, the editor of *Elle* magazine, was felled by a stroke so destructive that the only part of his body that could move was his left eyelid. Flicking that eyelid, he managed to signal the letters of the alphabet, and proceeded to write his autobiography, *The Diving Bell and the Butterfly*, with the last grand gesture of his life.

All of this is of acute and consoling interest to writers, whose odd existences are ordinarily strung between asking why we do it and doing it incessantly. The explanation I've been able to come up with has to do with freedom. You write a sentence, the basic unit of storytelling, and you are never sure where it will lead. The readers will not know where it leads either. Your adventure becomes theirs, eternally recapitulated in tandem—one wild ride together. Even when you come to the end of the sentence, that dot, it is still strangely inconclusive. I sometimes think one writes to find God in every sentence. But God (the ironist) always lives in the next sentence.

It is this freedom of the message sender and receiver that connects them— sailor to wife, the dying to the living. Writing has been so important in America, I think, because communication is the soul and engine of democracy. To write is to live according to one's terms. If you ask me to be serious, I will be frivolous. Magnanimous? Petty. Cynical? I will be a brazen believer in all things. Whatever you demand I will not give you—unless it is with the misty hope that what I give you is not what you ask for but what you want.

We use this freedom to break the silence, even of death, even when – in the depths of our darkest loneliness – we have no clear idea of why we reach out to one another with these frail, perishable chains of words. In the black chamber of the submarine, Kolesnikov noted, "I am writing blindly." Like everyone else.

Rosenblatt, Roger. "I Am Writing Blindly." *Time* (6 Nov. 2000). Rpt. in *The Prose Reader: Essays for Thinking, Reading, and Writing*. 9th ed. Eds. Kim Flachmann and Michael Flachmann. Boston: Pearson, 2011. 538-9. Print.

Discussion Questions for "Writing Blindly"

1. Rosenblatt states that "we are a narrative species," that communication via writing is instinctive in us, "like a biological fact." Do you agree with this claim? Why or why not?

2. Why do we bother? In those times when we absolutely have to tell someone something, why do we rely on writing, even its most primitive forms such as the text message or the brief email, the post-it, or even the cocktail napkin?

3. The author writes, "I sometimes think one writes to find God in every sentence. But God (the ironist) always lives in the next sentence." What is irony, and in what context is Rosenblatt using the term in his own writing? How does this relate to your experience in writing?

4. Rosenblatt calls writing "the soul and engine of democracy." What about writing makes it so important to this particular form of government? Is America a true democracy in the sense that Rosenblatt discusses the theory?

5. What is Rosenblatt's overall purpose? Why did he write this essay?

6. At the beginning of a semester of basic writing when students are asked to write their diagnostic essays, they often espouse their hatred of or insecurity with writing, yet this form of communication, as the author asserts, is a basic, even primal need we all share. What exactly are the roots of your fears and insecurities with formal academic writing? Are these obstacles something you are determined to overcome? Explain your answer.

MARY SHERRY—"IN PRAISE OF THE 'F' WORD"

Tens of thousands of 18-year-olds will graduate this year and be handed meaningless diplomas. These diplomas won't look any different from those awarded their luckier classmates. Their validity will be questioned only when their employers discover that these graduates are semiliterate.

Eventually a fortunate few will find their way into educational-repair shops—adult-literacy programs, such as the one where I teach basic grammar and writing. There, high-school graduates and high-school dropouts pursuing graduate-equivalency certificates will learn the skills they should have learned in school. They will also discover they have been cheated by our educational system.

As I teach, I learn a lot about our schools. Early in each session I ask my students to write about an unpleasant experience they had in school. No writers' block here! "I wish someone would have had made me stop doing drugs and made me study." "I liked to party and no one seemed to care." "I was a good kid and didn't cause any trouble, so they just passed me along even though I didn't read and couldn't write." And so on.

I am your basic do-gooder, and prior to teaching this class I blamed the poor academic skills our kids have today on drugs, divorce and other impediments to concentration necessary for doing well in school. But, as I rediscover each time I walk into the classroom, before a teacher can expect students to concentrate, he has to get their attention, no matter what distractions may be at hand. There are many ways to do this, and they have much to do with teaching style. However, if style alone won't do it, there is another way to show who holds the winning hand in the classroom. That is to reveal the trump card of failure.

I will never forget a teacher who played that card to get the attention of one of my children. Our youngest, a world-class charmer, did little to develop his intellectual talents but always got by. Until Mrs. Stifter.

Our son was a high-school senior when he had her for English. "He sits in the back of the room talking to his friends," she told me. "Why don't you move him to the front row?" I urged, believing the embarrassment would get him to settle down. Mrs. Stifter looked at me steely-eyed over her glasses."I don't move seniors," she said. "I flunk them." I was flustered. Our son's academic life flashed before my eyes. No teacher had ever threatened him with that before. I regained my composure and managed to say that I thought she was right. By the time I got home I was feeling pretty good about this. It was a radical approach for these times, but, well, why not? "She's going to flunk you," I told my son. I did not discuss it any further. Suddenly English became a priority in his life. He finished out the semester with an A.

I know one example doesn't make a case, but at night I see a parade of students who are angry and resentful for having been passed along until they could no longer even pretend to keep up. Of average intelligence or better, they eventually quit school, concluding they were too dumb to finish. "I should have been held back," is a comment I hear frequently. Even sadder are those students who are high-school graduates who say to me after a few weeks of class, "I don't know how I ever got a high-school diploma."

Passing students who have not mastered the work cheats them and the employers who expect graduates to have basic skills. We excuse this dishonest behavior by saying kids can't learn if they come from terrible environments. No one seems to stop to think that—no matter what environments they come from—most kids don't put school first on their list unless they perceive something is at stake. They'd rather be sailing.

Many students I see at night could give expert testimony on unemployment, chemical dependency, abusive relationships. In spite of these difficulties, they have decided to make education a priority. They are motivated by the desire for a better job or the need to hang on to the one they've got. They have a healthy fear of failure.

People of all ages can rise above their problems, but they need to have a reason to do so. Young people generally don't have the maturity to value education in the same way my adult students value it. But fear of failure, whether economic or academic, can motivate both. Flunking as a regular policy has just as much merit today as it did two generations ago. We must review the threat of flunking and see it as it really is--a positive teaching tool. It is an expression of confidence by both teachers and parents that the students have the ability to learn the material presented to them. However, making it work again would take a dedicated, caring conspiracy between teachers and parents. It would mean facing the tough reality that passing kids who haven't learned the material—while it might save them grief for the short term—dooms them to long-term illiteracy. It would mean that teachers would have to follow through on their threats, and parents would have to stand behind them, knowing their children's best interests are indeed at stake. This means no more doing Scott's assignments for him because he might fail. No more passing Jodi because she's such a nice kid.

This is a policy that worked in the past and can work today. A wise teacher, with the support of his parents, gave our son the opportunity to succeed—or fail. It's time we return this choice to all students.

Sherry, Mary. "In Praise of the 'F' Word." *Newsweek* 6 May 1991: 117-18. *Academic Search Premier.* Web.

Discussion Questions for "In Praise of the 'F' Word"

1. Sherry hooks her reader with the statistic that "[t]ens of thousands of 18-year-olds will graduate this year and be handed meaningless diplomas." What does she mean by this? What value do you place on your own high school diplomas? What value do you believe your college diplomas will hold?

2. What does it mean to be semi-literate? Do you believe you were adequately prepared for college level writing in high school or other classes you have taken? Do you believe you are semi-literate? Why or why not?

3. What is the main point of the essay? Can you find this main point explicitly stated anywhere in the text?

4. According to Sherry, what is wrong with passing students who have not mastered the material that earned them their diplomas? Do you agree with her assessment? Why or why not?

5. What is the "F" word? Do you think it is a valid source of motivation? What arguments does Sherry assert are valid reasons for failing students?

6. Recall the anecdote that Sherry brings into her essay about meeting a teacher who explained how she dealt with inadequate work and inappropriate behavior in the class room—"'I don't move seniors,' she said, 'I flunk them.'" Have you encountered this situation with a past teacher of your own? If you have, did it motivate you to improve? If you have not been in this situation, would this approach have motivated you to work harder?

7. Sherry wrote her essay in 1991. Do you think the problems she addresses are worse or better today? Explain your answer.

CHAPTER 2

MOVING FROM SENTENCES TO PARAGRAPHS

THE HUMBLE PARAGRAPH—WHAT IS IT?

If a sentence is an expression of thought, then a **paragraph** is the complete discussion of a limited subject through a series of sentences that serve the same idea. Whole in itself, the paragraph can stand alone, but it also often serves as the building block of all forms of **prose**, or the standard, conversational forms of speaking and writing. This basic unit is used to build essays, short stories, novels, and works of nonfiction. If you look at this book or any other, you will find that examples of these small but complete units of expression are the foundation of much larger ideas. They link together in a chain to inform, entertain, and argue much larger points. The paragraph is often greater than itself, meaning it is a piece of the puzzle that is the essence of clear communication, yet it is independent, a complete composition on its own. At first glance, this overview seems paradoxical, but consider how pervasive the concept of the paragraph is. This concept is not only the basis of writing but even rational thought.

Consider the paragraph in terms of the space you are in as you read this material. This might be the library, your dorm room, or a study hall. What elements in your area provide its theme? What makes a library, for example? The parts provided below could be used to define a library.

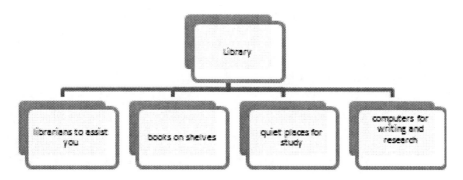

---

1 For more information on the definition and structure of sentences, see Unit II.

Each element, such as the shelved books, could be looked at as a **sentence**, one complete thought. Together, these elements complete the idea of the theme, subject, or topic—a library. From an even larger view, consider that the library is but one paragraph in a larger essay that is defining the idea of a college campus. Each building or department of the campus is also a paragraph that joins with the others to proclaim the concept of a university.

The Parts of a Paragraph

The idea of a paragraph is grand, even philosophic, but its role is basic. The function of a paragraph is to establish a clear subject, assert an opinion on the subject, adequately support the opinion, and conclude by reminding your reader of your subject. These functions are provided by the parts of the paragraph:

> **PARTS OF A PARAGRAPH:**
> 1. **Topic Sentence**
> 2. **Linking Sentence**
> 3. **Support**
> 4. **Concluding Sentence**

To break it down, a paragraph usually consists of seven to thirteen sentences that accomplish the following:

1. Identify a particular topic and direction through a topic sentence.

2. Link the topic sentence to the support through a transition or linking sentence.

3. Provide support for that direction.

4. Give examples to verify the support.

5. End with a closing sentence that restates the topic and direction.

NOTE: A paragraph of seven to thirteen sentences is a guideline, not a rule. What is important to understand is that a paragraph with sentences that have no relation to one another is merely a list. A paragraph without adequate support is too vague.

THE TOPIC SENTENCE—YOUR PARAGRAPH'S TRAVEL GUIDE

The topic sentence is the guide for your reader, letting him know what to expect as he travels through your writing. In short, the **topic sentence** summarizes or explains to your reader what the paragraph is about. This is crucial to keeping both you and your reader focused. Typically the first sentence of your paragraph, the topic sentence contains two key parts: topic and direction.

Topic and Direction—Your Destination and the Road to Your Destination

Both a clear topic and direction are necessary for a well-organized paragraph. The **topic** is the subject or idea you intend to discuss. The **direction** is your attitude or opinion of the subject. For example, if you were a commuter student writing a paragraph about your frustration over having to arrive on campus forty-five minutes early to find a parking spot, your topic would be the lack of parking available. The direction would be your frustration or anger about the lack of parking. When joining your topic to your direction, you might come up with a topic sentence like this one:

<u>**The lack of parking available at Rogers State University**</u> <u>**wastes my time.**</u>
             TOPIC   **DIRECTION**

Notice that the topic and direction in this topic sentence each can be identified as specific **parts of speech**, the elements that combine to express a complete thought. The topic contains the subject or a noun clause, and the direction contains the verb. Being able to identify the roles played by the parts of speech in a topic sentence can make it easier for you to determine whether your own topic sentences have all the parts necessary to begin a clear paragraph. This ability can also help you identify topics sentences in your reading.

WARNING: A topic sentence in Basic Writing and composition paragraphs should always be the first sentence. This placement demonstrates your understanding of the function and organization of this fundamental element of writing; however, more advanced writers may put their topic sentences in different areas of the paragraph, even at the end. Do not assume the first sentence of every paragraph you read is the topic sentence. Identify the topic sentence by its function and parts.

Exercise 1

Identify the topic and direction in the topic sentences below by underlining the topic once and the direction twice. Notice what parts of speech are identified in each.

Example: <u>Writing a complete paragraph</u> <u><u>takes time and patience.</u></u>

1. Bicycling helps me release tension and focus my thoughts.

2. Now that I know the parts of speech, I know how to write a complete sentence.

3. College requires much more personal responsibility than high school ever did.

4. *The Lord of the Rings* is my favorite fantasy series.

5. I learned that two plus two does not always equal four in philosophy.

6. Songs like "Shake that Laffy Taffy" prove that civilization is on the decline.

7. The clock in my room often makes me late for class.

8. Aside from color, all dishwashing soaps are the same.

9. I knew when Steve pushed my sister down that I would be in jail soon.

10. My English professor does not provide enough examples to make the material clear.

The Scope—Establishing the Boundaries of Your Topic Sentence

Remember a paragraph has a specific function to provide a complete discussion of a limited subject. A paragraph's **scope**, breadth, or range is determined by the topic sentence. A topic sentence that is too broad contains more than one subject or direction or states a fact will either exceed or not fulfill the scope of your paragraph.

First, a topic sentence that is **too broad** will not allow the writer to cover adequately the entire subject. For example, you could not possibly cover the possible causes of World War II in a paragraph or even an essay.

Second, a topic sentence that tries to cover **more than one subject** would confuse both the writer and his reader. If you write a topic sentence such as "Both Vans and Converse shoes appeal to nostalgia for the 1980s," you have two topics to discuss in a single paragraph. Although the two topics share shoe styles in common, neither of them can be sufficiently covered in one paragraph and would force your reader to jump back and forth between the two.

Third, a topic sentence that tries to cover **more than one direction** would be just as perplexing. Suppose you have written a topic sentence that covers two directions: "I like horror movies, but they give me nightmares." Although you may have both feelings about this type of movie, your direction is split causing your paragraph to be disjointed and confusing.

Finally, a topic sentence that is a **fact** or too narrow leaves no room for discussion. Take the following topic sentence, for instance: "As much as I want one, I cannot afford to buy a Mini-Cooper right now." Obviously, this is indisputable.

The only support you could provide is your bank statement and the sticker price of the car.

As mentioned earlier, a good topic sentence is your guide or anchor for your paragraph, giving it both a clear, singular topic and direction of a limited scope. Remember to sift through your prewriting to find one of each. Look at the prewriting below to refresh your memory:

- The trail was clear of obstructions.
- Since it was late spring, the air was still cool and breezy.
- The sun was out.
- The trees and flowers were in full bloom.

These ideas all speak of one particular place and the condition of that place and can be categorized into a topic sentence with one clear topic and direction that together become a comprehensive topic sentence.

As Laura and I stood at the entrance to Turkey Mountain, we realized we had a beautiful day of hiking ahead of us.

Exercise 2

Label the topic sentences below for one of the following errors: too broad, too many subjects, too many directions, or fact. If a topic sentence is of adequate scope, label it as "adequate scope."

Example: I have a meeting at noon.
FACT

1. A thesaurus and dictionary are both useful for Basic Writing.

2. Cell phones have changed the face of culture in many ways.

3. My favorite hobby is landscape photography.

4. Paleontologists have discovered that some dinosaurs thrived in cold climates.

5. I could not live without my computer or mp3 player.

6. The Bible is both enlightening and frightening to many parishioners.

7. Al Capone had his rivals killed on Valentine's Day of 1929.

8. Stem cell research could revolutionize medicine.

9. *The Catcher in the Rye* captures the essence of teen angst.

10. I like to study in the coffee shop at the library but am most comfortable writing at home.

THE TOPIC SENTENCE—A RECAP

As your paragraph's guide, the topic sentence is of utmost importance. All good topic sentences share these qualities:

1. They address **topic**, clearly stated in the topic sentence.
2. They provide a clear **direction**, which reveals a definite attitude or opinion of the topic.
3. They are restricted in **scope**, limiting the paragraph to one topic and direction, providing a topic that is not so broad it cannot be adequately covered in one paragraph, and consisting of a topic and direction that is not a mere statement of fact.

Exercise 3

Identify the topic and direction in the topic sentences below by underlining the topic once and the direction twice. Label the topic sentences below for one of the following errors: too broad, too many subjects, too many directions, or fact. If a topic sentence is of adequate scope, label it as "adequate scope."

Example: <u>Smoking is a hard habit to break</u>.
ADEQUATE SCOPE

1. My mother has been struck from behind in her car twice in the last two months.

2. Harry Potter and Gandalf are my two favorite wizards.

3. The trend of vampires in literature is baffling and ridiculous.

4. Keebler makes a good cracker.

5. The Renaissance is one of the most prolific periods of creativity in history.

THE LINKING SENTENCE—YOUR BRIDGE

Since the topic sentence, by nature, is the most general sentence in your paragraph and your support must be specific, you must include a **linking sentence** that bridges the gap between the two parts of your writing. Otherwise, your writing will be choppy, lacking coherence. Suppose you are writing about the poverty that is inherent in being a college student and want to write about how you deal with it to survive and accomplish your goals. You might come up with the following topic sentence:

> After two semesters of living at a subsistence level as a college student, I <u>have learned</u> <u>some tricks that allow me to thrive as a student.</u>

The support for this paragraph will probably consist of helpful examples of how the student lives on little money; however, the reader would need more details of the type of student this is before he can understand how to apply the lessons to his own situation. Without this information, the paragraph fails to address a specific audience and is too broad and, therefore, meaningless. A linking sentence, such as the one below, is needed to lead the reader smoothly from the topic sentence to the support.

After two semesters of living at a subsistence level as a college student, I have learned some tricks that allow me to thrive as a student. <u>I soon learned that sticking to a budget and, surprisingly, living in the dormitory both have their benefits.</u>

Now the reader knows the general lifestyle of the student and can decide for himself whether or not it is one he should adopt or whether the forthcoming information will be useful. Most importantly, the audience has been identified, and the evidence will have a context that gives it meaning.

Exercise 4

Write a linking sentence that would link the topic sentences below to the support that might be used for each of them.

Example: Often overlooked, the modest shrub marks the borders of our lives. ***It establishes property boundaries in an aesthetic way.***

1. Students use various methods to focus on their studies.
   _____
   _____
   _____

2. When Andrea saw the doctor's expression as he entered the waiting room, she knew her prognosis would not be good.
   _____
   _____
   _____

3. The number of sentences in a paragraph is not as important as its quality.
   _____
   _____
   _____

4. I need to learn to take better notes.
   _____
   _____
   _____

5. The supplemental reader to this course has improved my grammar.

_____

_____

_____

SUPPORT—WHAT MAKES YOUR WRITING USEFUL AND INTERESTING

Support, the details that comprise the body of your paragraph, is what makes writing entertaining and relatable to the reader's own experience. Without it, the ideas asserted i n the topic sentence are abstract with no practical application or substance. Worse yet, your writing is dull. A paragraph without adequate support is **undeveloped**.

Think of your topic sentence as an opinion or claim, an assertion that something is true or reasonable. You cannot expect your audience simply to take your word for this claim; you need evidence to support or back it up. For example, if you were to write a short paragraph about how the day was beautiful, you would have to back up this claim with evidence, undisputable and verifiable facts such as the sky is blue and cloudless; the temperature is a comfortable 72 degrees; a gentle breeze is blowing in from the south; and the birds are singing.

Of course, this is a simple demonstration, but these facts would support your claim that you have a nice day on your hands. Just as important, these facts bring your reader into the day with you. You are not just telling him about the day—you are showing it to him. You are allowing him to imagine this glorious day with you. Even at this basic level, your writing is interesting and useful.

Generating Support—Finding the Wellspring

One of the major issues Basic Writing students face is lack of support for paragraphs. For this reason, we writers should take a moment to consider where these examples come from. Most writers draw on their personal experience for support. After all, everyone is an expert on what he sees and hears and finds no shortage of it. Another source of support can be found in the observations of other people. As humans, we are social by nature and spend the majority of our days listening to the stories we tell one another about our experiences. A third source of support can be found media—in the television, movies, and novels we devour. These, after all, are only more (or less) sophisticated stories of personal experiences written by professionals. A fourth source of support is statistics and facts. By a certain age, we have all become experts, walking encyclopedias, on one subject or another and can use this information for support. When drawing from one or more these fountainheads of support, we find we have no excuse for not providing plenty of interesting details in our writing.

Personal Experience—Your Own Library

Personal experience is your own account, actions, and participation in the events you encounter daily. For Basic Writing, this should be your primary source of support for your paragraphs and essays. You can rest assured that any experiences that stick in your mind will be interesting to your reader. The topic sentence below, for example, would require its author to draw solely on personal experience:

> Visiting my sister and her children makes me wish for the peace and quiet of my own apartment.

What support is needed here? The chaos and clamor created by the sister's children would be needed. Examples of small children crying, banging pots and pans, activating noisy toys, and testing parents' boundaries would all provide support for the topic sentence and demonstrate the need for solitude.

Observations of Someone Else—Bearing Witness

Personal observations are the experiences you may witness or hear about but are not directly involved in. They are the events experienced by others. Again, these experiences have made an impression and will capture the attention of your reader:

> My brother, a radiology technician, relates his tales of grisly medical cases with relish.

You can imagine a sibling relating stories of exposed bone jutting from limbs and head wounds gushing blood and gray matter with a wry smile on his face while your own is white with terror. These would be all of the details needed to evoke the same feelings in your reader.

The Media—Our Common Source of Self-Superiority

Except for the technophobic hermit or the self-righteous scholar, most Americans spend more time than they would like to admit engaging with some form of mass communication. This **media** is any source that delivers information in spoken, visual, or written form, be it television, the internet, movies, music, or even a juicy novel. Although they vary in degrees of quality, these sources can all provide support for your writing and have become of a part of the popular culture your reader is well aware of. The topic sentence below is a clear demonstration of this fact:

> *Seinfeld* has produced many catch phrases that have become part of our vocabulary.

Most of us at some point have heard phrases like "yada yada yada," "re-gifter," "close-talker," "no soup for you," "bad-breaker-upper," and "not that there's anything wrong with that." Definitions and examples of their use could demonstrate a larger point about pop culture that would be interesting to you and your reader.

Facts and Statistics—Documented Evidence to Support Your Claim

Facts are indisputable certainties that can be verified with the senses. That you are reading this book is a fact, for example. Someone can watch you do it. Even more, this person can take a photograph of you doing it and test your knowledge. **Statistics** are mathematical interpretations of a series of events or phenomena. A quiz over the reading, for instance, can provide statistics for your instructor about how many students are doing their reading and retaining the material. Simply by reviewing the scores, a teacher can statistically gauge what percentage of the class is doing its work. An example of a topic sentence that relies on facts is provided below:

> Paul McCartney's announcement that he was quitting The Beatles signaled the end of the counter-culture movement.

To support this claim, the author must find evidence of how music, the prominent voice of culture at that time, changed. He would need examples of lyrics from The Beatles and compare them to those of emerging musicians such as Elton John, Billy Joel, and Harry Nilsson, who were more self-absorbed. The humble paragraph could illuminate the reader about the fickle nature of popular culture with such evidence.

WARNING: Sources such as the media and facts and statistics are considered outside sources. Any knowledge that you can link to a single source, you must document. In other words, if you quote, paraphrase, or summarize any specific outside sources, you must give full credit to them in an established format that allows the reader to find the information for himself. If you do not, you are committing **plagiarism**—*you are not giving full credit to your sources.*

That being said, much of the vernacular language we use in conversation has become common knowledge. Many facts and statistics have also been widely accepted. **Common knowledge** *is any information that has become so widespread or infused into your thinking that tracing it back to the original source would be impossible. This information is acceptable to use in your writing without documentation.*

On that note, this course is designed to help you become proficient in grammar usage and paragraph and essay writing. Since you will not be taught how to document sources properly until Composition I, you should either avoid using outside sources or seek your instructor's guidance before using any type of media, facts, or statistics as a source of support in your writing.

Exercise 5

For each of the topic sentences below, generate an example from personal experience, observations of others, the media, or facts and statistics. Be sure that the examples you come up with from the media and from facts and statistics are based on common knowledge.

Example: I knew I would have to keep the children entertained during the long ride to Colorado. <u>I began the trip by playing a game my father had played with me: Hawk. Each passenger would score a point for each hawk he or she spotted. This activity usually kept them occupied for at least a few hours.</u>
(personal experience)

1. Knowing how to dress properly is essential for a successful job interview.

   _____

   _____

   (personal experience)

2. My father prefers the company of horses to people.

   _____

   _____

   (observations of others)

3. I now use Facebook as my primary method of communication with friends and family.

   _____

   _____

   (media)

4. The iconic doll Barbie is grossly disproportionate to the female form of reality.

_____

_____

_____

(facts and statistics)

Two Kinds of Support—Interrelated Examples and Extended Examples

Gathering support in your prewriting is key to having a well-developed paragraph. When you begin drafting and revising, however, you must do more than simply drop in details. Support for paragraphs should be developed in one of two ways: through short interrelated examples or extended examples. The aim of either method is to remind your reader of the direction your paragraph is taking and provide evidence that validates your topic and direction. Short **interrelated examples** illustrate a point with three to five separate but related instances that support the topic sentence. **Extended examples** in a paragraph develop one instance, subject, or idea through a brief story or an involved description. Your choice of which to use depends on your purpose.

Interrelated Examples—The Friend to the Stand Alone Paragraph

A combination of major and minor supporting details to back up that support is required for short interrelated examples, which stand-alone paragraphs use almost exclusively to illustrate a point. **Major support** announces smaller opinions or subtopics of your paragraph, reminding the reader of your direction. **Minor support** provides evidence that these smaller opinions are reasonable. Moreover, they absorb the reader's attention. Both are necessary for clear, interesting writing.

From another perspective, without minor support, your major support has no meaning; moreover, without major support, your minor support has no clear relevance to your topic sentence. Again, you need both of these elements to fulfill your obligations to your reader; otherwise, your writing is bland and useless. The following paragraph, an attempt at using short interrelated examples, contains major supporting details but no minor details to make them real and interesting. See if you are inclined to accept the author's assertions or empathize with his predicament:

> My experience at the mall during the holiday season was tedious and irritating. All I wanted to do was finish my shopping, but the crowds and unfriendly store employees had other plans. At Barnes and Noble, I was met with rude customers and oblivious green-smocked staff. I surrendered and went to the food court where I had no chance of procuring a meager corn dog to muster my strength. With nothing to eat, I fought my way to a store I thought might be more user friendly, but I was intimidated by the frenzied teenagers who dragged their sheepish parents through the aisles of sweaters and khaki pants of the American Eagle. Finally, I went to Dillard's, but a weathered salesman hounded me to purchase loafers for his commission. I ran for the exit, but even under the expansive gray sky in the parking lot, I barely escaped with my life. The next time I shop for the holidays will be in July.

Certainly the hapless customer seems exasperated by his experience, but he provides no evidence, only opinion. He provides no examples of what makes the customers "rude," the teenagers "frenzied," or the parking lot hazardous. Since he does not provide this evidence, the reader can just as easily assume that he does not like shopping or even people. Furthermore, the reader has no real idea what the experience was like and will, therefore, not be inclined to accept his claims about the mall during the holidays. Notice the revisions made in the paragraph and determine whether you are more inclined to accept the author's claim and sympathize with him.

> My experience at the mall during the holiday season was tedious and irritating. All I wanted to do was finish my shopping, but the crowds and unfriendly store employees had other plans. At Barnes and Noble, I was met with rude customers and an oblivious green-smocked staff. A middle aged man sporting silver sideburns sneered over his glasses at me as he perused my book choice while I frantically waved for a sales girl chatting with her friends. I surrendered and went to the food court where I had no chance of procuring a meager corn dog to muster my strength. Three lines of hungry patrons blocked the counter of Corn Dog on a Stick brandishing their shopping bags like weapons and shields. With nothing to eat, I fought my way to a store I thought might be more user friendly, but I was intimidated by the frenzied teenagers who dragged their sheepish parents through the aisles of sweaters and khaki pants of the American Eagle. A sharp elbow shoved me into a sales rack as an exhausted mother frantically apologized, glancing toward her daughter. Finally, I went to Dillard's, but a weathered salesman hounded me to purchase loafers for his commission. The faded crease in his slacks and his stale breath revealed his

desperation. I ran for the exit, but even under the expansive gray sky in the parking lot, I barely escaped with my life. A Range Rover hovered behind me, coveting my spot, as I shuffled to my car. The next time I shop for the holidays will be in July.

The minor supporting details answer the questions the major supporting details seem to ask. Look at some of the major supporting details put in question form and determine whether the minor supporting details answer them:

- QUESTION 1: What makes the customers at the bookstore seem "rude" and the staff "oblivious"?
- ANSWER: A man "sneering" at my selection of book.
- ANSWER: A salesperson "chatting with her friends."

- QUESTION 2: Why couldn't the author get a corn dog?

- ANSWER: Lines of customers blocking the counter.

- ANSWER: Shopping bags being used as weapons.

- QUESTION 3: Why was he intimidated by the "frenzied teenagers" and "sheepish parents"?

- ANSWER: One of the teens drove an elbow into his back.

- ANSWER: The teen's mother apologized for her daughter's behavior.

If put into outline form, a paragraph of interrelated examples would look something like the one below:

```
┌─────────────────────────────────────────────────────────┐
│      OUTLINE OF PARAGRAPH WITH SHORT INTERRELATED EXAMPLES │
│          I.   Topic Sentence with Direction              │
│         II.   First Major Supporting Detail              │
│              a.  Minor Supporting Detail                 │
│              b.  Minor Supporting Detail                 │
│        III.   Second Major Supporting Detail             │
│              a.  Minor Supporting Detail                 │
│              b.  Minor Supporting Detail                 │
│         IV.   Third Major Supporting Detail              │
│              a.  Minor Supporting Detail                 │
│              b.  Minor Supporting Detail                 │
└─────────────────────────────────────────────────────────┘
```

Exercise 6

Using one of the topic sentences provided below, write a paragraph that includes a linking sentence and at least three to five short interrelated examples. Use a separate sheet of paper and be prepared to discuss your work.

1. Even from my limited experience, I have learned what topics to talk about on a first date.

2. The more I practice, the more I learn about why writing is important.

3. In five years, I hope to be successful at _____.

Extended Example—The Ambassador to the Essay

Unlike short interrelated examples, each of which illustrating an explicit point, **extended examples** tell a story or provide detailed description by only using what is understood, thus far, as minor supporting details. Of course, all paragraphs focus around a clear topic and direction, but this method of support falls mainly in the domain of the essay and may encompass more than one paragraph. The extended example usually serves to support a thesis statement, the sentence around which an essay is built. You will learn more about this kind of writing in the following chapter. For now, read the following example and see if you can tell the difference between a paragraph organized through short interrelated examples and one that develops by extended example.

> As I walked home from class, I noticed a strange object in the grass that filled me with dread. I knelt down and shaded my eyes to get a better look at it and grimaced. It was flesh colored and pear shaped, but it also had greenish black spots of mold infesting its edges. Red ants crawled over it as if delighted to discover this bounty. I took a pencil from my back pack and poked it through the hollow center. Lifting it closer to my face, I saw that a wax circled the hole through which my pencil protruded. An ant crawled up the pencil toward my fingers. At the same time, a stench swept into my flared nostrils. It smelled of putrid flesh. I threw both the pencil and the object down in disgust but hung over the thing as it lay atop the freshly cut lawn. As I pondered the curls and folds that lined its surface, I realized what it was. I had been holding an ear. Fighting my gag reflex, I pulled out a paper bag and flicked the ear into it. I then hurried to the campus police. My initial sense of foreboding had been confirmed, and I have kept my eyes forward ever since.

Notice that the paragraph of short interrelated examples and the paragraph of extended examples both possess a clear topic sentence, and both also have plenty of specific support. The paragraph of short interrelated examples, however, illustrates several separate events while the extended example develops one event into a full paragraph. In outline form, the extended example paragraph would look something like this:

OUTLINE OF PARAGRAPH WITH EXTENDED EXAMPLE

I. **Topic Sentence with Direction**
    a. **Minor Supporting Detail**
    b. **Minor Supporting Detail**
    c. **Minor Supporting Detail**
    d. **Minor Supporting Detail**
    e. **Minor Supporting Detail**

Exercise 7

Choose a new topic sentence and write a paragraph that includes a linking sentence and an extended example. Use a separate sheet of paper and be prepared to discuss your work.

1. Even from my limited experience, I have learned what topics to talk about on a first date.

2. The more I practice, the more I learn about why writing is important.

3. In five years, I hope to be successful at _____.

REVIEW OF COHERENCE AND UNITY: *Now that you have learned about the two methods of providing support, you must refresh your memory on coherence and unity (see Chapter 1: The Writing Process).*

Coherence, linking the ideas in the sentences of your paragraph, is achieved primarily through the use of transitions, the repetition of key words and phrases, and changes in sentence structure. Transitions are words and phrases in a sentence that allude to previous ideas or subjects before moving to new ones, linking the sentences together. They accomplish this through time signals, words that compare and contrast, and words that emphasize meaning.

Unity in a paragraph means that all of your support directly relates to both parts of your topic sentence: topic and direction. As you revise your paragraph, you must eliminate any phrases or sentences that sacrifice the unity of your writing or consider whether they should be placed in a separate paragraph if you are writing an essay.

Order—Organizing Your Support

Even a coherent and unified paragraph can be improved by ensuring that your support is in some sort of **order**. Order is the progression of ideas, details, or events in a way that is logical to your reader and emphasizes your point. A paragraph can be organized in one or more of several ways: chronologically, spatially, and emphatically.

Chronological order is the organization of events or actions in a paragraph according to time. This is accomplished by not only placing events in the order they happened but also by using transitions known as **time signals**. Time signals encompass a whole range of words and phrases such as the ones listed below:

TIME SIGNALS		
first	second	finally
next	meanwhile	after
before	later	until
noon	afternoon	four o'clock

Spatial order is the organizing of objects from your point of view, moving logically through the space you are in. For example, if you were to describe the room you are in now, you might start with the object nearest to you such as a clock or desk and move clockwise through the space to describe each item of interest. Transitions such as those provided below can help your reader follow your eye as you move to each object.

SPATIAL SIGNALS		
behind	above	below
beside	next to	underneath
across	from	on top of
on	near	parallel to

Emphatic Order stresses the importance of the details you are providing in your support. In academic writing, much as in storytelling, your most important ideas are presented in order of their significance, saving the most significant ones for last or providing your most important details first. In addition, transitions can be used to emphasize the weight of each detail. Examples are provided below:

EMPHATIC SIGNALS		
as a matter of fact	best of all	finally
as a result	furthermore	consequently
still	above all	in addition
in fact	moreover	therefore

Notice that a combination of the orders described can be used to organize support in a paragraph, or you can stick to one. Which of them you use depends on your topic and direction.

NOTE: You may have guessed by now that writing can be organized in more ways than have been, thus far, discussed, and the transitions that can be used to support thes e methods of organization are infinite. Chapter 4 of this book will present other patterns for organizing as this class puts the final touches on your preparation for Composition I.

Exercise 8

Rewrite the paragraph below to organize the support in the order you believe is most logical. Supply transitions and repeat key words and phrases where needed to improve coherence. Eliminate any phrases or sentences that detract from unity by crossing them out.

Enamored of the endurance possessed by many of his favorite superheroes, Jason sought to gain their power. He even began electrocuting himself with his mother's blow dryer. He began lifting weights every morning before class. He practiced balancing himself on the telephone lines. He bought and borrowed dozens of illuminated watches and sat for hours in a room to expose himself to their radiation. He helped elderly men and women carry their groceries to their cars. He fought amateur boxers at the local gym. He rode his mountain bike on the most dangerous trails. He used his chest as a target at the batting cages. He had a friend, the owner of a 1988 Chevy Lumina, back over his thighs. Because of these activities, Jason felt he was gaining some of the endurance that defined many of his favorite superheroes.

SUPPORT—A RECAP

The heart of your paragraph, support is what makes your writing interesting and useful. The following characteristics of support are indications of whether your paragraph is complete and organized:

1. Paragraphs without adequate support are **undeveloped**, meaning they are neither interesting nor relevant to your reader.

2. Support may be generated from a variety of sources: **personal experience**, the **observations of someone else**, the **media**, and **facts and statistics**.

3. Support for a paragraph is provided in one of two methods: short interrelated examples and extended example.

    a. Short **interrelated examples** support the topic sentence with three to five details. These details are interrelated with **major support,** which extends the topic and direction, and **minor support**, which provides evidence for the major details.

    b. An **extended example** supports the topic sentence by developing a single event, idea, or subject with lots of details.

4. **Coherence** in a paragraph is essential to emphasizing the relationship between sentences of support. Coherence is maintained through the use of transitions, words and phrases that link ideas, the repetition of key words, and sentence variety.

5. Careful scrutiny of a paragraph ensures that it has **unity**; all support directly relates to the topic sentence.

6. Support in a paragraph is placed in a specific **order** that makes sense and emphasizes key details. Transitions are often used to accent the different methods of organization

    a. **Chronological order** moves the reader through time.

    b. **Spatial order** moves the reader through a given limited environment.

    c. **Emphatic order** arranges the details by increasing or decreasing importance.

THE CONCLUDING SENTENCE—BRINGING CLOSURE TO YOUR PARAGRAPH

Just as the topic sentence introduces your topic and direction, so does your concluding sentence restate these elements in a new and interesting way that brings closure to your paragraph. Like bookends, the topic sentence and concluding sentence effectively announce the beginning and ending of your paragraph. Look at the outline of a paragraph below, and see if you can identify the need for a concluding sentence:

I. Topic Sentence: Now that I am in college, I have to budget more carefully the time I have during weekends.
II. Major Support: Spending less time with friends
   a. Stuffing all my fun into a Friday night at the movies or restaurant with friends
   b. Having to decline offers to go out after Friday
III. Major Support: Spending Saturdays completing the assigned reading
   a. Reading history in the morning at my desk
   b. Reading English into the afternoon and evening at the library
IV. Major Support: Finishing my homework on Sunday
   a. Doing my algebra exercises
   b. Writing an essay

As you can see, the list of things to do during a typical weekend for a college student is endless. So far, only the topic sentence has set the limits for this paragraph. A concluding sentence is needed to remind the reader of the topic ("the time I have during weekends") and direction ("I have to budget more carefully") and bring a sense of finality to the paragraph:

Because of all the school work I have, I have to plan carefully my weekends.

Notice that the concluding sentence echoes the topic sentence but does not restate it word for word.

 Exercise 9
Provide a concluding sentence for each of the topic sentences below. You may find it necessary to prewrite for supporting details.

Example: My laptop is the possession I value most.
Because it is an endless source of entertainment and invaluable to my work, I value my laptop above my other possessions.

1. Although I am not religious, meditation is helping me to understand myself.

   _____
   _____
   _____

2. Sheila began to understand the importance of sleep after taking her final exam in biology.

   _____
   _____
   _____

3. I wonder why the teacher wants me to complete the exercises in the textbook.

   _____
   _____
   _____

4. Without Simon, the quality of *American Idol* is in jeopardy.

   _____
   _____
   _____

5. My adventure at the grocery store is responsible for my fear of ham.

   _____
   _____
   _____

CHAPTER EXAM—WHAT DO YOU KNOW?

1. In your own words, define the term "paragraph."

   _____

   _____

   _____

2. Explain why the topic sentence below is not suitable for a paragraph.
   Skiing and snowboarding are my two favorite winter activities.

   _____

   _____

   _____

3. From which source are most likely to find the most support for a paragraph?

   _____

   _____

   _____

4. In your own words, explain why support for a paragraph is so important.

   _____

   _____

   _____

5. In your own words, explain the difference between interrelated examples and an extended example.

   _____

   _____

   _____

6. In your own words, explain what is considered common knowledge.

   _____

   _____

   _____

7. Describe three ways that you can improve coherence in a paragraph.

_____
_____
_____

8. Provide five examples of time signals.

_____
_____
_____

9. What are the two functions of a concluding sentence?

_____
_____
_____

10. Name and arrange the parts of a paragraph in the order they appear.

_____
_____
_____

SHERMAN ALEXIE – "THE JOY OF READING AND WRITING: SUPERMAN AND ME"

I learned to read with a *Superman* comic book. Simple enough, I suppose. I cannot recall which particular *Superman* comic book I read, nor can I remember which villain he fought in that issue. I cannot remember the plot nor the means by which I obtained the comic book. What I can remember is this: I was three years old, a Spokane Indian boy living with his family on the Spokane Indian Reservation in eastern Washington state. We were poor by most standards, but one of my parents usually managed to find some minimum-wage job or another, which made us middle-class by reservation standards. I had a brother and three sisters. We lived on a combination of irregular paychecks, hope, fear, and government surplus food.

My father, who is one of the few Indians who went to Catholic school on purpose, was an avid reader of westerns, spy thrillers, murder mysteries, gangster epics, basketball player biographies, and anything else he could find. He bought his books by the pound at Dutch's Pawn Shop, Goodwill, Salvation Army, and Value Village. When he had extra money, he bought new novels at supermarkets, convenience stores, and hospital gift shops. Our house was filled with books. They were stacked in crazy piles in the bathroom, bedrooms, and living room. In a fit of unemployment-inspired creative energy, my father built a set of bookshelves and soon filled them with a random assortment of books about the Kennedy assassination, Watergate, the Vietnam War, and the entire twenty-three-book series of the Apache westerns. My father loved books, and since I loved my father with an aching devotion, I decided to love books as well.

I can remember picking up my father's books before I could read. The words themselves were mostly foreign, but I still remember the exact moment when I first understood, with a sudden clarity, the purpose of a paragraph. I didn't have the vocabulary to say "paragraph," but I realized that a paragraph was a fence that held words. The words inside a paragraph worked together for a common purpose. They had some specific reason for being inside the same fence. This knowledge delighted me. I began to think of everything in terms of paragraphs. Our reservation was a small paragraph within the United States. My family's house was a paragraph, distinct from the other paragraphs of the LeBrets to the north, the Fords to the south, and the Tribal School to the west. Inside our house, each family member existed as a separate paragraph but still had genetics and common experiences to link us. Now, using this logic, I can see my changed family as an essay of seven paragraphs: mother, father, older brother, the deceased sister, my younger twin sisters, and our adopted little brother.

At the same time, I was seeing the world in paragraphs. I also picked up the *Superman* comic book. Each panel, complete with picture, dialogue, and narrative, was a three-dimensional paragraph. In one panel, Superman breaks through a door. His suit is read, blue, and yellow. The brown door shatters into many pieces. I look at the narrative above the picture. I cannot read the words, but I assume it tells me that "Superman is breaking down the door." Words, dialogue, also float out of Superman's mouth. Because he is breaking down the door, I assume he says, "I am breaking down the door." Once again, I pretend to read the words and say aloud, "I am breaking down the door." In this way, I learned to read.

This might be an interesting story all by itself. A little Indian boy teaches himself to read at an early age and advances quickly. He reads *Grapes of Wrath* in kindergarten when other children are struggling through Dick and Jane. If he'd been anything but an Indian boy living on the reservation, he might have been called a prodigy. But he is an Indian boy living on the reservation and is simply an oddity. He grows into a man who often speaks of his childhood in the third person, as if it will somehow dull the pain and make him sound more modest about his talents.

A smart Indian is a dangerous person, widely feared and ridiculed by Indians and non-Indians alike. I fought with my classmates on a daily basis. They wanted me to stay quiet when the non-Indian teacher asked for answers, for volunteers, for help. We were Indian children who were expected to be stupid. Most lived up to those expectations inside the classroom but subverted them on the outside. They struggled with basic reading in school but could remember how to sing a few dozen powwow songs. They were monosyllabic in front of their non-Indian teachers but could tell complicated stories and jokes at the dinner table. They submissively ducked their heads when confronted by a non-Indian adult but would slug it out with the Indian bully who was ten years older. As Indian children, we were expected to fail in the non-Indian world. Those who failed were ceremonially accepted by other Indians and appropriately pitied by non-Indians.

I refused to fail. I was smart. I was arrogant. I was lucky. I read books late into the night, until I could barely keep my eyes open. I read books at recess, then during lunch, and in the few minutes left after I had finished my classroom assignments. I read books in the car when my family traveled to powwows or basketball games. In shopping malls, I ran to the bookstores and read bits and pieces of as many books as I could. I read the books my father brought home from the pawnshops and secondhand. I read the books I borrowed from the library. I read the backs of cereal boxes. I read the newspaper. I read the bulletins posted on the walls of the school, the clinic, the tribal offices, the post office. I read junk mail. I read auto-repair manuals. I read magazines. I read anything that had words and paragraphs. I read with equal parts joy and desperation. I loved those books, but I also knew that love had only one purpose. I was trying to save my life.

Despite all the books I read, I am still surprised I became a writer. I was going to be a pediatrician. These days, I write novels, short stories, and poems. I visit schools and teach creative writing to Indian kids. In all my years in the reservation school system, I was never taught how to write poetry, short stories, or novels. I was certainly never taught that Indians wrote poetry, short stories, or novels. Writing was something beyond Indians. I cannot recall a single time that a guest teacher visited the reservation. There must have been visiting teachers. Who were they? Where are they now? Do they exist? I visit the schools as often as possible. The Indian kids crowd the classroom. Many are writing their own poems, short stories, and novels. They have read my books. They have read many other books. They look at me with bright eyes and arrogant wonder. They are trying to save their lives. Then there are the sullen and already defeated Indian kids who sit in the back rows and ignore me with theatrical precision. The pages of their notebooks are empty. They carry neither pencil nor pen. They stare out the window. They refuse and resist. "Books," I say to them. "Books," I say. I throw my weight against their locked doors. The door holds. I am smart. I am arrogant. I am lucky. I am trying to save our lives.

Alexie, Sherman. "The Joy of Reading and Writing: Superman and Me." *The Los Angeles Times* (19 Apr 1998). Rpt. in *The Prose Reader: Essays for Thinking, Reading, and Writing.* 9th ed. Eds. Kim Flachmann and Michael Flachmann. Boston: Pearson, 2011. 445-8. Print.

Discussion Questions for "The Joy of Reading and Writing: Superman and Me."

1. What is Alexie's purpose for writing this essay?

2. How does Alexie learn to read? Why is this skill so valuable to him?

3. How does Alexie come to understand the concept of a paragraph? How does he use what he learns to better himself and others?

4. Why does Alexie say that a smart Indian is a "dangerous person" (par. 6)? Those who are not well-read often have an innate fear or hatred for those who are, labeling them as communist, liberal, or socialist. Have you received such attacks or dealt them out. How does being informed and thinking for yourself separate you from others?

5. How is Alexie "trying to save lives"? Most Americans are literate, but that is not necessarily a saving grace. How can reading save you? What can critical reading and writing skills do for you?

6. Describe the first major breakthrough you had with reading or writing. How did this first revelation make you feel? How have you built on this foundation since then, or what skills would you like to improve in your comprehension of the written form?

CHAPTER 3

MOVING FROM PARAGRAPHS TO ESSAYS

MASTERING ONE, MASTERING BOTH

Most academic writing comes in two forms: the paragraph and the essay. In structure and in content, the stand-alone paragraph discussed in Chapter 2 can be seen as the miniature of the basic essay. The comparison below illustrates this point:

PARAGRAPH/ESSAY COMPARISON

Paragraph	*Essay*
Focused on one topic	Focused on one subject
Has three major parts:	Has three parts:
Topic sentence with direction	Introduction with thesis statement
Supporting details	Supporting body paragraphs
Concluding sentence	Conclusion

Hopefully, by now, you have become familiar with the paragraph format, so moving to the essay format should not be as challenging as it otherwise would have been. If you are not confident in your knowledge of the structure of a stand-alone paragraph, you should carefully review the material in Chapter 2 before moving on with this chapter. The stand-alone paragraph is the basic building block of all academic writing and writing in general; as such, you need to be confident in your ability to produce a well-written stand-alone paragraph before moving on to the full essay.

Moving from Paragraphs to Essays: Building on a Foundation

As has been emphasized, every element in a well-written paragraph has a corresponding element in a well-written essay. Below you will see in greater detail how each part of a paragraph corresponds to a part of an essay that performs a similar function:

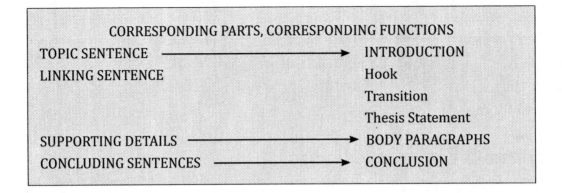

THE INTRODUCTION—GETTING YOUR READER'S ATTENTION

Have you ever been in situation where you *had* to get someone's attention? Did you stand there quietly, or did you wave your arms back and forth like human windshield wipers? Did you quietly whisper the individual's name, or did you let loose with a hearty "Hey you!"? Each culture has its own rules for how politely yet effectively to get an individual's attention, and academic writing is no different. How many times have you lost interest in a book or in a movie because it failed to get your attention? Did you keep reading or watching, hoping it would get better, or did you abandon it in favor of something else, perhaps thinking that your time would be better spent doing something else. Technically, the fault for this does not lie with you but with the writer; the writer's major responsibility is to capture and then to keep his audience's attention. As a writer, you are no different; fortunately, you have rules and formats to follow in order to get your reader's attention, and the best place to get your reader's attention is in your essay's introduction.

An **introduction (or introductory paragraph)** contains more than just the thesis statement that will anchor your essay. This beginning paragraph of your essay is perhaps the most important because it sets the tone for the rest of your work. A good introductory paragraph consists of three very important parts:

PARTS OF AN INTRODUCTION

The **hook** or **lead-in**

The **transition** or **bridge**

The **thesis statement** that has direction and lists the main points to be covered in the essay.

The Hook – Grabbing Your Reader's Attention

Most of us have hundreds if not thousands of things vying for our attention every day, so if you want your reader to pay attention to what you are about to say, you have to get your reader's attention. This is done through a device called a **hook**. Experienced fishermen know that, in order to lure a fish, you have to do more than just drop a line in the water and hope a fish will come by; to capture a fish's attention, you have to put something on that line that will entice that fish to check out what is at the end of *your* line. In writing, your hook is the first chance— and possibly the only chance—you will get to entice your reader; a cleverly written hook can make your reader want to read more, but a weak or ineffective hook can alienate or bore your reader.

Hooks are constructed using any one of a number of techniques. Which of these techniques you use will depend in large part on your topic and your audience. These techniques include the following:

TYPES OF HOOKS
HOOK 1: personal examples
HOOK 2: quotations
HOOK 3: facts or statistics
HOOK 4: questions
HOOK 5: current events
HOOK 6: a contrast to the thesis statement

Hook 1: Personal Examples—Using a personal example, your own experience or the observations of others, as a hook can often put a human face on a very large or complex issue; it can also give you as the writer a certain level of expertise, showing the reader that you have first-hand knowledge of the subject matter. However, in order to be effective, your personal example must be:

- **Pertinent to the topic**—The most gripping example will not be effective if it has nothing to do with your essay's topic. If no clear connection exists with the topic, your reader may well feel that you are trying to manipulate his or her feelings, which could make your reader disregard anything else you have to say.

- **Appropriate in its tone**—A hilarious personal anecdote would not be appropriate as a hook if your topic is a gravely serious issue.

Hook 2: Quotations—Using a quotation from a famous person or a quotation that your audience will be familiar with can certainly get your audience's attention; however, as with personal examples, you must consider some drawbacks and cautions when contemplating a quotation as a hook:

- **Will this quotation be familiar to my reader?** You should not assume that, just because *you* are familiar with a quotation, your audience will be familiar with it. Just because you found it in a book that claims to have "Familiar" quotations in it does *not* guarantee your reader will recognize it.

- **Will the person attributed with this quotation be familiar to my reader?** The exact quotation may not be familiar to your audience, but the person who originated the quotation may be.

- **Is this quotation or this person pertinent to my topic?** This is, perhaps, the most important consideration for the use of any quotation. Using a very familiar quotation from a widely known celebrity will have little impact if the quotation in question is not pertinent to your topic; in fact, relying solely on an individual's celebrity to sway your reader can be very detrimental to your reader's perception of both you and your writing.

Hook 3: Facts or Statistics—Using a fact or a statistic as your hook can be effective in capturing your reader's attention. However, this particular type of hook can be the most dangerous for two reasons: first, once you have stated a fact, often very little else can be said; and second, statistics can be manipulated in such a way that they can be made to say anything the writer wants them to. Like the two previous hook types discussed, using facts or statistics comes with questions that you as the writer must answer:

- **Is this fact or statistic pertinent to my topic**? The fact or statistic you use must be closely related to your topic or must be an important part of the issue you plan to address.

- **Can I, if the need arises, attribute this fact or statistic to a reliable source or expert in this particular field?** If you can provide this information for your reader, it can greatly enhance the fact's or statistic's importance and believability.

Hook 4: Questions—Using this technique as a hook can get your reader's attention by posing the kinds of questions that, hopefully, will get your reader thinking about issues or problems that your essay will address and answer. However, this technique also comes with certain drawbacks:

- **Rhetorical or unanswerable questions** can alienate your reader by posing problems that realistically cannot be addressed. For example, one writer started his essay with the question "What if we all walked around like apes?" Since this is not within the realm of possibility,

---

1. A problem with using facts and/or statistics as hooks comes in the area of academic dishonesty or plagiarism: if the fact or statistic you are using is not considered "common knowledge" (something your reader can be reasonably expected to know), you must tell your audience where you got this information—which calls for attribution and citation (two areas that you will become more familiar with when you move on to your next composition class)—or you could be accused of plagiarism. (See section on common knowledge and plagiarism in Chapter 2.)

this question only serves to make the reader question the writer's believability.

- **Too many questions** can alienate your readers by overwhelming them with more questions than your essay could possibly answer.

Hook 5: Current Events—Using this hook can focus your reader's attention to the connection between a current event and the topic of your essay. On the other hand, as with other hook techniques, utilizing a current event that has no or a very weak connection to your topic can alienate your audience. Therefore, when contemplating this particular type of hook, make sure that the current event is common knowledge to your reader and directly connected (or connectable) to your topic.

Hook 6: Contrast to Your Thesis Statement – Using this technique can get your reader's attention by setting up a direct contrast to the main point you intend to make. For example, if *your* thesis statement is going to take a stand on global warming, your hook could bring up the existence of opinions that global warming does not, in fact, exist.

Exercise 1

Here are some topics that you might encounter in an academic setting (for instance, Composition I). Which type of hook might best be used for each? Give an example of that hook—plus a brief explanation of why you think that particular hook would best serve in that particular instance:

1. You have been asked to write an essay about the perils of modern-day advertising.

   _____

   _____

   _____

   _____

---

2. For more information regarding common knowledge, see Chapter 2.

2. You have been asked to write an essay describing an incident that influenced you the most in your choice of profession.

_____

_____

_____

_____

3. You have been asked to write an essay describing an academic or athletic talent that you have developed and explain how that talent will help you as a college student. _____

_____

_____

_____

4. You have decided to apply for a scholarship sponsored by a large Oklahoma corporation, and part of that application process is to write and to submit an essay on the topic "How My College Education Can Help Oklahoma."

_____

_____

_____

_____

The Transition—Moving the Reader toward the Thesis Statement

Once you have the reader's attention with your hook, you cannot just jump straight into your thesis statement; you must provide a **transition**, a word or phrase that provides a connection between two ideas, that eases the reader into your upcoming thesis statement. This transition acts much like a funnel: when you have a lot of liquid that you have to get into a small hole, pouring it straight from a much larger container into that small hole can often result in very little of the liquid making it to its intended target. In these instances, we often use a funnel to channel that liquid to where we want it to go. Accordingly, a transition in your introductory paragraph can channel your reader's attention to where *you* want it to go.

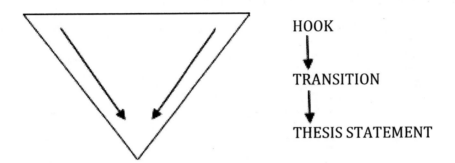

HOOK

↓

TRANSITION

↓

THESIS STATEMENT

This transition allows you to give more detail (if necessary) and start preparing your reader for the most important aspect of your introductory paragraph: **the thesis statement**. It functions as a bridge between the attention-grabber of the hook and the meat of the introduction, the thesis statement; therefore, its absence or the absence of an effective transition makes your writing unclear and gives your reader a valid excuse to stop reading.

Since this transition is so important, you must as a writer ensure that your transition:

- Is pertinent to the hook.
- Is a logical extension of the hook.
- Leads the reader logically and unobtrusively to the thesis statement.

Exercise 2

Here are the topics that you worked on earlier in this chapter. You decided which hook might be most effective for each example; now you need

to fashion a transition that moves the reader out of the hook and toward the upcoming thesis statement:

1. You have been asked to write an essay about the perils of modern-day advertising.

   _____

   _____

   _____

   _____

2. You have been asked to write an essay describing an incident that influenced you the most in your choice of profession.

   _____

   _____

   _____

   _____

3. You have been asked to write an essay describing an academic or athletic talent that you have developed and explain how that talent will help you as a college student. _____

   _____

   _____

   _____

   _____

4. You have decided to apply for a scholarship sponsored by a large Oklahoma corporation, and part of that application process is to write and to submit an essay on the topic "How My College Education Can Help Oklahoma."

   _____

   _____

_____

_____

The Thesis Statement—The Anchor of Your Essay

We stated earlier that paragraphs cover only one topic. Essays, however, due to their length, are a little broader in scope. The writing process for an essay is also very much like the writing process for a paragraph, but instead of generating topic sentences, you must now think in much larger terms. Your topic sentence for a paragraph might be "Puerto Rico, my favorite vacation spot, is beautiful," but that is much too narrow for an entire essay; thesis statements broaden your scope to include more than one topic within the confines of an essay's **subject**, what your essay is about, and allows you to  preview for the reader the main points you will cover in your essay. In a basic five-paragraph essay, you will preview three main points; each of those three main points then will correspond to a body paragraph. For example, to broaden the scope of the vacation spot topic sentence, you might want to include other favorite vacation spots: My three favorite vacation spots are Puerto Rico, Yellowstone National Park, and Gettysburg. Whereas a topic sentence is narrow in scope, covering only one vacation spot, a thesis statement can cover much more territory (literally and figuratively).

A good thesis statement not only tells what the essay is going to be about (the subject) but also gives the reader the **direction**, your attitude or opinion about your subject, that the essay will take—as well as the three points the writer is going to use in defending or supporting that direction. If the thesis statement does not provide a clear direction, then it becomes merely a statement of fact, not a thesis statement. A "thesis" is a proposition to be proved—and, as the writer, your job is to provide that proof.

Characteristics of an Effective Thesis Statement

Like a paragraph's topic sentence, an essay's thesis statement tells readers what to expect. An effective thesis statement has two important characteristics:

1. A good thesis statement makes a point about a topic; for this reason, it must do more than state a fact or announce what you plan to write about.

   - A statement of fact takes no position and gives you nothing to develop in your essay. Look at the example below, and see if you agree:

     My new Chevy Eco cost $13,599.

     This sentence merely gives the reader a fact that can be easily verified by looking at the sticker on the car and gives the writer no room for discussion or further development.

   - An announcement gives the reader no idea of what position or direction you will take on your subject. Announcements often take the form of "In this essay, I will discuss" or "This essay will cover" and does little if anything to tell the reader what direction the essay will take. For example, the thesis statement below merely trumpets the writer's vague intent:

     In this essay, I will discuss my choice of major.

     This poorly worded thesis statement has no direction nor does it preview the points the writer intends to cover; instead, it merely calls unwarranted attention to the writer.

2. A good thesis statement is clearly worded and specific.

   - Vague thesis statements give very little indication to the reader just exactly what will be covered in the essay. In the statement below, the writer's use of vague terms may leave the reader wondering just exactly what the subject and direction will be:

I will make it through Basic Writing even if it takes a little more time to study I will pick my professor's brain until I get what I need, and if I still do not figure it out, go see a tutor regularly.

Aside from grammar issues, this statement provides no clear topic or direction and leads the reader to wonder just what, exactly, the writer's main points are.

Exercise 3

Take a look at the following statements and determine if they are good thesis statements (TS) or simply statements of fact (SF) or announcements (A):

___ 1. Many older students are returning to college.

___ 2. Hummingbirds, the world's smallest birds, are amazing creatures.

___ 3. Television shows do not portray real life.

___ 4. In this paper, I will discuss why students should not cheat.

___ 5. Schools should establish policies regarding smoking on campus.

For those statements that were either statements of fact or announcements, change them to make them more effective thesis statements:

_____

_____

_____

_____

_____

_____

A Few More Words about Direction

Not only does a thesis statement give the reader the subject to be covered, but also it gives the reader a **direction** that performs the following functions:

1. It tells the reader what specifically about that subject the writer intends to cover

2. It reveals what the writer's stand on the topic will be

3. It clearly states what specific aspect of the subject matter the writer will addressing.

These direction words often take the form of adjectives ("good," "bad," "amazing," "boring," etc.) or words (verbs like "should" or "ought to," etc.) that indicate a value judgment on the writer's part. If we take one of the sentences from the previous exercise, we can start to see how direction takes shape:

> Hummingbirds, the world's smallest birds, are amazing creatures.

Rather than simply state that hummingbirds are the world's smallest birds (which would be a statement of fact), the writer here is making a claim: that hummingbirds are **amazing**.

Exercise 4

In the following examples, indicate whether the statement has direction (D) or no direction (ND). If direction can be found, underline the direction word.

___ 1. Pit bulls, despite their reputation, actually make good pets.

___ 2. When budgeting money, college students need to keep some important things in mind.

___ 3. A person has many choices when deciding on what car to buy.

___ 4. Laptops are superior to iPads.

___ 5. Her bookshelves are filled with novels and biographies.

Rewrite those statements that have no direction:

_____

_____

_____

_____

_____

_____

A Few More Words about Support Points

Not only do effective thesis statements have a subject and direction, they also have a brief list of the evidence the writer intends to use to support his or her statement—also known as **support points**. These points also give the reader a preview of what the body paragraphs of the essay will cover.

If we go back to our hummingbird example—Hummingbirds, the world's smallest birds, are amazing creatures.—our support points, then, would tell the reader *why* these birds are amazing, what specifically about them could be classified that way, and what the reader can expect the body of the essay to cover. The example below illustrates what support points can add to a thesis statement:

> Hummingbirds, the world's smallest birds, are amazing creatures because they can hover, can eat their own weight in one day, and can help in the pollination process of flowers and plants.

Exercise 5

Read the following thesis statements. First, <u>circle the most general idea</u> (topic and direction). Then <u>underline</u> the support points that complete the thesis statement.

1. Restoring an old house can be gratifying, unnerving, and surprising.

2. Speaking two languages can be advantageous when a person seeks a job, travels in another country, or assists foreign people.

3. When interacting with a disabled person, a person needs to be empathetic, realistic, and knowledgeable.

4. I appreciate my mother-in-law because she accepts me into the family, is generous, and treats me like a friend.

5. Learning about our prehistoric past involves studying historical archives, visiting archaeological museums, and interpreting new findings.

6. Exercise helps people sleep, lowers their blood pressure, and increases their ability to remember.

7. Artists today may exhibit and sell their work at local fairs, galleries, and private sales.

8. A good financial aid package, a part-time job, and a budget can ease financial difficulties for students.

9. Car manufacturers appeal to people's interests in comfort, appearance, and power.

10. Many college lecture halls today include sophisticated overhead projection systems, laptop projection systems, and Internet access.

Making Your Support Points Parallel

 You may have noticed in the exercise above that all of the support points shown in each statement are in **parallel structure**—that is, they all match grammatically. (For more on parallel st ructure, see Unit II.) If we look at an example—Her new car is better than her old one because it has cruise control, a five-disc CD player, and has a four-cylinder engine.—we see that the first two support points ("cruise control" and "a five-disc CD player") are nouns or noun phrases; however, the last support point begins with a verb ("has"). This results in the support points that are not in parallel structure.

To correct this, you might find it easier to look for the one point that is different than the other two and correct it to match the other points. In the above example, taking "has" out of the last phrase leaves you with a noun phrase that will be in parallel structure with the first two points:

Her new car is better than her old one because it has cruise control, a five-disc CD player, and a four-cylinder engine

Exercise 6

Carefully read the following thesis sentences. Revise each thesis sentence so that the points previewed are in parallel form. You may need to add, delete, or alter a word or words.

1.   When buying children's toys, parents need to be sure the toys are colorful, safe, appropriate, and have durability.

2.   Ray spent his life working hard all day, to socialize in the evening, and sleeping well at night.

3.   His summers are spent jet-skiing at the lake, surfing at the beach, and he even sails on the ocean.

4.   An afternoon in an art museum can be fun, inexpensive, and have educational benefits.

5.   Raising children requires time, having patience, and money.

6.   Jerry's retirement years were pleasant because he had bought land, invested in stocks, and saving some money.

7.   His knowledge, he had social skills, and age helped make him successful at his job.

8.   Adobe buildings are strong, simple, look attractive, and practical.

9.   Individuals, families, and listening to friends all provide motivation to get a college degree.

10.   Comforting a child, to provide a pleasant home environment, and teaching a child are all aspects of parenting.

Coordinating Your Support Points

Support points must also be **coordinate**—all of equal value without overlapping—and **subordinate**—**all** logically a part of the subject of the thesis statement. Effective support points also are general in nature; this leaves the writer with greater room to provide specific details in the body paragraph that discusses that point. For example, take a look at the following sentence:

> His apartment is interesting because of its décor, its location, and the neighborhood's history.

These support points may be in parallel structure, but they are not all coordinate and subordinate. The first two—décor and location—refer only to the apartment; however, the third—the neighborhood's history—is much broader in scope and might lead a writer to stray from the subject, "his apartment". Additionally, the neighborhood's history and the apartment's location may overlap. In other words, they are covering the same sub-topic. In order to make these points coordinate and subordinate, the last one needs to be narrowed in its scope:

> His apartment is interesting because of its décor, its location, and its history.

These support points now are focused solely on the apartment, are logically a part of the subject (subordinate), and are all of equal value without overlapping (coordinate), as well as being in parallel structure.

Exercise 7

Carefully read the following thesis sentences. Some of the coordinate ideas are faulty because they overlap (have almost the same meaning) or are not coordinate (equal). Cross out the overlapping or uncoordinate idea, making sure that you reword (or move words) where necessary.

1.   Eating popcorn, seeing the animals, watching the clowns, enjoying the elephants, and reading a program are memories from the circus.

2.   A person running for public office needs money, emotional support from friends and family, personal endurance, and stamina.

3.   Jean's favorite activities are collecting coins, painting pictures, restoring old telephones, and painting with oils.

4.   After work, Harry drives home safely, watches the news, works in the yard, cooks supper, and watches television.

5.   Cooperation, strength, speed, intelligence, and willingness to work together are qualities of a good football player.

6.   Addictive eating disorders can destroy a person physically, mentally, socially, and psychologically.

7.   Being prepared to fish at the lake means having a license, fishing gear and bait, a cooler with food and drinks, sunblock, and fishing hooks.

8.   A teacher should have patience, kindness, compassion, and knowledge.

9.   Air pollution can irritate eyes and noses, cause lung problems, damage plants, damage buildings, and destroy outer layers of stone buildings.

10.   Before buying a computer, people should consider personal needs, expenses, available software, computer capabilities, and costs.

Exercise 8

Here are the topics that you worked on earlier in this chapter. So far, you have composed a hook and a transition for each topic; now, you need to add a thesis statement *with support points and direction* that will provide the direction for the rest of your essay:

1. You have been asked to write an essay about the perils of modern-day advertising.

     _____

     _____

     _____

     _____

2. You have been asked to write an essay describing an incident that influenced you the most in your choice of profession.

   _____

   _____

   _____

   _____

3. You have been asked to write an essay describing an academic or athletic talent that you have developed and explain how that talent will help you as a college student. _____

   _____

   _____

   _____

   _____

4. You have decided to apply for a scholarship sponsored by a large Oklahoma corporation, and part of that application process is to write and to submit an essay on the topic "How My College Education Can Help Oklahoma."

   _____

   _____

   _____

   _____

Once you have these three important parts—the hook, the transition, and the thesis statement—put together, you have an introduction (or introductory paragraph) that will effectively prepare your reader for the body paragraphs to follow.

Exercise 9

Previously, you determined a hook, a transition, and a thesis statement for each of these topics. Now the time has come to put the entire introductory paragraph together; write an introductory paragraph for each of the following:

1. You have been asked to write an essay about the perils of modern-day advertising.

   _____

   _____

   _____

   _____

   _____

   _____

   _____

2. You have been asked to write an essay describing an incident that influenced you the most in your choice of profession.

   _____

   _____

   _____

   _____

   _____

   _____

   _____

   _____

   _____

3. You have been asked to write an essay describing an academic or athletic talent that you have developed and explain how that talent will help you as a college student.

_____

_____

_____

_____

_____

_____

_____

_____

_____

4. You have decided to apply for a scholarship sponsored by a large Oklahoma corporation, and part of that application process is to write and to submit an essay on the topic "How My College Education Can Help Oklahoma."

_____

_____

_____

_____

_____

_____

_____

BODY PARAGRAPHS: SUPPORTING YOUR THESIS STATEMENT

The body of your essay is where you provide your reader with the details that support your thesis statement. The three points you listed at the end of your thesis statement become the topics for each of these paragraphs, as shown in the chart below:

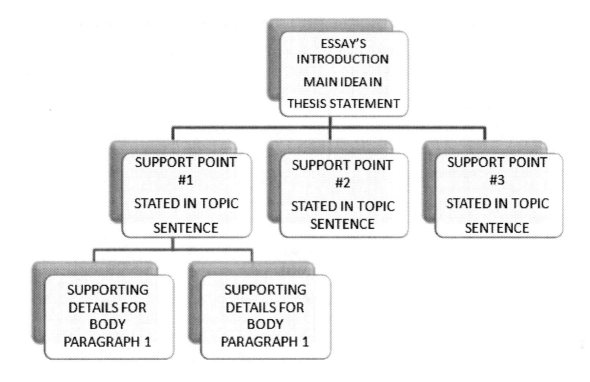

Once you start the body of your essay, your paragraphs should follow the pattern shown earlier in Chapter 2:

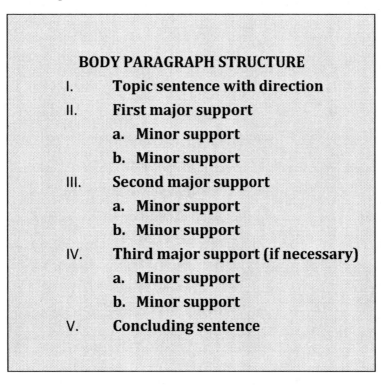

As you can tell from this outline, each body paragraph must have sufficient supporting detail to fully cover each point given in your thesis statement in what could be called the **"equal time" rule**—each point should be given the same amount of support as the others.

For example, a student given the assignment of writing an essay about the advantages of living in a dorm has outlined her body paragraphs as follows:

    I.   Body paragraph 1: Close to campus services
        a. Close to Library
        b. Close to labs and computer centers
        c. Close to classrooms
    II.   Body paragraph 2: Close to fellow students
        a. Making new friends
        b. Studying with classmates
    III.   Body paragraph 3: Close to cafeteria
        a. Good food

She realizes that two of her body paragraphs are not as fully developed as the first. This writer must do some additional brainstorming or freewriting to come up with additional support for the last two points. For the second paragraph, she might want to add that the proximity to fellow students can be convenient if she has to miss class for some reason; having classmates nearby can be a source for missed lecture notes or handouts. What else can be said about the school cafeteria besides "good food"? This writer may have restricted herself too much on this point, and it may be best to broaden the scope of this particular point. Instead of just talking about the cafeteria, she instead might make this point about the Student Center—which houses the cafeteria and other sometimes essential things like a convenience store and bookstore. Her revised outline, then, would look like this example:

    I.   Body paragraph 1: Close to campus services
        a. Close to Library
        b. Close to labs and computer centers
        c. Close to classrooms
    II.   Body paragraph 2: Close to fellow students
        a. Making new friends
        b. Studying with classmates
        c. Getting missed class notes/handouts

III.   Body paragraph 3: Close to Student Center
   a.   Good food at the cafeteria
   b.   Essentials available at the Convenience Store
   c.   Bookstore nearby

Now her outline clearly shows that each body paragraph is going to have the same amount of support with no two (or three) points overlapping.

NOTE: Although the introduction and conclusion paragraphs of an essay will not follow the same structure as the stand-alone paragraph, each of your three body paragraphs for a basic five-paragraph essay will mimic the exact structure of a stand-alone paragraph. In other words, each body paragraph should have a topic sentence, a linking sentence, support, and a concluding sentence.

Exercise 10

Using the examples we have been working on previously in this chapter and using the support points stated in your previously constructed thesis statements, construct a rough outline of what your body paragraphs will cover.

1.   You have been asked to write an essay about the perils of modern-day advertising.

_____

_____

_____

_____

_____

_____

_____

2. You have been asked to write an essay describing an incident that influenced you the most in your choice of profession.

_____

_____

_____

_____

_____

_____

_____

_____

_____

3. You have been asked to write an essay describing an academic or athletic talent that you have developed and explain how that talent will help you as a college student.

_____

_____

_____

_____

_____

_____

_____

_____

_____

4. You have decided to apply for a scholarship sponsored by a large Oklahoma corporation, and part of that application process is to write and to submit an essay on the topic "How My College Education Can Help Oklahoma."

_____

_____

_____

_____

_____

_____

_____

THE CONCLUDING PARAGRAPH: BRINGING CLOSURE TO YOUR ESSAY

The last paragraph in a five-paragraph essay model is the **concluding paragraph** or **conclusion**. This paragraph has a very specific role in your essay: it brings your essay to a satisfactory close for your reader—and for you. Like its paragraph counterpart (the concluding sentence), your concluding paragraph clearly brings all the points you have been discussing to a close; without it, the reader is left to wonder what he or she is supposed to carry away from your essay. Therefore, your concluding paragraph is just as important as your introductory paragraph and has the same basic elements – but in reverse:

CORRESPONDING PARTS, CORRESPONDING FUNCTIONS	
INTRODUCTION	**CONCLUSION**
Hook ————————————▶	**Restatement of Thesis**
Transition ————————▶	**Transition**
Thesis Statement ————▶	**Hook**

In this way the reader is eased out of your essay just as he or she was eased into it; by mirroring your introductory paragraph, you provide for your reader a "wrap-up" that makes sense and gives your essay closure.

Characteristics of an Effective Conclusion

While your conclusion should be a mirror image of your introductory paragraph, you need to make a few modifications:

1. Your conclusion should include a **restatement** of your thesis statement, wording it in a different way while retaining the main idea, the direction, and the three points. Many college writers basically "cut and paste" their thesis statements into their conclusions; this is <u>not</u> restating it.

2. Your conclusion should also include a **strong transition** which moves the reader from the restated thesis statement to the end of the essay. You might want to reword the transition you used in your introduction, or you may choose to use a different transition.

3. Your conclusion should end with **a reminder of the hook** you used to begin your essay. This reminder need not be long and involved, but it should be the same type of hook you used to get your reader's attention in your introduction.

If your conclusion contains these three vital aspects—and in this order—your reader will be more likely to perceive your essay as a finished work rather than something that suddenly comes to a halt with no warning.

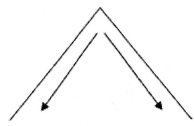

RESTATEMENT OF THESIS

TRANSITION

REMINDER OF HOOK

Just as certain things should not appear in your introductory paragraph, these same things should not be a part of your concluding paragraph, such as the following:

1. *An "announcement" of what the main idea of your essay was.* Statements such as "As the reader can clearly see" or "This essay has shown (or covered)" are problematic on two levels. First, what if you *have not* clearly shown or covered for your reader what you claim to have? If you reader can respond with "No, you really have *not*," you have just effectively ruined your entire essay. Second, just as announcements in your thesis statement are potentially alienating for your reader, repeating those same announcements in your concluding paragraph can be just as disconcerting.

2. *The introduction of new material.* You have just spent four (or more) paragraphs putting forward your main idea; the concluding paragraph is *not* the place to throw in any points you forgot to include earlier in the essay. If those points are important to understanding your main idea, then you should make them a separate body paragraph (complete with sufficient support) and *then* go into your concluding paragraph.

3. *A statement or idea that is in direct contrast to the main idea.* The last paragraph of your essay is not the place to switch the entire focus of your essay. For example, if you have spent four paragraphs arguing why tuition rates should be lowered, you should not then in your concluding paragraph come out in favor of increased tuition. If for some reason you *have* changed your mind, then you should go back through the rest of your essay and change your body paragraphs and your introduction to indicate this shift in your stand or change in your thinking.

4. *An apology.* Apologizing for what you have just written makes the readers wonder why they wasted their time; if what you have to say is important (why else would you have written?), then you should not apologize for what you have said. Even though in some cultures this is seen as good manners, in academic writing apologizing for your stand or for what you have said could be construed as weakness on the writer's part.

Exercise 11

Using the examples you have been working on previously in this chapter, construct a *concluding paragraph* based on what you have written for each example so far:

1. You have been asked to write an essay about the perils of modern-day advertising.

    _____

    _____

_____

_____

_____

_____

_____

_____

2. You have been asked to write an essay describing an incident that influenced you the most in your choice of profession.

_____

_____

_____

_____

_____

_____

_____

_____

_____

3. You have been asked to write an essay describing an academic or athletic talent that you have developed and explain how that talent will help you as a college student.

_____

_____

_____

_____

_____

_____

_____

_____

_____

4. You have decided to apply for a scholarship sponsored by a large Oklahoma corporation, and part of that application process is to write and to submit an essay on the topic "How My College Education Can Help Oklahoma."

_____

_____

_____

_____

_____

_____

_____

PUTTING ALL THE PIECES TOGETHER: ASSEMBLING AN ESSAY

We have been talking about each section of the basic five-paragraph essay separately; the time has come to put it all together. The diagram below illustrates how each part of the essay interrelates with the others. What we have not spent much time on in this chapter are two essential aspects of any piece of writing: unity and coherence (see Chapters 1 and 2). In an essay, unity is achieved when all support relates directly to the corresponding topic sentence of a body paragraph and all body paragraphs directly relate to the thesis statement. As with unity, coherence has been discussed in previous chapters. The writer should note, however, that in addition to using different signals within your support, the topic sentence of each body paragraph should refer to the ideas of the previous body paragraph before stating its own topic and direction. You will see this addition to the topic sentence noted in the diagram below.

THE STRUCTURE OF A COHESIVE, UNIFIED ESSAY

Introduction	• Hook • Transition • Thesis Statement
Body Paragraph	• Topic Sentence with transition • Support • Concluding Sentence
Body Paragraph	• Topic Sentence with transition • Support • Concluding Sentence
Body Paragraph	• Topic Sentence with transition • Support • Concluding Sentence
Conclusion	• Restate Thesis Statement • Echo hook • End with obvious closure that leaves essay with sense of completeness

Putting Together Your Own Essay: Following the Process

Now that we have discussed the various parts of an essay, the next step is to actually put one together—to apply what you have learned by going through the process. Throughout this chapter, we have looked at four different topics:

1. You have been asked to write an essay about the perils of modern-day advertising.

2. You have been asked to write an essay describing an incident that influenced you the most in your choice of profession.

3. You have been asked to write an essay describing an academic or athletic talent that you have developed and explain how that talent will help you as a college student.

4. You have decided to apply for a scholarship sponsored by a large Oklahoma corporation, and part of that application process is to write and to submit an essay on the topic "How My College Education Can Help Oklahoma."

The next step, then, is to start assembling the pieces of your essay that you have produced so far—the introductory paragraph, an outline for your body paragraphs, and the concluding paragraph. For additional help in fleshing out the outline for your body paragraphs, see Chapter 2, "Moving from Sentences to Paragraphs."

A CHECKLIST FOR ESSAYS

How can you tell if what you have is an essay? Many student writers, by the time they finish a writing assignment, are so time-invested in the project that they cannot see what they have written objectively – and sometimes this leads to very important aspects of a well-written essay being weak or being absent. What follows is a checklist to help you determine where your essay is strong or where your essay needs further work.

CHECKLIST FOR AN ESSAY ASSIGNMENT

Rhetorical Pattern:

- Does your essay conform to the kind of essay requested in the assignment?

Content:

- **Introduction**
  - Does your introduction have an effective hook?
  - Do you have a smooth transition between the hook and the thesis statement?
  - Does your thesis statement have a topic and direction?
  - Does your thesis statement preview the main points of the essay?
  - Is your voice (or word choices) appropriate for the purpose and audience of your essay?

- **Support Paragraphs**
  - Does each body or support paragraph have a clear topic sentence that introduces one of the main points?
  - Does each body or support paragraph have sufficient supporting detail (major *and* minor support)?
  - Do all the sentences in your body or support paragraphs relate back to and support the topic sentences?
  - Do you have coherence within your body or support paragraphs?
  - Do you have coherence *between* your body or support paragraphs?
  - Does each of your body or support paragraphs end with a concluding sentence that brings a sense of closure to the paragraph?

- **Conclusion**
  - Does your concluding paragraph reaffirm the main idea of the essay?
  - Does your concluding paragraph mirror your introduction?
    - Restatement of thesis statement?
    - Effective transition?
    - Reminder of hook used in introduction?
  - Does your concluding paragraph give a sense of closure to your entire essay?

Mechanics and Grammar:
- **Mechanics**
  - o Do you practice sentence variety (combination of simple, compound, and complex sentences)?
  - o Do you have a consistent point of view throughout your essay?
  - o Is you verb tense consistent throughout your essay?
  - o Have all sentence fragments, run-ons (or fused sentences), and comma splices been corrected?
  - o Have all agreement problems been corrected?
    - ▪ Subject/Verb Agreement?
    - ▪ Pronoun/Antecedent Agreement?
    - ▪ Dangling Modifiers?
  - o Is your essay in the proper format (as outlined in the assignment)?
- **Grammar**
  - o Is spelling correct throughout your essay? (Do *not* trust Spell Check.)
  - o Have all punctuation problems (misplaced commas, misused semi-colons, etc.) been corrected?
  - o Have all homonym problems been corrected (*there/their/ they're, its/it's, weather/whether*, etc.)?

PAUL MCHENRY ROBERTS – "HOW TO SAY NOTHING IN FIVE HUNDRED WORDS"

It's Friday afternoon, and you have almost survived another week of classes. You are just looking forward dreamily to the weekend when the English instructor says: "For Monday you will turn in a five hundred-word composition on college football."

Well, that puts a good hole in the weekend. You don't have any strong views on college football one way or the other. You get rather excited during the season and go to all the home games and find it rather more fun than not. On the other hand, the class has been reading Robert Hutchins in the anthology and perhaps Shaw's "Eighty-Yard Run," and from the class discussion you have got the idea that the instructor thinks college football is for the birds. You are no fool. You can figure out what side to take.

After dinner you get out the portable typewriter that you got for high school graduation. You might as well get it over with and enjoy Saturday and Sunday. Five hundred words is about two double-spaced pages with normal margins. You put in a sheet of paper, think up a title, and you're off:

WHY COLLEGE FOOTBALL SHOULD BE ABOLISHED

College football should be abolished because it's bad for the school and also for the players. The players are so busy practicing that they don't have any time for their studies.

This, you feel, is a mighty good start. The only trouble is that it's only thirty-two words. You still have four hundred and sixty-eight to go, and you've pretty well exhausted the subject. It comes to you that you do your best thinking in the morning, so you put away the typewriter and go to the movies. But the next morning you have to do your washing and some math problems, and in the afternoon you go to the game. The English instructor turns up too, and you wonder if you've taken the right side after all. Saturday night you have a date, and Sunday morning you have to go to church. (You can't let English assignments interfere with your religion.) What with one thing and another, it's ten o'clock Sunday night before you get out the typewriter again. You make a pot of coffee and start to fill out your views on college football. Put a little meat on the bones.

WHY COLLEGE FOOTBALL SHOULD BE ABOLISHED

In my opinion, it seems to me that college football should be abolished. The reason why I think this to be true is because I feel that football is bad for the colleges in nearly every respect. As Robert Hutchins says in his article in our anthology in which he discusses college football, it would be better if the colleges had race horses and had races with one another, because then the horses would not have to attend classes. I firmly agree with Mr. Hutchins on this point, and I am sure that many other students would agree too.

One reason why it seems to me that college football is bad is that it has become too commercial. In the olden times when people played football just for the fun of it, maybe college football was all right, but they do not play college football just for the fun of it now as they used to in the old days. Nowadays college football is what you might call a big business. Maybe this is not true at all schools, and I don't think it is especially true here at State, but certainly this is the case at most colleges and universities in America nowadays, as Mr. Hutchins points out in his very interesting article. Actually the coaches and alumni go around to the high schools and offer the high school stars large salaries to come to their colleges and play football for them. There was one case where a high school star was offered a convertible if he would play football for a certain college.

Another reason for abolishing college football is that it is bad for the players. They do not have time to get a college education, because they are so busy playing football. A football player has to practice every afternoon from three to six and then he is so tired that he can't concentrate on his studies. He just feels like dropping off to sleep after dinner, and then the next day he goes to his classes without having studied and maybe he fails the test.

(Good ripe stuff so far, but you're still a hundred and fifty-one words from home. One more push.)

Also I think college football is bad for the colleges and the universities because not very many students get to participate in it. Out of a college of ten thousand students only seventy-five or a hundred play football, if that many. Football is what you might call a spectator sport. That means that most people go to watch it but do not play it themselves.

(Four hundred and fifteen. Well, you still have the conclusion, and when you retype it, you can make the margins a little wider.)

These are the reasons why I agree with Mr. Hutchins that college football should be abolished in American colleges and universities.

On Monday you turn it in, moderately hopeful, and on Friday it comes back marked "weak in content" and sporting a big "D." This essay is exaggerated a little, not much. The English instructor will recognize it as reasonably typical of what an assignment on college football will bring in. He knows that nearly half of the class will contrive in five hundred words to say that college football is too commercial and bad for the players. Most of the other half will inform him that college football builds character and prepares one for life and brings prestige to the school. As he reads paper after paper all saying the same thing in almost the same words, all bloodless, five hundred words dripping out of nothing, he wonders how he allowed himself to get trapped into teaching English when he might have had a happy and interesting life as an electrician or a confidence man.

Well, you may ask, what can you do about it? The subject is one on which you have few convictions and little information. Can you be expected to make a dull subject interesting? As a matter of fact, this is precisely what you are expected to do. This is the writer's essential task. All subjects, except sex, are dull until somebody makes them interesting. The writer's job is to find the argument, the approach, the angle, the wording that will take the reader with him. This is seldom easy, and it is particularly hard in subjects that have been much discussed: College Football, Fraternities, Popular Music, Is Chivalry Dead?, and the like. You will feel that there is nothing you can do with such subjects except repeat the old bromides. But there are some things you can do which will make your papers, if not throbbingly alive, at least less insufferably tedious than they might otherwise be.

AVOID THE OBVIOUS CONTENT

Say the assignment is college football. Say that you've decided to be against it. Begin by putting down the arguments that come to your mind: it is too commercial, it takes the students' minds off their studies, it is hard on the players, it makes the university a kind of circus instead of an intellectual center, for most schools it is financially ruinous. Can you think of any more arguments, just off hand? All right. Now when you write your paper, make sure that you don't use any of the material on this list. If these are the points that leap to your mind, they will leap to everyone else's too, and whether you get a "C" or a "D" may depend on whether the instructor reads your paper early when he is fresh and tolerant or late, when the sentence "In my opinion, college football has become too commercial," inexorably repeated, has bought him to the brink of lunacy.

Be against college football for some reason or reasons of your own. If they are keen and perceptive ones, that's splendid. But even if they are trivial or foolish or indefensible, you are still ahead so long as they are not everybody else's reasons too. Be against it because the colleges don't spend enough money on it to make it worthwhile, because it is bad for the characters of the spectators, because the players are forced to attend classes, because the football stars hog all the beautiful women, because it competes with baseball and is therefore un-American and possibly Communist-inspired. There are lots of more or less unused reasons for being against college football.

Sometimes it is a good idea to sum up and dispose of the trite and conventional points before going on to your own. This has the advantage of indicating to the reader that you are going to be neither trite nor conventional. Something like this: *We are often told that college football should be abolished because it has become too commercial or because it is bad for the players. These arguments are no doubt very cogent, but they don't really go to the heart of the matter.*

Then you go to the heart of the matter.

TAKE THE LESS USUAL SIDE

One rather simple way of getting into your paper is to take the side of the argument that most of the citizens will want to avoid. If the assignment is an essay on dogs, you can, if you choose, explain that dogs are faithful and lovable companions, intelligent, useful as guardians of the house and protectors of children, indispensable in police work -- in short, when all is said and done, man's best friends. Or you can suggest that those big brown eyes conceal, more often than not, a vacuity of mind and an inconstancy of purpose; that the dogs you have known most intimately have been mangy, ill-tempered brutes, incapable of instruction; and that only your nobility of mind and fear of arrest prevent you from kicking the flea-ridden animals when you pass them on the street. Naturally personal convictions will sometimes dictate your approach. If the assigned subject is "Is Methodism Rewarding to the Individual?" and you are a pious Methodist, you have really no choice. But few assigned subjects, if any, will fall in this category.

Most of them will lie in broad areas of discussion with much to be said on both sides. They are intellectual exercises, and it is legitimate to argue now one way and now another, as debaters do in similar circumstances. Always take the side that looks to you hardest, least defensible. It will almost always turn out to be easier to write interestingly on that side.

This general advice applies where you have a choice of subjects. If you are to choose among "The Value of Fraternities" and "My Favorite High School Teacher" and "What I Think About Beetles," by all means plump for the beetles. By the time the instructor gets to your paper, he will be up to his ears in tedious tales about a French teacher at Bloombury High and assertions about how fraternities build character and prepare one for life. Your views on beetles, whatever they are, are bound to be a refreshing change.

Don't worry too much about figuring out what the instructor thinks about the subject so that you can cuddle up with him. Chances are his views are no stronger than yours. If he does have convictions and you oppose him, his problem is to keep from grading you higher than you deserve in order to show he is not biased. This doesn't mean that you should always cantankerously dissent from what the instructor says; that gets tiresome too. And if the subject assigned is "My Pet Peeve," do not begin, "My pet peeve is the English instructor who assigns papers on 'my pet peeve.'" This was still funny during the War of 1812, but it has sort of lost its edge since then. It is in general good manners to avoid personalities.

SLIP OUT OF ABSTRACTION

If you will study the essay on college football [near the beginning of this essay], you will perceive that one reason for its appalling dullness is that it never gets down to particulars. It is just a series of not very glittering generalities: "football is bad for the colleges," "it has become too commercial," "football is big business," "it is bad for the players," and so on. Such round phrases thudding against the reader's brain are unlikely to convince him, though they may well render him unconscious.

If you want the reader to believe that college football is bad for the players, you have to do more than say so. You have to display the evil. Take your roommate, Alfred Simkins, the second-string center. Picture poor old Alfy coming home from football practice every evening, bruised and aching, agonizingly tired, scarcely able to shovel the mashed potatoes into his mouth. Let us see him staggering up to the room, getting out his econ textbook, peering desperately at it with his good eye, falling asleep and failing the test in the morning. Let us share his unbearable tension as Saturday draws near. Will he fail, be demoted, lose his monthly allowance, be forced to return to the coal mines? And if he succeeds, what will be his reward? Perhaps a slight ripple of applause when the third-string center replaces him, a moment of elation in the locker room if the team wins, of despair if it loses. What will he look back on when he graduates from college? Toil and torn ligaments. And what will be his future? He is not good enough for pro football, and he is too obscure and weak in econ to succeed in stocks and bonds. College football is tearing the heart from Alfy Simkins and, when it finishes with him, will callously toss aside the shattered hulk.

This is no doubt a weak enough argument for the abolition of college football, but it is a sight better than saying, in three or four variations, that college football (in your opinion) is bad for the players.

Look at the work of any professional writer and notice how constantly he is moving from the generality, the abstract statement, to the concrete example, the facts and figures, the illustrations. If he is writing on juvenile delinquency, he does not just tell you that juveniles are (it seems to him) delinquent and that (in his opinion) something should be done about it. He shows you juveniles being delinquent, tearing up movie theatres in Buffalo, stabbing high school principals in Dallas, smoking marijuana in Palo Alto. And more than likely he is moving toward some specific remedy, not just a general wringing of the hands.

It is no doubt possible to be too concrete, too illustrative or anecdotal, but few inexperienced writers err this way. For most the soundest advice is to be seeking always for the picture, to be always turning general remarks into seeable examples. Don't say, "Sororities teach girls the social graces." Say, "Sorority life teaches a girl how to carry on a conversation while pouring tea, without sloshing the tea into the saucer." Don't say, "I like certain kinds of popular music very much." Say, "Whenever I hear Gerber Sprinklittle play 'Mississippi Man' on the trombone, my socks creep up my ankles."

GET RID OF OBVIOUS PADDING

The student toiling away at his weekly English theme is too often tormented by a figure: five hundred words. How, he asks himself, is he to achieve this staggering total? Obviously by never using one word when he can somehow work in ten. He is therefore seldom content with a plain statement like "Fast driving is dangerous." This has only four words in it. He takes thought, and the sentence becomes: *In my opinion, fast driving is dangerous.*

Better, but he can do better still: *In my opinion, fast driving would seem to be rather dangerous.* If he is really adept, it may come out: *In my humble opinion, though I do not claim to be an expert on this complicated subject, test driving, in most circumstances, would seem to be rather dangerous in many respects, or at least so it would seem to me.*

Thus four words have been turned into forty, and not an iota of content has been added. Now this is a way to go about reaching five hundred words, and if you are content with a "D" grade, it is as good a way as any. But if you aim higher, you must work differently. Instead of stuffing your sentences with straw, you must try steadily to get rid of the padding, to make your sentences lean and tough. If you are really working at it, your first draft will greatly exceed the required total, and then you will work it down, thus:

It is thought in some quarters that fraternities do not contribute as much as might be expected to campus life.
vs.
Some people think that fraternities contribute little to campus life.

The average doctor who practices in small towns or in the country must toil night and day to heal the sick.
vs.
Most country doctors work long hours.

When I was a little girl, I suffered from shyness and embarrassment in the presence of others.
vs.
I was a shy little girl.

It is absolutely necessary for the person employed as a marine fireman to give the matter of steam pressure his undivided attention at all times.
vs.
The fireman has to keep his eye on the steam gauge.

You may ask how you can arrive at five hundred words at this rate. Simple. You dig up more real content. Instead of taking a couple of obvious points off the surface of the topic and then circling warily around them for six paragraphs, you work in and explore, figure out the details. You illustrate. You say that fast driving is dangerous, and then you prove it. How long does it take to stop a car at forty and at eighty? How far can you see at night? What happens when a tire blows? What happens in a head-on collision at fifty miles an hour? Pretty soon your paper will be full of broken glass and blood and headless torsos, and reaching five hundred words will not really be a problem.

CALL A FOOL A FOOL

Some of the padding in freshman themes is to be blamed not on anxiety about the word minimum but on excessive timidity. The student writes, "In my opinion, the principal of my high school acted in ways that I believe every unbiased person would have to call foolish." This isn't exactly what he means. What he means is, "My high school principal was a fool." If he was a fool, call him a fool. Hedging the thing about with "in-my-opinion's" and "it-seems-to-me's" and "as-I-see-it's" and "at-least-from-my-point-of-view's" gains you nothing. Delete these phrases whenever they creep into your paper.

The student's tendency to hedge stems from a modesty that in other circumstances would be commendable. He is, he realizes, young and inexperienced, and he half suspects that he is dopey and fuzzy minded beyond the average. Probably only too true. But it doesn't help to announce your incompetence six times in every paragraph. Decide what you want to say and say it as vigorously as possible, without apology and in plain words.

Linguistic diffidence can take various forms. One is what we call euphemism. This is the tendency to call a spade "a certain garden implement" or women's underwear "unmentionables." It is stronger in some eras than others and in some people than others but it always operates more or less in subjects that are touchy or taboo: death, sex, madness, and so on. Thus we shrink from saying "He died last night" but say instead "passed away," "left us," "joined his Maker," "went to his reward." Or we try to take off the tension with a lighter cliché: "kicked the bucket," "cashed in his chips," "handed in his dinner pail." We have found all sorts of ways to avoid saying mad: "mentally ill," "touched," "not quite right upstairs," "feebleminded," "innocent," "simple," "off his trolley," "not in his right mind." Even such a now plain word as insane began as a euphemism with the meaning "not healthy."

Modern science, particularly psychology, contributes many polysyllables in which we can wrap our thoughts and blunt their force. To many writers there is no such thing as a bad schoolboy. Schoolboys are maladjusted or unoriented or misunderstood or in the need of guidance or lacking in continued success toward satisfactory integration of the personality as a social unit, but they are never bad. Psychology no doubt makes us better men and women, more sympathetic and tolerant, but it doesn't make writing any easier.

Had Shakespeare been confronted with psychology, "To be or not to be" might have come out, "To continue as a social unit or not to do so. That is the personality problem. Whether 'tis a better sign of integration at the conscious level to display a psychic tolerance toward the maladjustments and repressions induced by one's lack of orientation in one's environment or --" but Hamlet would never have finished the soliloquy.

Writing in the modern world, you cannot altogether avoid modern jargon. Nor, in an effort to get away from euphemism, should you salt your paper with four-letter words. But you can do much if you will mount guard against those roundabout phrases, those echoing polysyllables that tend to slip into your writing to rob it of its crispness and force.

BEWARE OF PAT EXPRESSIONS

Other things being equal, avoid phrases like "other things being equal." Those sentences that come to you whole, or in two or three doughy lumps, are sure to be bad sentences. They are no creation of yours but pieces of common thought floating in the community soup. Pat expressions are hard, often impossible, to avoid, because they come too easily to be noticed and seem too necessary to be dispensed with. No writer avoids them altogether, but good writers avoid them more often than poor writers.

By "pat expressions" we mean such tags as "to all practical intents and purposes," "the pure and simple truth," "from where I sit," "the time of his life," "to the ends of the earth," "in the twinkling of an eye," "as sure as you're born," "over my dead body," "under cover of darkness," "took the easy way out," "when all is said and done," "told him time and time again," "parted the best of friends," "stand up and be counted," "gave him the best years of her life," "worked her fingers to the bone." Like other clichés, these expressions were once forceful. Now we should use them only when we can't possibly think of anything else.

Some pat expressions stand like a wall between the writer and thought. Such a one is "the American way of life." Many student writers feel that when they have said that something accords with the American way of life or does not they have exhausted the subject. Actually, they have stopped at the highest level of abstraction. The American way of life is the complicated set of bonds between a hundred and eighty million ways. All of us know this when we think about it, but the tag phrase too often keeps us from thinking about it.

So with many another phrase dear to the politician: "this great land of ours," "the man in the street," "our national heritage." These may prove our patriotism or give a clue to our political beliefs, but otherwise they add nothing to the paper except words.

COLORFUL WORDS

The writer builds with words, and no builder uses a raw material more slippery and elusive and treacherous. A writer's work is a constant struggle to get the right word in the right place, to find that particular word that will convey his meaning exactly, that will persuade the reader or soothe him or startle or amuse him. He never succeeds altogether—sometimes he feels that he scarcely succeeds at all—but such successes as he has are what make the thing worth doing.

There is no book of rules for this game. One progresses through everlasting experiment on the basis of ever-widening experience. There are few useful generalizations that one can make about words as words, but there are perhaps a few. Some words are what we call "colorful." By this we mean that they are calculated to produce a picture or induce an emotion. They are dressy instead of plain, specific instead of general, loud instead of soft. Thus, in place of "Her heart beat," we may write, "her heart **pounded, throbbed, fluttered, danced**." Instead of "He sat in his chair," we may say, "he **lounged, sprawled, coiled**." Instead of "It was hot," we may say, "It was **blistering, sultry, muggy, suffocating, steamy, wilting**."

However, it should not be supposed that the fancy word is always better. Often it is as well to write "Her heart beat" or "It was hot" if that is all it did or all it was. Ages differ in how they like their prose. The nineteenth century liked it rich and smoky. The twentieth has usually preferred it lean and cool. The twentieth century writer, like all writers, is forever seeking the exact word, but he is wary of sounding feverish. He tends to pitch it low, to understate it, to throw it away. He knows that if he gets too colorful, the audience is likely to giggle. See how this strikes you: "As the rich, golden glow of the sunset died away along the eternal western hills, Angela's limpid blue eyes looked softly and trustingly into Montague's flashing brown ones, and her heart pounded like a drum in time with the joyous song surging in her soul." Some people like that sort of thing, but most modern readers would say, "Good grief," and turn on the television.

COLORED WORDS

Some words we would call not so much colorful as colored—that is, loaded with associations, good or bad. All words—except perhaps structure words—have associations of some sort. We have said that the meaning of a word is the sum of the contexts in which it occurs. When we hear a word, we hear with it an echo of all the situations in which we have heard it before.

In some words, these echoes are obvious and discussible. The word *mother*, for example, has, for most people, agreeable associations. When you hear *mother* you probably think of home, safety, love, food, and various other pleasant things. If one writes, "She was like a mother to me," he gets an effect which he would not get in "She was like an aunt to me." The advertiser makes use of the associations of *mother* by working it in when he talks about his product. The politician works it in when he talks about himself. So also with such words as *home, liberty, fireside, contentment, patriot, tenderness, sacrifice, childlike, manly, bluff, limpid*. All of these words are loaded with associations that would be rather hard to indicate in a straightforward definition. There is more than a literal difference between "They sat around the fireside" and "They sat around the stove."

They might have been equally warm and happy around the stove, but *fireside* suggests leisure, grace, quiet tradition, congenial company, and *stove* does not. Conversely, some words have bad associations. *Mother* suggests pleasant things, but *mother-in-law* does not. Many mothers-in-law are heroically lovable and some mothers drink gin all day and beat their children insensible, but these facts of life are beside the point. The point is that *mother* sounds good and *mother-in-law* does not.

Or consider the word *intellectual*. This would seem to be a complimentary term, but in point of fact it is not, for it has picked up associations of impracticality and ineffectuality and general dopiness. So also such words as *liberal, reactionary, Communist, socialist, capitalist, radical, schoolteacher, truck driver; operator, salesman, huckster, speculator*. These convey meaning on the literal level, but beyond that—sometimes in some places—they convey contempt on the part of the speaker.

The question of whether to use loaded words or not depends on what is being written. The scientist, the scholar, try to avoid them; for the poet, the advertising writer, the public speaker, they are standard equipment. But every writer should take care that they do not substitute for thought. If you write, "Anyone who thinks that is nothing but a Socialist (or Communist or capitalist)" you have said nothing except that you don't like people who think that, and such remarks are effective only with the most naive readers. It is always a bad mistake to think your readers more naive than they really are.

COLORLESS WORDS

But probably most student writers come to grief not with words that are colorful or those that are colored but with those that have no color at all. A pet example is ***nice***, a word we would find it hard to dispense with in casual conversation but which is no longer capable of adding much to a description. Colorless words are those of such general meaning that in a particular sentence they mean nothing. Slang adjectives like cool ("That's real cool") tend to explode all over the language. They are applied to everything, lose their original force, and quickly die.

Beware also of nouns of very general meaning, like ***circumstances, cases, instances, aspects, factors, relationships, attitudes, eventualities***, etc. In most circumstances you will find that those cases of writing which contain too many instances of words like these will in this and other aspects have factors leading to unsatisfactory relationships with the reader resulting in unfavorable attitudes on his part and perhaps other eventualities, like a grade of "D." Notice also what "etc." means. It means "I'd like to make this list longer, but I can't think of any more examples."

Roberts, Paul. "How to Say Nothing in 500 Words." *The Longman Reader*. 7th ed. Ed. Judith Nadell, John Langan, and Eliza A. Comodromos. New York: Pearson, 2005. 316-26. Print.

Discussion Questions for "How to Say Nothing in 500 Words"

1. In your own words, what is the thesis of the essay?

2. Roberts begins his essay with a hook that tells a story about a fictional student and a fictional writing assignment before recommending how to produce stronger, more efficient writing. Is the hook effective, or have you mistaken the hook for the topic of the essay? If you found it confusing, how would you rearrange the essay or what type of hook would you substitute for the original? If, instead, you found it effective, explain why you did.

3. Which of Roberts' suggestion do you find most useful. Explain why.

4. Despite the essay's title, Roberts wants writers—especially college writers—to make their writing styles more compact and effective. Did the title initially throw you off track? If so, how? Now that you have read the essay, what device is he employing in the title?

5. Based on this essay, you may not be surprised to learn that the author was an English teacher. His advice comes from years of experience reading student essays. In response to these essays, Roberts emphasizes that original, concise, and colorful writing is the most effective and interesting. If you were to put yourself in his place and evaluate your own writing, what weaknesses (not including grammar) would you find? How would you strive to eliminate these weaknesses?

ADDING TOOLS TO THE WRITER'S TOOLBOX

To conclude your preparation for college composition, this chapter provides a brief introduction to the kinds of essays – or *genres*, rhetorical patterns – you may encounter once you leave this class. Introductory composition courses are devoted almost exclusively to the patterns we are touching on here. After all, if you are preparing to travel to a strange city or country, then you may want to check into the kinds of places and things you are likely to see or encounter there. You might also consider these different *genres* as tools in a writer's toolbox: a well-stocked toolbox ensures that you have whatever you need to address any challenge. All college writing falls into one of nine categories:

RHETORICAL PATTERNS OF ACADEMIC WRITING
1. **Description**
2. **Narration**
3. **Illustration**
4. **Comparison/Contrast**
5. **Classification / Division**
6. **Definition**
7. **Cause and Effect (Cause / Consequence)**
8. **Process analysis**
9. **Argumentation**

Depending on your major and the courses you intend to take, you may encounter one or more of these types of essays more than others; for example, if you are a nursing major, you may not be asked to write an illustration essay but *may* be

asked to write up what happened during a patient's visit, which requires narration, or to describe a patient's symptoms, which requires description. On the other hand, if you are a business administration major, you may be asked to write a report giving examples o f solid business models (illustration) or an essay charting the causes or consequences of certain business decisions (cause/effect). Many times, you will find that each of these types of writing can be used to build an entire essay.

However, before you worry needlessly about having to learn about *all* of these, you need to realize that, in some cases, these different rhetorical patterns can be used in varying combinations to produce larger writing projects. A writer putting together a research project may find herself utilizing definition to define the issue being researched, comparison and/or contrast to show how the issue is either similar to or different from other issues, and argument to get the reader to agree that action about this issue should be taken. In the readings you have been covering for this semester, you should notice that no essay utilizes only of the patterns; instead, the authors utilize a combination of the patterns to emphasize their purposes, even if one pattern is primarily used. In order to utilize fully these rhetorical patterns, you need to first understand how and in what situations each can be used (separately or together).

DESCRIPTION—USING YOUR SENSES

Description allows the writer to paint a picture for the reader—of a person, a place, a thing, an event, or even a concept or idea—in such a way that the reader can visualize the subject matter as though he or she is *with* the writer. This type of writing involves using **sensory details**—hearing, touch, sight, smell, and taste—as well as **figurative language**—parts of speech that rely on comparisons using sensory details—to appeal to the reader's imagination. However, merely describing something is not enough: you must focus your description around a **dominant impression**, an emotion or attitude you have about your subject, giving your writing direction.

Appealing to one of the reader's five senses is often challenging because we often do not stop and think about what we are actually seeing and hearing or smelling and tasting; appealing to your reader's senses requires that you think beyond such generalizations as "good" or "bad" ("How did it taste?" "Bad." "How was the movie?" "Good."). How *would* you describe the fragrances from a garden or the aromas coming from a first-class kitchen? This task is even more daunting when you factor in those in your audience who perhaps are not possessed of the senses you plan to appeal to; how would you describe the smell of burning rubber to someone who cannot smell, or how would you describe the sound of your favorite band to someone who cannot hear? These challenges should cause us as writers to think carefully (and sometimes creatively) when asked to write a description. Good descriptive writing *shows* the reader what is being experienced rather than simply telling her. Be careful to avoid words of opinion when concrete sensory details can do a much better job of putting the reader into the world you are creating.

APPEALING TO THE SENSES USING SENSORY DETAILS

Taste
> When I bit my tongue, a coppery taste filled my mouth.

Smell
> The recycling plant surprisingly smelled of lilacs and honeysuckle but with a deep undertone of rotting flesh.

Touch
> The Braille letters were only small, smooth bumps to me, but to my friend, Brenda, they opened the world of language.

Sound
> Dave Grohl of the Foo Fighters belted out emotionally charged lyrics with his scratchy screams that left my right ear ringing for several hours after the concert.

Sight
> The Washington Monument jutted into the gray sky, holding erect against the buffeting winds.

Along with appealing to a reader's five senses, a writer also has figurative language at his or her disposal. The use of sensory details is an excellent device when describing the physical world, but a description of the abstract world of thoughts, emotions, and ideas requires figurative language. In fact, more sophisticated descriptions of the physical world often rely on this type of language. Figurative language allows the writer to compare something potentially unknown to the reader to something that is more likely to be in the reader's knowledge base; to paraphrase Aristotle, figurative language allows the writer to make the unfamiliar familiar through such devices as **similes, metaphors**, and **personification**, which are defined below:

USING SENSORY DETAILS IN FIGURATIVE LANGUAGE

Metaphor: a direct comparison of two unlike things.
My car is a lemon, squirting oil all over the highway four days after purchase.

Simile: a comparison of two unlike things using "like" or "as"
Getting a final draft of an essay together is like landing a man on the moon.

Personification: giving human attributes to an inanimate object
The dark house loomed over the boy, its black eyes staring him down.

NARRATION—TELLING TALES OUT OF SCHOOL (AND IN)

A **narrative** is, basically, a story—a relating of events that have a specific focus. To be successful, narratives must have certain elements: characters, narrative point, and conflict. In academic writing, you may not be asked to compose many narrative essays in which you "make up" a story; however, you may, on occasion, be asked to write about something that actually happened to you or provide anecdotes, small stories used to support larger points, in essays. Even in this kind of assignment, you must make sure that your story has a specific **narrative point**, or reason for telling the story, to make and that your story contains **conflict** - a problem experienced by the main character that must be solved. Like all essays, narratives must have clear organization (usually chronological) as well as striking and engaging descriptions.

A good narrative has a very definite structure: **exposition**, in which the setting and characters are introduced; **rising action,** in which the main character(s) encounter the conflict, building to the **climax,** the moment when the conflict is resolved; and **falling action**, the resolution or end of the story, tying all loose ends. The parts of a narrative or story can be diagrammed as follows:

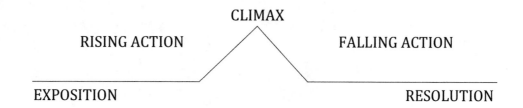

When you read your favorite novel or short story, you should notice, however, that no story is complete with vivid description. Narratives, especially personal ones, may be difficult to write, but they can add a very powerful aspect to your essay. For example, writing about the continuing effects of Hurricane Katrina on the Gulf Coast becomes much more believable when you add a narrative about an individual who daily copes with those effects. In this way, you can put a human face on a potentially abstract or unimaginable problem.

ILLUSTRATION—SHOW; DO NOT TELL

Illustration, also known as exemplification, can be used when a writer wants to explain something by using examples to illustrate his meaning. Illustration can be utilized in a wide variety of other rhetorical patterns and relies heavily on the same kinds of descriptive o r figurative language described above.

Examples, as discussed in previous chapters, generally can be broken down into two major categories: short, interrelated examples and extended examples. No concrete rules exist regarding which category to use in specific instances; this is a decision that you as a writer must make based on the topic of your essay, the support you need to provide, and the overall effect you want to have on your audience. For instance, if you are writing an essay about different kinds of cell phone applications, you might want to use short, interrelated examples to accommodate the wide variety of the subject matter; however, if you are writing an essay about the effects of the recent oil spill on the Louisiana Gulf Coast environment, an extended example might be more compelling and would allow you the latitude to paint a very powerful picture for your reader.

Notice that exemplification is borrowing from narration to complete an extended example. What cannot be stressed enough is that as you use the rhetorical patterns more, you will find that they often mix. The main concern of this text is that you recognize each pattern and use them to serve your point.

If you have decided to include examples in your essay, keep these three guidelines in mind:

1. Make sure that the examples you have chosen are *relevant, representative, accurate, specific, and striking*:

   - Relevant—they pertain to the subject matter;
   - Representative—they represent other similar examples about that subject matter;

- Accurate—they can be backed up with support or research;
- Specific—they cover only certain aspects or facets of the subject being discussed;
- Striking—they capture the reader's attention.

2. Make sure that you use *clear* transitions between these examples.

3. Make sure that you *limit* overly specific details; include only the amount of detail to make the connection with the subject clear to the reader. Overly detailed examples tend to distract the reader from the main point, and they can give the writer an excuse to drift away from the overall focus.

E.B. WHITE—"ONCE MORE TO THE LAKE"

August, 1941

One summer, along about 1904, my father rented a camp on a lake in Maine and took us all there for the month of August. We all got ringworm from some kittens and had to rub Pond's Extract on our arms and legs night and morning, and my father rolled over in a canoe with all his clothes on; but outside of that the vacation was a success and from then on none of us ever thought there was any place in the world like that lake in Maine. We returned summer after summer—always on August 1st for one month. I have since become a salt-water man, but sometimes in summer there are days when the restlessness of the tides and the fearful cold of the sea water and the incessant wind which blows across the afternoon and into the evening make me wish for the placidity of a lake in the woods. A few weeks ago this feeling got so strong I bought myself a couple of bass hooks and a spinner and returned to the lake where we used to go, for a week's fishing and to revisit old haunts.

I took along my son, who had never had any fresh water up his nose and who had seen lily pads only from train windows. On the journey over to the lake I began to wonder what it would be like. I wondered how time would have marred this unique, this holy spot—the coves and streams, the hills that the sun set behind, the camps and the paths behind the camps. I was sure that the tarred road would have found it out and I wondered in what other ways it would be desolated. It is strange how much you can remember about places like that once you allow your mind to return into the grooves which lead back. You remember one thing, and that suddenly reminds you of another thing. I guess I remembered clearest of all the early mornings, when the lake was cool and motionless, remembered how the bedroom smelled of the lumber it was made of and of the wet woods whose scent entered through the screen. The partitions in the camp were thin and did not extend clear to the top of the rooms, and as I was always the first up I would dress softly so as not to wake the others, and sneak out into the sweet outdoors and start out in the canoe, keeping close along the shore in the long shadows of the pines. I remembered being very careful never to rub my paddle against the gunwale for fear of disturbing the stillness of the cathedral.

The lake had never been what you would call a wild lake. There were cottages sprinkled around the shores, and it was in farming although the shores of the lake were quite heavily wooded. Some of the cottages were owned by nearby farmers, and you would live at the shore and eat your meals at the farmhouse. That's what our family did. But although it wasn't wild, it was a fairly large and undisturbed lake and there were places in it which, to a child at least, seemed infinitely remote and primeval.

I was right about the tar: it led to within half a mile of the shore. But when I got back there, with my boy, and we settled into a camp near a farmhouse and into the kind of summertime I had known, I could tell that it was going to be pretty much the same as it had been before—I knew it, lying in bed the first morning, smelling the bedroom, and hearing the boy sneak quietly out and go off along the shore in a boat. I began to sustain the illusion that he was I, and therefore, by simple transposition, that I was my father. This sensation persisted, kept cropping up all the time we were there. It was not an entirely new feeling, but in this setting it grew much stronger. I seemed to be living a dual existence. I would be in the middle of some simple act, I would be picking up a bait box or laying down a table fork, or I would be saying something, and suddenly it would be not I but my father who was saying the words or making the gesture. It gave me a creepy sensation.

We went fishing the first morning. I felt the same damp moss covering the worms in the bait can, and saw the dragonfly alight on the tip of my rod as it hovered a few inches from the surface of the water. It was the arrival of this fly that convinced me beyond any doubt that everything was as it always had been, that the years were a mirage and there had been no years. The small waves were the same, chucking the rowboat under the chin as we fished at anchor, and the boat was the same boat, the same color green and the ribs broken in the same places, and under the floor-boards the same freshwater leavings and debris—the dead helgramite, the wisps of moss, the rusty discarded fishhook, the dried blood from yesterday's catch. We stared silently at the tips of our rods, at the dragonflies that came and wells. I lowered the tip of mine into the water, tentatively, pensively dislodging the fly, which darted two feet away, poised, darted two feet back, and came to rest again a little farther up the rod. There had been no years between the ducking of this dragonfly and the other one—the one that was part of memory. I looked at the boy, who was silently watching his fly, and it was my hands that held his rod, my eyes watching. I felt dizzy and didn't know which rod I was at the end of.

We caught two bass, hauling them in briskly as though they were mackerel, pulling them over the side of the boat in a businesslike manner without any landing net, and stunning them with a blow on the back of the head. When we got back for a swim before lunch, the lake was exactly where we had left it, the same number of inches from the dock, and there was only the merest suggestion of a breeze. This seemed an utterly enchanted sea, this lake you could leave to its own devices for a few hours and come back to, and find that it had not stirred, this constant and trustworthy body of water. In the shallows, the dark, water-soaked sticks and twigs, smooth and old, were undulating in clusters on the bottom against the clean ribbed sand, and the track of the mussel was plain. A school of minnows swam by, each minnow with its small, individual shadow, doubling the attendance, so clear and sharp in the sunlight. Some of the other campers were in swimming, along the shore, one of them with a cake of soap, and the water felt thin and clear and insubstantial. Over the years there had been this person with the cake of soap, this cultist, and here he was. There had been no years.

Up to the farmhouse to dinner through the teeming, dusty field, the road under our sneakers was only a two-track road. The middle track was missing, the one with the marks of the hooves and the splotches of dried, flaky manure. There had always been three tracks to choose from in choosing which track to walk in; now the choice was narrowed down to two. For a moment I missed terribly the middle alternative. But the way led past the tennis court, and something about the way it lay there in the sun reassured me; the tape had loosened along the backline, the alleys were green with plantains and other weeds, and the net (installed in June and removed in September) sagged in the dry noon, and the whole place steamed with midday heat and hunger and emptiness. There was a choice of pie for dessert, and one was blueberry and one was apple, and the waitresses were the same country girls, there having been no passage of time, only the illusion of it as in a dropped curtain--the waitresses were still fifteen; their hair had been washed, that was the only difference—they had been to the movies and seen the pretty girls with the clean hair.

Summertime, oh summertime, pattern of life indelible, the fade proof lake, the woods unshatterable, the pasture with the sweet fern and the juniper forever and ever, summer without end; this was the background, and the life along the shore was the design, the cottages with their innocent and tranquil design, their tiny docks with the flagpole and the American flag floating against the white clouds in the blue sky, the little paths over the roots of the trees leading from camp to camp and the paths leading back to the outhouses and the can of lime for sprinkling, and at the souvenir counters at the store the miniature birch-bark canoes and the post cards that showed things looking a little better than they looked. This was the American family at play, escaping the city heat, wondering whether the newcomers at the camp at the head of the cove were "common" or "nice," wondering whether it was true that the people who drove up for Sunday dinner at the farmhouse were turned away because there wasn't enough chicken.

It seemed to me, as I kept remembering all this, that those times and those summers had been infinitely precious and worth saving. There had been jollity and peace and goodness. The arriving (at the beginning of August) had been so big a business in itself, at the railway station the farm wagon drawn up, the first smell of the pine-laden air, the first glimpse of the smiling farmer, and the great importance of the trunks and your father's enormous authority in such matters, and the feel of the wagon under you for the long ten-mile haul, and at the top of the last long hill catching the first view of the lake after eleven months of not seeing this cherished body of water. The shouts and cries of the other campers when they saw you, and the trunks to be unpacked, to give up their rich burden. (Arriving was less exciting nowadays, when you sneaked up in your car and parked it under a tree near the camp and took out the bags and in five minutes it was all over, no fuss, no loud wonderful fuss about trunks.)

Peace and goodness and jollity. The only thing that was wrong now, really, was the sound of the place, an unfamiliar nervous sound of the outboard motors. This was the note that jarred, the one thing that would sometimes break the illusion and set the years moving. In those other summertimes, all motors were inboard; and when they were at a little distance, the noise they made was a sedative, an ingredient of summer sleep. They were one-cylinder and two-cylinder engines, and some were make-and-break and some were jump-spark, but they all made a sleepy sound across the lake. The one-lungers throbbed and fluttered, and the twin-cylinder ones purred and purred, and that was a quiet sound too. But now the campers all had outboards. In the daytime, in the hot mornings, these motors made a petulant, irritable sound; at night, in the still evening when the afterglow lit the water, they whined about one's ears like mosquitoes. My boy loved our rented outboard, and his great desire was to achieve single-handed mastery over it, and authority, and he soon learned the trick of choking it a little (but not too much), and the adjustment of the needle valve. Watching him I would remember the things you could do with the old one-cylinder engine with the heavy flywheel, how you could have it eating out of your hand if you got really close to it spiritually. Motor boats in those days didn't have clutches, and you would make a landing by shutting off the motor at the proper time and coasting in with a dead rudder. But there was a way of reversing them, if you learned the trick, by cutting the switch and putting it on again exactly on the final dying revolution of the flywheel, so that it would kick back against compression and begin reversing. Approaching a dock in a strong following breeze, it was difficult to slow up sufficiently by the ordinary coasting method, and if a boy felt he had complete mastery over his motor, he was tempted to keep it running beyond its time and then reverse it a few feet from the dock. It took a cool nerve, because if you threw the switch a twentieth of a second too soon you would catch the flywheel when it still had speed enough to go up past center, and the boat would leap ahead, charging bull-fashion at the dock.

We had a good week at the camp. The bass were biting well and the sun shone endlessly, day after day. We would be tired at night and lie down in the accumulated heat of the little bedrooms after the long hot day and the breeze would stir almost imperceptibly outside and the smell of the swamp drift in through the rusty screens. Sleep would come easily and in the morning the red squirrel would be on the roof, tapping out his gay routine. I kept remembering everything, lying in bed in the mornings—the small steamboat that had a long rounded stern like the lip of a Ubangi, and how quietly she ran on the moonlight sails, when the older boys played their mandolins and the girls sang and we ate doughnuts dipped in sugar, and how sweet the music was on the water in the shining night, and what it had felt like to think about girls then. After breakfast we would go up to the store and the things were in the same place—the minnows in a bottle, the plugs and spinners disarranged and pawed over by the youngsters from the boys' camp, the fig newtons and the Beeman's gum. Outside, the road was tarred and cars stood in front of the store. Inside, all was just as it had always been, except there was more Coca Cola and not so much Moxie and root beer and birch beer and sarsaparilla. We would walk out with a bottle of pop apiece and sometimes the pop would backfire up our noses and hurt. We explored the streams, quietly, where the turtles slid off the sunny logs and dug their way into the soft bottom; and we lay on the town wharf and fed worms to the tame bass. Everywhere we went I had trouble making out which was I, the one walking at my side, the one walking in my pants.

One afternoon while we were there at that lake a thunderstorm came up. It was like the revival of an old melodrama that I had seen long ago with childish awe. The second-act climax of the drama of the electrical disturbance over a lake in America had not changed in any important respect. This was the big scene, still the big scene. The whole thing was so familiar, the first feeling of oppression and heat and a general air around camp of not wanting to go very far away. In mid-afternoon (it was all the same) a curious darkening of the sky, and a lull in everything that had made life tick; and then the way the boats suddenly swung the other way at their moorings with the coming of a breeze out of the new quarter, and the premonitory rumble. Then the kettle drum, then the snare, then the bass drum and cymbals, then crackling light against the dark, and the gods grinning and licking their chops in the hills. Afterward the calm, the rain steadily rustling in the calm lake, the return of light and hope and spirits, and the campers running out in joy and relief to go swimming in the rain, their bright cries perpetuating the deathless joke about how they were getting simply drenched, and the children screaming with delight at the new sensation of bathing in the rain, and the joke about getting drenched linking the generations in a strong indestructible chain. And the comedian who waded in carrying an umbrella.

When the others went swimming my son said he was going in too. He pulled his dripping trunks from the line where they had hung all through the shower, and wrung them out. Languidly, and with no thought of going in, I watched him, his hard little body, skinny and bare, saw him wince slightly as he pulled up around his vitals the small, soggy, icy garment. As he buckled the swollen belt suddenly my groin felt the chill of death.

White, E. B. "Once More to the Lake." *One Man's Meat.* Gardiner, Maine: Tilbury House Pub., 1941. Rpt. in *Making Sense: A Real-World Rhetorical Reader.* New York: Bedford, 2005. 118-25. Print.

Discussion Questions for "Once More to the Lake"

1. What is White's narrative point? Why does he spend so much time telling his readers about a family vacation?

2. Find examples of description in this essay that employ each of the five senses. What effect does the vivid imagery have on you the reader?

3. What motifs does White use in the essay to emphasize his narrative point?

4. What examples of figurative language are used in the essay? Can you find any examples of extended metaphor?

5. The story ends with an unusual description of the boy's body, even his "vitals." Why does the author use this description to end the narrative? How does it resolve the conflict?

6. Hopefully you have discovered that beneath the surface of White's narrative lies a deep underlying meaning. What significance can you derive from the endless cycle of father and son visiting this "cathedral"? How does his use of description help to emphasize this point?

COMPARISON/CONTRAST—SHOWING SIMILARITIES AND DIFFERENCES

Comparison/contrast is often the most misunderstood of the rhetorical patterns and can trip up student writers if they are not careful. Imagine that you are looking at an essay test question that asks you to "compare the causes of the American Revolution to the causes of the Civil War." What is this actually asking you to compose? **Comparison** essays look only at *similarities*—how two or more things are *alike*. On the other hand, **contrast** essays look only at *differences*. Therefore, the essay test question is asking you to tell about how the causes of these two conflicts were alike, and your response should be limited to that. At times, these two types can be utilized together; in any instance, the wording of the question will tell you which one your instructor wants you to address, so read the question or assignment carefully.

Comparison or contrast essays can be organized in two ways, and which one you choose will depend on where you want the focus of your essay to be. **Subject-by-subject** organization takes each thing being compared or contrasted and discusses each difference or similarity one subject at a time as shown below:

SUBJECT-BY-SUBJECT

I. **Subject 1**
   a. **Difference or Similarity**
   b. **Difference or Similarity**
   c. **Difference or Similarity**

II. **Subject 2**
   a. **Difference or Similarity**
   b. **Difference or Similarity**
   c. **Difference or Similarity**

Point-by-point organization takes each similarity or difference and discusses them one point at a time.

> **POINT-BY-POINT:**
> I. **Point (Difference or Similarity) 1**
>   a. **Subject 1**
>   b. **Subject 2**
> II. **Point (Difference or Similarity) 2**
>   a. **Subject 1**
>   b. **Subject 2**
> III. **Point (Difference or Similarity) 3**
>   a. **Subject 1**
>   b. **Subject 2**

CLASSIFICATION/DIVISION—CATEGORIZING YOUR WORLD

Whether we realize it or not, we are surrounded by classifications every day. Even your local newspaper has a specific section called the "Classifieds." What is unique about this particular section? It contains advertisements and notices that are organized by clearly identified categories; you would not expect to find an advertisement for a bass boat for sale next to a notice about an upcoming estate auction. Similarly, **classification** essays group subject matter into already defined and established categories. Division separates groups into their individual parts. How you classify or divide a group is determined by your purpose, or **ruling principle.**

Classification/division essays primarily have two different types of organization: showing why something should—or should *not*—be grouped within a certain category or showing in what order, based on importance for example, things within a category should be listed. For example, you might want to write an essay about the men you consider to be the three top baseball players of all time; on the other hand, you might want to write an essay about why Lady Gaga should or should not be considered a pop music icon.

In *either* case, you must show the criteria that you use to make this decision. In the example about the three top baseball players, you must tell your reader what specific criteria you are using to evaluate these individuals and how they meet those criteria. In the Lady Gaga example, you must show your reader that the pop star possesses or has exhibited the qualities or accomplishments generally accepted and expected from already acknowledged icons. In either case, the criteria could be your own or those already established and agreed upon by experts in that particular field; in either case, you *must* make these criteria clear to your reader.

DEFINITION—WHAT DOES THAT MEAN?

Definition, simply put, explains what a term or concept means. Many beginning academic writers rely on dictionary definitions as a way of introducing a topic to their readers. What they may not know is that this particular method is *not* the most effective way of beginning an essay and, in fact, it may diminish their believability in the eyes of their reading audience. These definitions *do* have a place in academic writing, however, and should be utilized when you are trying to define a concept or issue or general term in a way that the reader may not have thought of before; similarly, a dictionary definition should be used when *your* definition of the issue or term being discussed is radically different than one found in a dictionary – and that difference is the main focus of your essay.

When dealing with definitions, writers need to remember that words have two very different meanings:

TWO TYPES OF MEANING IN DEFINITION

Denotative meaning—a definition found in a dictionary; this language is often *objective* and neutral or void of emotion.

Connotative meaning—a definition that is *subjective* and emotionally charged and based on your personal experiences and prior knowledge.

Since words have such varying meanings, a writer must make clear which meaning is being discussed and must keep in mind that readers' connotative meanings may affect how they respond to what is written. In doing so, a writer keeps the reader's viewpoint in mind, making concessions and addressing differences as needed.

Definitions also come in various forms. These forms help both the writer and reader come to a clear point. One of the forms of definition actually reveals a weakness in the writer's own thinking and should be avoided (see if you can recognize it). Brief definitions and examples of these forms are shown below:

Stipulative definition—restricts the meaning of a term by letting the reader know exactly what the author means in order to limit the scope of the discussion.

> The term romance when applied to literature suggests an era of writing when science and technology were rejected in favor of nature as a sublime force.

Definition by negation—tells the reader what a term does not mean in order to make clear what he is trying to focus on.

> College is not a time for frivolity, a time for continuing potentially harmful habits for high school, nor a time for rejecting all avenues of fun.

Etymology—reveals to the reader the history or origin of a word in order to make its present meaning clearer.

> For centuries, gay has merely meant to be happy, of good cheer and disposition, or frolicsome.

Circular definition—using a root of the word you are trying to define in the definition itself or using a definition so vague that no meaning can be attributed to the word.

> Poetry is work written by a poet.

> Death is the state of no longer being alive.

DAVE BARRY—"GUYS VS. MEN"

This book is about guys. It's not a book about men. There are already way too many books about men, and most of them are *way* too serious.

Men itself is a serious word, not to mention *manhood* and *manly*. Such words make being male sound like a very important activity, as opposed to what it primarily consists of, namely, possessing a set of minor and frequently unreliable organs.

But men tend to attach great significance to Manhood. This results in certain characteristically masculine, by which I mean stupid, behavioral patterns that can produce unfortunate results such as violent crime, war, spitting, and ice hockey. These things have given males a bad name. And the "Men's Movement," which is supposed to bring out the more positive aspects of Manliness, seems to be densely populated with loons and goobers.

So I'm saying that there's another way to look at males, not as aggressive macho dominators, not as sensitive, liberated, hugging drummers, but as *guys*.

And what, exactly, do I mean by "guys"? I don't know. I haven't thought that much about it. One of the major characteristics of guyhood is that we guys don't spend a lot of time pondering our deep innermost feelings. There is a serious question in my mind about whether guys actually *have* deep innermost feelings, unless you count, for example, loyalty to the Detroit Tigers or fear of bridal showers.

But although I can't define exactly what it means to be a guy, I can describe certain guy characteristics, such as:

GUYS LIKE NEAT STUFF

By "neat," I mean "mechanical and unnecessarily complex." I'll give you an example. Right now I'm typing these words on an *extremely* powerful computer. It's the latest in a line of maybe ten computers I've owned, each one more powerful than the last. My computer is chock full of RAM and ROM and bytes and megahertzes and various other items that enable a computer to kick data-processing butt. It is probably capable of supervising the entire U.S. air-defense apparatus while simultaneously processing the tax return of every resident of Ohio. I use it mainly to write a newspaper column. This is an activity wherein I sit and stare at the screen for maybe ten minutes, then, using only my forefingers, slowly type something like:

Henry Kissinger looks like a big wart.

I stare at this for another ten minutes, have an inspiration, then amplify the original thought as follows:

Henry Kissinger looks like a big fat wart.

Then I stare at that for another ten minutes, pondering whether I should try to work in the concept of "hairy."

This is absurdly simple work for my computer. It sits there, humming impatiently, bored to death, passing the time between keystrokes via brain-teaser activities such as developing a Unified Field Theory of the universe and translating the complete works of Shakespeare into rap.

In other words, this computer is absurdly overqualified to work for me, and yet soon, I guarantee, I will buy an *even more powerful* one. I won't be able to stop myself. I'm a guy.

Probably the ultimate example of the fundamental guy drive to have neat stuff is the Space Shuttle. Granted, the guys in charge of this program *claim* it has a Higher Scientific Purpose, namely to see how humans function in space. But of course we have known for years how humans function in space. They float around and say things like, "Looks real good, Houston!"

No, the real reason for the existence of the Space Shuttle is that it is one humongous and spectacularly gizmo-intensive item of hardware. Guys can tinker with it practically forever, and occasionally even get it to work, and use it to place *other* complex mechanical items into orbit, where they almost immediately break, which provides a great excuse to send the Space Shuttle up *again*. It's Guy Heaven.

Other results of the guy need to have stuff are Star Wars, the recreational boating industry, monorails, nuclear weapons, and wristwatches that indicate the phase of the moon. I am not saying that women haven't been involved in the development or use of this stuff. I'm saying that, without guys, this stuff probably would not exist, just as, without women, virtually every piece of furniture in the world would still be in its original position. Guys do not have a basic need to rearrange furniture. Whereas a woman who could cheerfully use the same computer for fifty-three years will rearrange her furniture on almost a weekly basis, sometimes in the dead of night. She'll be sound asleep in bed, and suddenly, at 2 a.m., she'll be awakened by the urgent thought: *The blue-green sofa needs to go perpendicular to the wall instead of parallel, and it needs to go there* **right now.** So she'll get up and move it, which of course necessitates moving other furniture, and soon she has rearranged her entire living room, shifting great big heavy pieces that ordinarily would require several burly men to lift, because there are few forces in Nature more powerful than a woman who needs to rearrange furniture. Every so often a guy will wake up to discover that, because of his wife's overnight efforts, he now lives in an entirely different house.

(I realize that I'm making gender-based generalizations here, but my feeling is that if God did not want us to make gender-based generalizations, She would not have given us genders.)

GUYS LIKE A REALLY POINTLESS CHALLENGE

Not long ago, I was sitting in my office at the *Miami Herald*'s Sunday magazine, *Tropic*, reading my fan mail, when I heard several of my guy coworkers in the hallway talking about how fast they could run the forty-yard dash. These are guys in their thirties and forties who work in journalism, where the most demanding physical requirement is the ability to digest vending-machine food. In other words, these guys have absolutely no need to run the forty-yard dash.

But one of them, Mike Wilson, was writing a story about a star high-school football player who could run it in 4.38 seconds. Now if Mike had written a story about, say, a star high-school poet, none of my guy co-workers would have suddenly decided to find out how well they could write sonnets. But when Mike turned in his story, they became *deeply* concerned about how fast they could run the forty-yard dash. They were so concerned that the magazine editor, Tom Shroder, decided that they should get a stopwatch and go out to a nearby park and find out. Which they did, a bunch of guys taking off their shoes and running around barefoot in a public park on company time.

This is what I heard them talking about, out in the hall. I heard Tom, who was thirty-eight years old, saying that his time in the forty had been 5.75 seconds. And I thought to myself: This is ridiculous. These are middle-aged guys, supposedly adults, and they're out there *bragging* about their performance in this stupid juvenile footrace. Finally, I couldn't stand it anymore.

"Hey!" I shouted. *"I could beat 5.75 seconds."*

So we went out to the park and measured off forty yards, and the guys told me that I had three chances to make my best time. On the first try my time was 5.78 seconds, just three-hundredths of a second slower than Tom's, even though, at forty-five, I was seven years older than he. So I just *knew* I'd beat him on the second attempt if I ran really, really hard, which I did for a solid ten yards, at which point my left hamstring muscle, which had not yet shifted into Spring Mode from Mail-Reading Mode, went, and I quote, "pop."

I had to be helped off the field. I was in considerable pain, and I was obviously not going to be able to walk right for weeks. The other guys were very sympathetic, especially Tom, who took the time to call me at home, where I was sitting with an ice pack on my leg and twenty-three Advil in my bloodstream, so he could express his concern.

"Just remember," he said, *"you didn't beat my time."*

There are countless other examples of guys rising to meet pointless challenges. Virtually all sports fall into this category as well as a large part of U.S. foreign policy. ("I'll be you can't capture Manuel Noriega." ***"Oh yeah??"***)

GUYS DO NOT HAVE A RIGID AND WELL-DEFINED MORAL CODE

This is not the same as saying that guys are bad. Guys *are* capable of doing bad things, but this generally happens when they try to be Men and start becoming manly and aggressive and stupid. When they're being just plain guys, they aren't so much actively evil as they are lost. Because guys have never really grasped the Basic Human Moral Code, which I believe was invented by women millions of years ago when all the guys were out engaging in some other activity, such as seeing who could burp the loudest. When they came back, there were certain rules that they were expected to follow unless they wanted to get into Big Trouble, and they have been trying to follow these rules ever since, with extremely irregular results. Because guys have never *internalized* these rules. Guys are similar to my small auxiliary backup dog, Zippy, a guy dog who has been told numerous times that he is not supposed to (1) get into the kitchen garbage or (2) poop on the floor. He knows that these are the rules, but he has never really understood *why*, and sometimes he gets to thinking: Sure, I am *ordinarily* not supposed to get into the garbage, but obviously this rule is not meant to apply when there are certain extenuating circumstances, such as (1) somebody just threw away some perfectly good seven-week-old Kung Pao Chicken, and (2) I am home alone.

And so when the humans come home, the kitchen floor has been transformed into Garbage-Fest USA, and Zippy, who usually comes rushing up, is off in a corner disguised in a wig and sunglasses, hoping to get into the Federal Bad Dog Relocation Program before the humans discover the scene of the crime.

When I yell at him, he frequently becomes so upset that he poops on the floor.

Morally, most guys are just like Zippy, only taller and usually less hairy. Guys are *aware* of the rules of moral behavior, but they have trouble keeping these rules in the forefronts of their minds at certain times, especially the present. This is especially true in the area of faithfulness to one's mate. I realize, of course, that there are countless examples of guys being faithful to their mates until they die, usually as a result of being eaten by their mates immediately after copulation. Guys outside of the spider community, however, do not have a terrific record of faithfulness.

I'm not saying guys are scum. I'm saying that many guys who consider themselves to be committed to their marriages will stray if they are confronted with overwhelming temptation, defined as "virtually any temptation."

Okay, so maybe I *am* saying guys are scum. But they're not *mean spirited* scum. And few of them – even when they are out of town on business trips, far from their wives, and have a clear-cut opportunity – will poop on the floor.

GUYS ARE NOT GREAT AT COMMUNICATING THEIR INTIMATE FEELINGS, ASSUMING THEY HAVE ANY

This is an aspect of guyhood that is very frustrating to women. A guy will be reading the newspaper, and the phone will ring; he'll answer it, listen for ten minutes, hang up, and resume reading. Finally his wife will say "Who was that?"

And he'll say, "Phil Wonkerman's mom."

(Phil is an old friend they haven't heard from in seventeen years.)

And the wife will say, "Well?"

And the guy will say, "Well what?"

And the wife will say, "What did she *say*?"

And the guy will say, "She said Phil is fine," making it clear by his tone of voice that, although he does not wish to be rude, he is trying to read the newspaper, and he happens to be right in the middle of an important panel of "Calvin and Hobbes."

But the wife, ignoring this, will say, "That's *all* she said?"

And she will not let up. She will continue to ask district-attorney-style questions, forcing the guy to recount the conversation until she's satisfied that she has the entire story, which is that Phil just got out of prison after serving a sentence for a murder he committed when he became a drug addict because of the guilt he felt when his wife died in a freak submarine accident while Phil was having an affair with a nun, but now he's all straightened out and has a good job as a trapeze artist and is almost through with the surgical part of his sex change and recently became happily engaged to marry a prominent member of the Grateful Dead, so in other words he is fine, which is *exactly* what the guy told her in the first place, but is that enough? No. She wants to hear *every single detail*.

Or let's say two couples get together after a long separation. The two women will have a conversation, lasting several days, during which they discuss virtually every significant event that has occurred in their lives and the lives of those they care about, sharing their innermost thoughts, analyzing and probing, inevitably coming to a deeper understanding of each other, and a strengthening of a cherished friendship. Whereas the guys will watch the play-offs.

This is not to say the guys won't share their feelings. Sometimes they'll get quite emotional.

"That's not a *foul*??" they'll say.

Or "**You're telling me that's not a *foul*??**"

I have a good friend, Gene, and one time, when he was going through a major medical development in his life, we spent a weekend together. During this time Gene and I talked a lot and enjoyed each other's company immensely, but – this is true—the most intimate personal statement he made to me is that he has reached Level 24 of a video game called "Arkanoid." He had even seen the Evil Presence, although he refused to tell me what it looks like. We're very close, but there's a limit.

You may think that my friends and I are Neanderthals, and that a lot of guys are different. This is true. A lot of guys don't use words at all. They communicate entirely by nonverbal methods, such as sharing bait.

Are you starting to see what I mean by "gayness"? I'm basically talking about the part of the male psyche that is less serious and/or aggressive than the Manly Manhood part, but still essentially very male. My feeling is that the world would be a much better place if more males would stop trying so hard to be Men and instead settle for being Guys. Think of the historical problems that could have been avoided if more males had been able to keep their genderhood in its proper perspective, both in themselves and in others. ("Hey, Adolph, just because you happen to possess a set of minor and frequently unreliable organs, that is no reason to invade Poland.")

And think how much happier women would be if, instead of endlessly fretting about what the males in their lives are thinking, they could relax, secure in the knowledge that the correct answer is *very little*.

Yes, what we need, on the part of both genders, is more understanding of gayness. And that is why I wrote this book. I intend to explore in detail every major facet of guyhood, including the historical facet, the sociological facet, the physiological facet, the psychosexual facet, and the facet of how come guys spit so much. Every statement of fact you will read in this book is either based on actual laboratory tests, or else I made it up. But you can trust me. I'm a guy.

EXAMPLE CHART

MEN	*GUYS*
Vince Lombardi	Joe Namath
Oliver North	Gilligan
Hemingway	Gary Larson
Columbus	Whichever astronaut hit the first golf ball on the Moon
Superman	Bart Simpson
Doberman pinschers	Labrador retrievers
Abbott	Costello
Captain Ahab	Captain Kangaroo
Satan	Snidely Whiplash
The pope	Willard Scott
Germany	Italy
Geraldo	Katie Couric

STIMULUS-RESPONSE COMPARISON CHART: WOMEN VS. MEN VS. GUYS

Stimulus	*Typical Woman*	*Typical Man*	*Typical Guy*
An untamed river in the wilderness.	Contemplate its beauty.	Build a dam.	See who can pee the farthest off the dam.
A child who is sent home from school for being disruptive in class.	Talk to the child in an effort to determine the cause.	Threaten to send the child to military school.	Teach the child how to make armpit farts.
Human mortality	Religious faith	The pyramids	Bungee jumping

Barry, Dave. "Guys vs. Men." *Dave Barry's Complete Guide to Guys.* New York: Random House, 1995. Rpt. in *Making Sense: A Real-World Rhetorical Reader.* 2d ed. Ed. Cheryl Glenn. New York: Bedford, 2005. 399-406. Print.

Discussion Questions for "Guys Vs. Men"

1. Dave Barry is a humorist, someone who uses various forms of humor (satire, caricature, etc.) to get a point across to the reader—sometimes a very serious point. What is Barry's point in this essay? How can you tell if his point is a serious one or one to be considered as unserious?

2. How does Barry use comparison/contrast to emphasize his point? Which method of organization is he using? What other rhetorical patterns is he employing? Provide specific examples from the text.

3. Many of Barry's supporting details are in the form of anecdotes. Discuss how Barry weaves these stories into a cohesive whole. Provide specific examples of the transitions he uses from the text.

4. In addition to his main point, the author is also making a larger comment on middle class society. What statement is he making about suburban men and their relationship to women? What implications is he making about middle class women who suffer these "loons and goobers"?

5. For the men: Are you a man or a guy? Explain your answer and provide specific examples to support your claim.

6. For the women: Are you surrounded by men or guys? Explain your answer and provide specific examples to support your claim.

CAUSE AND EFFECT (CAUSE/CONSEQUENCE)—THE RESULTS ARE IN

Cause and effect (or cause and consequence) essays often pose the biggest challenge for academic writers; we often see causes and effects as logical when, perhaps, the conclusions we make are not as solid as we may believe. Therefore, cause and effect (cause and consequence) essays must be handled carefully and must be constructed in such a way that causal or consequence chains are clearly defined for the reader.

Cause and effect essays trace the causes and effects of certain events or situations and can be constructed in one of two ways:

CAUSE AND EFFECT DEFINED

Cause—this method starts with an event and works backward to show the reasons for it.

> The events of September 11, 2001, were caused by growing tension with the Middle Eastern allies, inattention to dissidents who should have been known threats, and complacency.

Effect—this method starts with an event and works forward to show what potential effects or consequences may occur because of that event.

> Ironically, global climate change will eventually result in coastal flooding, the cessation of the ocean's currents, and the next ice age.

Essentially, the cause and effect pattern can be said to be a form of argument. Using this pattern, you are asserting that certain cause or effects are your own logical conclusions, and you are trying to convince the reader your conclusions are valid. The complexity of this pattern lies in the fact that the writer must construct the chain of events so carefully that the reader can *logically* follow it and see the possibility of the cause or effect (or consequence) being argued; a poorly constructed cause/effect or cause/consequence essay can ruin a writer's believability.

PROCESS ANALYSIS—EXPLAINING HOW TO MAKE THE CHEESE

All of us have had the uncomfortable experience of trying to assemble something or do something or go somewhere using a set of directions that are virtually impossible to follow or understand. Others may have not-so-pleasant memories of trying to follow a recipe only to find out, once the charred hockey puck that was supposed to be a pizza comes out of the oven, that you misread the directions. If your assignment is to explain to your reader how to do something or how *you* did something, you are writing a **process analysis** essay.

Process essays come in two general forms: **informational**—how *you* did it—and **directional**—how the *reader* should do it. For example, an instructional process essay might take the form of a chemistry lab report, outlining and detailing the steps you followed in an experiment; on the other hand, a directional process essay might take the form of a speech you have been asked to give about the steps necessary to apply for financial aid. *Instructional* process essays are always written from a first-person perspective while *directional* process essays are always directed at the reader through the use of second person point-of-view or the use of the imperative (command) mode—where the subject ("you") is implied but not directly stated.

 NOTE: Directional process analysis writing is virtually the only instance in academic writing when using second person is acceptable.

ARGUMENT—YOU SHOULD READ THIS

The word "argument" has very definite connotations (some of them distinctly negative) for all of us; we tend to equate "argument" with raised voices, hurled insults, threats of violence, and, later, rather awkward explanations of how and why you ended up on an episode of *Cops.* Often, we see argument as a "win or lose" proposition and resort to any means necessary to get people to agree with us. We view argument negatively because it has come so far from its original purpose. **Argument** is the use of logical, well-reasoned discourse to discuss and come to agreement (or *consensus*) about problems.

Another misconception about argument is that it is synonymous with persuasion. In reality, argument and persuasion have two very different outcomes in mind:

> ## THE DIFFERENCE OF OPINION
>
> **Argument**—agreement that a problem exists.
> **Persuasion**—agreement about what to do about the problem.

Perhaps an example will make this difference clearer. Imagine that you have been summoned to serve on a jury for a capital murder trial. On the first day of the trial, once everyone is in his or her appointed place, the judge calls on the prosecuting attorney to give her opening remarks. She approaches the podium and says, "Your Honor, ladies and gentlemen of the jury, the People of Oklahoma demand the death penalty in this case," at which point she turns and walks back to her seat. What is wrong with this scenario? What part of the process has she forgotten about? *First*, she must prove that the defendant is guilty; *then*, once guilt has been established, she can make her case for the death penalty. Argument, then, is like the evidence phase of a trial; the arguer—*you*—have to place before your "jury" (your reader) the evidence you have to get the reader to agree with you that a problem exists; after that, then, once you have persuaded your reader that the problem exists, you can put forward your recommendations for how to handle or solve the problem.

CHARACTERISTICS OF ARGUMENT AND PERSUASION

Argument:
- Seeks consensus that a problem exists and should be dealt with
- Takes a stand on an issue or question, either to argue that a problem exists or to add your vote
- Helps the writer or the audience come to a conclusion

Persuasion:
- Moves your reader to action – once argument proves a problem exists
- Details possible ways to fix the problem, usually ending in recommending one over the others
- Convinces others to accept your conclusion

THINGS TO REMEMBER ABOUT RHETORICAL PATTERNS

- There's no *one correct* pattern of development; which one you choose will be determined by the purpose of your writing and the wording of the assignment.

- These different patterns can be used individually (as the sole focus of an essay) or together (as building blocks within an essay).

Knowing how to utilize these tools correctly and successfully will broaden your abilities as a writer.

Determining What You Are Being Asked to Write

Perhaps the biggest challenge for any college writer is determining what exactly he or she is being asked to produce. With all of these rhetorical patterns to choose from, how can you know whether you are being asked to write an argument or a classification essay? The easiest way to figure this out is to take the time needed to dissect the assignment or the prompt, looking for key words that will give you clues as to what your instructor expects. Some of these key words are rather straight-forward ("define," "argue," or "describe") while others may be bit harder to decipher.

What follows is a brief list of words that can tip you off regarding the kind of essay you should produce:

Key Word(s)	Rhetorical Pattern Required
Define	Definition
Discuss	Illustration, Definition, Description
Take a stand on	Argument
Relate an experience	Narration
Describe	Description
Evaluate	Classification, Argument
Rank, Rate	Classification
Describe the process	Process (either informational or directional)
What steps...	Process (either informational or directional)
Give examples of	Illustration
What are the differences	Contrast
What are the similarities	Comparison
What consequences	Cause/Effect
What produced	Cause/Effect
Define	Definition
Explain	Illustration, Definition

While this is by no means an exhaustive list, if you are still unsure about what the assignment is asking you to write, *ask your instructor.* It will save you time and frustration to get any clarification needed from your instructor, and your instructor would rather make sure you are certain than penalize you later for turning in an essay that does not meet the assignment.

Exercise 1

For each of the following essay prompts, determine which rhetorical pattern will best address the question and produce the desired essay *and* which rhetorical patterns might be employed in each (if applicable):

1. Relate an experience that changed how you view your hometown. _____

   _____

   _____

   _____

2. Which of the following movies would you include on a list of the Top 10 Movies of All Time, and why?: *Citizen Kane, Titanic, Young Frankenstein, How the West Was Won, Kill Bill, Harry Potter and the Half-Blood Prince,* or *Airplane!*_____

   _____

   _____

   _____

3. Trace the consequences of the Volstead Act of 1920. _____

   _____

   _____

   _____

4. Describe your favorite place to relax. _____

   _____

   _____

   _____

5. Take a stand on whether or not admissions standards should be raised for public universities in Oklahoma. _____

   _____

   _____

   _____

6. Write an essay explaining the steps involved in applying for federal financial aid. _____

   _____

   _____

7. Contrast the causes of the American Revolution and the causes of the French Revolution. _____

_____

_____

_____

STEPHEN KING—"WHY WE CRAVE HORROR MOVIES"

I think that we're all mentally ill; those of us outside the asylum only hide it a little better—and maybe not all that much better, after all. We've all known people who talk to themselves, people who sometimes squinch their faces into horrible grimaces when they believe no one is watching, people who have some hysterical fear—of snakes, the dark, the tight place, the long drop . . . and, of course, those final worms and grubs that are waiting so patiently underground.

When we pay our four or five bucks and seat ourselves at tenth-row center in a theater showing a horror movie, we are daring the nightmare.

Why? Some of the reasons are simple and obvious. To show that we can, that we are not afraid, that we can ride this roller coaster. Which is not to say that a really good horror movie may not surprise a scream out of us at some point, the way we may scream when the roller coaster twists through a complete 360 or plows through a lake at the bottom of the drop. And horror movies, like roller coasters, have always been the special province of the young; by the time one turns 40 or 50, one's appetite for double twists or 360-degree loops may be considerably depleted.

We also go to reestablish our feelings of essential normality; the horror movie is innately conservative, even reactionary. Freda Jackson as the horrible melting woman in *Die, Monster, Die!* confirms for us that no matter how far we may be removed from the beauty of a Robert Redford or a Diana Ross, we are still light years from true ugliness.

And we go to have fun.

Ah, but this is where the ground starts to slope away, isn't it? Because this is a very peculiar sort of fun, indeed. The fun comes from seeing others menaced—sometimes killed. One critic has suggested that if pro football has become the voyeur's version of combat, then the horror film has become the modern version of the public lynching.

It is true that the mythic, "fairy-tale" horror film intends to take away the shades of gray . . . It urges us to put away our more civilized and adult penchant for analysis and to become children again, seeing things in pure blacks and whites. It may be that horror movies provide psychic relief on this level because this invitation to lapse into simplicity, irrationality, and even outright madness is extended so rarely. We are told we may allow our emotions a free rein . . . or no rein at all.

If we are all insane, then sanity becomes a matter of degree. If your insanity leads you to carve up women, like Jack the Ripper or the Cleveland Torso Murderer, we clap you away in the funny farm (but neither of those two amateur-night surgeons was ever caught, heh-heh-heh); if, on the other hand, your insanity leads you only to talk to yourself when you're under stress or to pick your nose on your morning bus, then you are left alone to go about your business . . . though it is doubtful that you will ever be invited to the best parties.

The potential lyncher is in almost all of us (excluding saints, past and present; but then, most saints have been crazy in their own ways), and every now and then, he has to be let loose to scream and roll around in the grass. Our emotions and our fears form their own body, and we recognize that it demands its own exercise to maintain proper muscle tone. Certain of these emotional muscles are accepted—even exalted—in civilized society; they are, of course, the emotions that tend to maintain the status quo of civilization itself. Love, friendship, loyalty, kindness—these are all the emotions that we applaud, emotions that have been immortalized in the couplets of Hallmark cards and in the verses (I don't dare call it poetry) of Leonard Nimoy.

When we exhibit these emotions, society showers us with positive reinforcement; we learn this even before we get out of diapers. When, as children, we hug our rotten little puke of a sister and give her a kiss, all the aunts and uncles smile and twit and cry. 'Isn't he the sweetest little thing?" Such coveted treats as chocolate-covered graham crackers often follow. But if we deliberately slam the rotten little puke of a sister's fingers in the door, sanctions follow—angry remonstrance from parents, aunts, and uncles; instead of a chocolate-covered graham cracker, a spanking.

But anticivilization emotions don't go away, and they demand periodic exercise. We have such "sick" jokes as, "What's the difference between a truckload of bowling balls and a truckload of dead babies?" (You can't unload a truckload of bowling balls with a pitchfork . . . a joke, by the way, that I heard originally from a ten-year-old.) Such a joke may surprise a laugh or a grin out of us even as we recoil, a possibility that confirms the thesis: If we share a brotherhood of man, then we also share an insanity of man. None of which is intended as a defense of either the sick joke or insanity but merely as an explanation of why the best horror films, like the best fairy tales, manage to be reactionary, anarchistic, and revolutionary, all at the same time.

The mythic horror movie, like the sick joke, has a dirty job to do. It deliberately appeals to all that is worst in us. It is morbidity unchained, our most base instincts let free, our nastiest fantasies realized . . . and it all happens, fittingly enough, in the dark. For those reasons, good liberals often shy away from horror films. For myself, I like to see the most aggressive of them – *Dawn of the Dead*, for instance—as lifting a trap door in the civilized forebrain and throwing a basket of raw meat to the hungry alligators swimming around in that subterranean river beneath.

Why bother? Because it keeps them from getting out, man. It keeps them down there and me up here. It was Lennon and McCartney who said that all you need is love, and I would agree with that.

As long as you keep the gators fed.

King, Stephen. "Why We Crave Horror Movies." *Playboy* (1982). Rpt. in *The Prose Reader: Essays for Thinking, Reading, and Writing*. 9th ed. Eds. Kim Flachmann and Michael Flachmann. Boston: Pearson, 2011. 434-7. Print.

Discussion Questions for "Why We Crave Horror Movies"

1. As the author of books on which many horror movies have been based (*Carrie*, *The Shining*, *The Green Mile*, *Cujo*, and others), King has a definite perspective on this genre. What is his thesis? Is it implied or directly stated?

2. How does he answer the question posed in the title? What three things, according to King, explain why we go to horror movies? Do you agree with these assertions? Explain why or why not. If you go to horror movies, why do you go? If you do not go, are you scared or disinterested or even repulsed?

3. Does the author's essay primarily follow the cause pattern, the effect pattern, or both? What clues did you find to help you decide? If he emphasizes one over the other, which one is emphasized, and how does this pattern serve his overall claim?

4. "Every now and then," King writes, "[the potential lyncher in all of us] has to be let loose to scream and roll around in the grass." Based on King's argument, what might happen if this does not occur? What outlets do you have other than horror films, to help occasionally tame your beast?

5. Stephen King claims that the horror film "is innately conservative, even reactionary." How can a genre that is centered on death, destruction, pain, and "anarchy" be considered conservative in any way? Describe the narrative arc of one of your favorite films, and explain whether or not you agree with King's assessment.

MARK TWAIN—"THE DAMNED HUMAN RACE"

I have been studying the traits and dispositions of the "lower animals" (so-called), and contrasting them with the traits and dispositions of man. I find the result humiliating to me. For it obliges me to renounce my allegiance to the Darwinian theory of the Ascent of Man from the Lower Animals; since it now seems plain to me that the theory ought to be vacated in favor of a new and truer one, this new and truer one to be named the *Des*cent of Man from the Higher Animals.

In proceeding toward this unpleasant conclusion I have not guessed or speculated or conjectured, but have used what is commonly called the scientific method. That is to say, I have subjected every postulate that presented itself to the crucial test of actual experiment, and have adopted it or rejected it according to the result. Thus I verified and established each step of my course in its turn before advancing to the next. These experiments were made painstakingly in the London Zoological Gardens, and covered many months of painstaking and fatiguing work.

Before particularizing any of the experiments, I wish to state one or two things which seem to more properly belong in this place than further along. This in the interest of clearness. The massed experiments established to my satisfaction certain generalizations, to wit:

1. That the human race is of one distinct species. It exhibits slight variations--in color, stature, mental caliber, and so on--due to climate, environment, and so forth; but it is a species by itself, and not to be confounded with any other.
2. That the quadrupeds are a distinct family, also. This family exibits variations--in color, size, food preferences and so on; but it is a family by itself.
3. That the other families--the birds, the fishes, the insects, the reptiles, etc.-- are more or less distinct, also. They are in the procession. They are links in the chain which stretches down from the higher animals to man at the bottom.

Some of my experiments were quite curious. In the course of my reading I had come across a case where, many years ago, some hunters on our Great Plains organized a buffalo hunt for the entertainment of an English earl—that and to provide some fresh meat for his larder. They had charming sport. They killed seventy-two of those great animals; and ate part of one of them and left the seventy-one to rot. In order to determine the difference between an anaconda and an earl—if any—I caused seven young calves to be turned into the anaconda's cage. The grateful reptile immediately crushed one of them and swallowed it, then lay back satisfied. It showed no further interest in the calves, and no disposition to harm them. I tried this experiment with other anacondas; always with the same result. The fact stood proven that the difference between an earl and an anaconda is that the earl is cruel and the anaconda isn't; and that the earl wantonly destroys what he has no use for, but the anaconda doesn't. This seemed to suggest that the anaconda was not descended from the earl. It also seemed to suggest that the earl was descended from the anaconda, and had lost a great deal in the translation.

I was aware that many men who have accumulated more millions of money than they can ever use have shown a rabid hunger for more, and have not scrupled to cheat the ignorant and the helpless out of their poor servings in order to partially appease that appetite. I furnished a hundred different kinds of wild and tame animals the opportunity to accumulate vast stores of food, but none of them would do it. The squirrels and bees and certain birds made accumulations, but stopped when they had gathered a winter's supply, and could not be persuaded to add to it either honestly or by chicane. In order to bolster up a tottering reputation the ant pretended to store up supplies, but I was not deceived. I know the ant. These experiments convinced me that there is this difference between man and the higher animals: he is avaricious and miserly, they are not.

In the course of my experiments I convinced myself that among the animals man is the only one that harbors insults and injuries, broods over them, waits till a chance offers, then takes revenge. The passion of revenge is unknown to the higher animals.

Roosters keep harems, but it is by consent of their concubines; therefore no harm is done. Men keep harems, but it is by brute force, privileged by atrocious laws which the other sex were allowed no hand in making. In this matter man occupies a far lower place than the rooster. Cats are loose in their morals, but not consciously so. Man, in his descent from the cat, has brought the cat's looseness with him but has left the unconsciousness behind—the saving grace which excuses the cat. The cat is innocent, man is not.

Indecency, vulgarity, obscenity—these are strictly confined to man; he invented them. Among the higher animals there is no trace of them. They hide nothing; they are not ashamed. Man, with his soiled mind, covers himself. He will not even enter a drawing room with his breast and back naked, so alive are he and his mates to indecent suggestion. Man is "The Animal that Laughs." But so does the monkey, as Mr. Darwin pointed out; and so does the Australian bird that is called the laughing jackass. No—Man is the only Animal that Blushes. He is the only one that does it—or has occasion to.

At the head of this article[1] we see how "three monks were burnt to death" a few weeks ago, and a prior "put to death with atrocious cruelty." Do we inquire into the details? No; or we should find out that the prior was subjected to unprintable mutilations. Man—when he is a North American Indian—gouges out his prisoner's eyes; when he is King John, with a nephew to render untroublesome, he uses a red-hot iron; when he is a religious zealot dealing with heretics in the

---

10. *Note*: Twain's original article began with references to and clippings from telegrams that reported atrocities occurring in Crete.

Middle Ages, he skins his captive alive and scatters salt on his back; in the first Richard's time he shuts up a multitude of Jew families in a tower and sets fire to it; in Columbus's time he captures a family of Spanish Jews and—but *that* is not printable; in our day in England a man is fined ten shillings for beating his mother nearly to death with a chair, and another man is finded forty shillings for having four pheasant eggs in his possession without being able to satisfactorily explain how he got them. Of all the animals, man is the only one that is cruel. He is the only one that inflicts pain for the pleasure of doing it. It is a trait that is not known to the higher animals. The cat plays with the frightened mouse; but she has this excuse, that she does not know that the mouse is suffering. The cat is moderate—unhumanly moderate: she only scares the mouse, she does not hurt it; she doesn't dig out its eyes, or tear off its skin, or drive splinters under its nails—man-fashion; when she is done playing with it she makes a sudden meal of it and puts it out of its trouble. Man is the Cruel Animal. He alone is of that distinction.

The higher animals engage in individual fights, but never in organized masses. Man is the only animal that deals in that atrocity of atrocities, War. He is the only one that gathers his brethren about him and goes forth in cold blood and with calm pulse to exterminate his kind. He is the only animal that for sordid wages will march out, as the Hessians did in our Revolution, and as the boyish Prince Napoleon did in the Zulu war, and help to slaughter strangers of his own species who have done him no harm and with whom he has no quarrel.

Man is the only animal that robs his helpless fellow of his country—takes possession of it and drives him out of it or destroys him. Man has done this in all the ages. There is not an acre of ground on the globe that is in possession of its rightful owner, or that has not been taken away from owner after owner, cycle after cycle, by force and bloodshed.

Man is the only Slave. And he is the only animal who enslaves. He has always been a slave in one form or another, and has always held other slaves in bondage under him in one way or another. In our day he is always some man's slave for wages, and does that man's work; and this slave has other slaves under him for minor wages, and they do *his* work. The higher animals are the only ones who exclusively do their own work and provide their own living.

Man is the only Patriot. He sets himself apart in his own country, under his own flag, and sneers at the other nations, and keeps multitudinous uniformed assassins on hand at heavy expense to grab slices of other people's countries, and keep *them* from grabbing slices of *his*. And in the intervals between campaigns he washes the blood off his hands and works for "the universal brotherhood of man"—with his mouth.

Man is the Religious Animal. He is the only Religious Animal. He is the only animal that has the True Religion—several of them. He is the only animal that loves his neighbor as himself, and cuts his throat if his theology isn't straight. He has made a graveyard of the globe in trying his honest best to smooth his brother's path to happiness and heaven. He was at it in the time of the Caesars, he was at it in Mahomet's time, he was at it in the time of the Inquisition, he was at it in France a couple of centuries, he was at it in England in Mary's day, he has been at it ever since he first saw the light, he is at it today in Crete—as per the telegrams quoted above—he will be at it somewhere else tomorrow. The higher animals have no religion. And we are told that they are going to be left out, in the Hereafter. I wonder why? It seems questionable taste.

Man is the Reasoning Animal. Such is the claim. I think it is open to dispute. Indeed, my experiments have proven to me that he is the Unreasoning Animal. Note his history, as sketched above. It seems plain to me that whatever he is his is *not* a reasoning animal. His record is the fantastic record of a maniac. I consider that the strongest count against his intelligence is the fact that with that record back of him he blandly sets himself up as the head animal of the lot: whereas by his own standards he is the bottom one.

In truth, man is incurably foolish. Simple things which the other animals easily learn, he is incapable of learning. Among my experiments was this. In an hour I taught a cat and a dog to be friends. I put them in a cage. In another hour I taught them to be friends with a rabbit. In the course of two days I was able to add a fox, a goose, a squirrel and some doves. Finally a monkey. They lived together in peace; even affectionately.

Next, in another cage I confined an Irish Catholic from Tipperary, and as soon as he seemed tame I added a Scotch Presbytarian from Aberdeen. Next a Turk from Constantinople; a Greek Christian from Crete; an Armenian; a Methodist from the wilds of Arkansas; a Buddhist from China; a Brahman from Benares. Finally, a Salvation Army Colonel from Wapping. Then I stayed away two whole days. When I came back to note results, the cage of Higher Animals was all right, but in the other there was but a chaos of gory odds and ends of turbans and fezzes and plaids and bones and flesh—not a specimen left alive. These Reasoning Animals had disagreed on a theological detail and carried the matter to a Higher Court.

One is obliged to concede that in true loftiness of character, Man cannot claim to approach even the meanest of the Higher Animals. It is plain that he is constitutionally incapable of approaching that altitude; that he is constitutionally afflicted with a Defect which must make such approach forever impossible, for it is manifest that this defect is permanent in him, indestructible, ineradicable. I find this Defect to be *the Moral Sense*. He is the only animal that has it. It is the secret of his degradation. It is the quality *which enables him to do wrong*. It has no other office. It is incapable of performing any other function. It could never have been intended to perform any other. Without it, man could do no wrong. He would rise at once to the level of the Higher Animals.

Since the Moral Sense has but one office, the one capacity—to enable man to do wrong—it is plainly without value to him. It is as valueless to him as is disease. In fact, it manifestly *is* a disease. *Rabies* is bad, but it is not so bad as this disease. Rabies enables a man to do a bad, but it is not so bad as this disease. Rabies enables a man to do a thing which he could not do when in a healthy state: kill his neighbor with a poisonous bite. No one is the better man for having rabies. The Moral Sense enables a man to do wrong. It enables him to do wrong in a thousand ways. Rabies is an innocent disease, compared to the Moral Sense. No one, then, can be the better man for having the Moral Sense. What, now, do we find the Primal Curse to have been? Plainly what it was in the beginning: the infliction upon man of the Moral Sense; the ability to distinguish good from evil; and with it, necessarily, the ability to *do* evil; for there can be no evil act without the presence of consciousness of it in the doer of it.

And so I find that we have descended and degenerated, from some far ancestor— some microscopic atom wandering at its pleasure between the mighty horizons of a drop of water perchance—insect by insect, animal by animal, reptile by reptile, down the long highway of smirchless innocence, till we have reached the bottom stage of development--namable as the Human Being. Below us—nothing. Nothing but the Frenchman.

There is only one possible stage below the Moral Sense; that is the Immoral Sense. The Frenchman has it. Man is but a little lower than the angels This definitely locates him. He is between the angels and the French.

Man seems to be a rickety poor sort of a thing, any way you take him; a kind of British Museum of infirmities and inferiorities. He is always undergoing repairs. A machine that was as unreliable as he is would have no market. On top of his specialty—the Moral Sense—are piled a multitude of minor infirmities; such a multitude, indeed, that one may broadly call them countless. The higher animals get their teeth without pain or inconvenience. Man gets his through months and months of cruel torture; and at a time of life when he is but ill able to bear it. As soon as he has got them they must all be pulled out again, for they were of no value in the first place, not worth the loss of a night's rest. The second set will answer for a while, by being reinforced occasionally with rubber or plugged up with gold; but he will never ger a set which can really be depended on till a dentist makes him one. This set will be called "false" teeth—as if he had ever worn any other kind.

In a wild state—a natural state—the Higher Animals have a few diseases; diseases of little consequence; the main one is old age. But man starts in as a child and lives on diseases till the end, as a regular diet. He has mumps, measles, whooping cough, croup, tonsillitis, diptheria, scarlet fever, almost as a matter of course. Afterward, as he goes along, his life continues to be threatened at every turn: by colds, coughs, asthma, bronchitis, itch, cholera, cancer, consumption, yellow fever, bilious fever, typhus fevers, hay fever, ague, chilblains, piles, inflammation of the entrails, indigestion, toothache, earache, deafness, dumbness, blindness, influenza, chicken pox, cowpox, smallpox, liver compliant, constipation, bloody flux, warts, pimples, boils, carbuncles, abscesses, bunions, corns, tumors, fistulas, pneumonia, softening of the brain, melancholia and fifteen other kinds of insanity; dysentery, jaundice, diseases of the heart, the bones, the skin, the scalp, the spleen, the kidneys, the nerves, the brain, the blood; scrofula, paralysis, leprosy, neuralgia, palsy, fits, headache, thirteen kinds of rheumatism, forty-six of gout, and a formidable supply of gross and unprintable disorders of one sort and another. Also—but why continue the list? The mere names of the agents appointed to keep this shackly machine out of repair would hide him from sight if printed on his body in the smallest type known to the founder's art. He is but a basket of pestilent corruption provided for the support and entertainment of swarming armies of bacilli—armies commissioned to rot him and destroy him, and each army equipped with a special detail of the work. The process of waylaying him, persecuting him, rotting him, killing him, begins with his first breath, and there is no mercy, no pity, no truce till he draws his last one.

Look at the workmanship of him, in certain of its particulars. What are his tonsils for? They perform no useful function; they have no value. They have no business there. They are but a trap. They have but the one office, the one industry: to provide tonsillitis and quinsy and such things for the possessor of them. And what is the vermiform appendix for? It has no value; it cannot perform any useful service. It is but an ambuscaded enemy whose sole interest in life is to lie in wait for stray grapeseeds and employ them to breed strangulated hernia. And what are the male's mammals for? For business, they are out of the question; as an ornament, they are a mistake. What is his beard for? It performs no useful function; it is a nuisance and a discomfort; all nations hate it; all nations persecute it with a razor. And because it is a nuisance and a discomfort, Nature never allows the supply of it to fall short, in any man's case, between puberty and the grave. You never see a man baldheaded on his chin. But his hair! It is a graceful ornament, it is a comfort, it is the best of all protections against certain perilous ailments, man prizes it above emeralds and rubies. And because of these things Nature puts it on, half the time, so that it won't stay. Man's sight, smell, hearing, sense of locality—how inferior they are. The condor sees a corpse at five miles; man has no telescope that can do it. The bloodhound follows a scent that is two days old. The robin hears the earthworm burrowing his course under the ground. The cat, deported in a closed basket, finds its way home again through twenty miles of country which it has never seen.

Certain functions lodged in the other sex perform in a lamentably inferior way as compared with the performance of the same functions in the Higher Animals. In the human being, menstruation, gestation and parturition are terms which stand for horrors. In the Higher Animals these things are hardly even inconveniences.

For style, look at the Bengal tiger—that ideal of grace, beauty, physical perfection, majesty. And then look at Man—that poor thing. He is the Animal of the Wig, the Trepanned Skull, the Ear Trumpet, the Glass Eye, the Pasteboard Nose, the Porcelain Teeth, the Silver Windpipe, the Wooden

Leg—a creature that is mended and patched all over, from top to bottom. If he can't get renewals of his bric-a-brac in the next world, what will he look like?

He has just one stupendous superiority. In his intellect he is supreme. The Higher Animals cannot touch him there. It is curious, it is noteworthy, that no heaven has ever been offered him wherein his one sole superiority was provided with a chance to enjoy itself. Even when he himself has imagined a heaven, he has never made provision in it for intellectual joys. It is a striking omission. It seems a tacit confession that heavens are provided for the Higher Animals alone. This is matter for thought; and for serious thought. And it is full of a grim suggestion: that we are not as important, perhaps, as we had all along supposed we were.

Twain, Mark. "The Damned Human Race." *Letters from the Earth by Mark Twain*. Ed. Bernard DeVoto. New York: Perennial Pr, 1962. Rpt. in *The Longman Reader*. 7th ed. Eds. Judith Nadell, John Langan, and Eliza A. Comodromos. New York: Pearson, 2005. 525-31. Print.

Discussion Questions for "The Damned Human Race"

1. Which rhetorical pattern does Twain's essay primarily fall under? Use specific evidence from the text to justify your answer.

2. Twain was by no means a scientist. Why then did he organize and write this essay as a "scientific report"?

3. Humor can help a writer make a very serious point; satire has as its goal the focusing of attention on a serious subject in order to start a discussion about or incite change in a distressing situation. In that respect, how successful is Twain's use of humor in support of his thesis?

4. This essay was written in the late nineteenth century—in part as a reaction to what was happening at the time. Based on everything that has happened since then, how different would Twain's conclusions be today? Justify your answer using specific current events.

5. What is Twain's thesis? How does his use of contrived evidence and humor support it?

6. What examples of satire can you find in the media today? How do they help shape the socio-political debate and keep governments and people in check?

UNIT II

A HANDBOOK FOR WRITING IN
A NEW LANGUAGE

In many respects, writers do not have to deal with a bunch of rules that govern what they write; in fact, the nature of writing itself encourages creativity and introspection. However, this is not true for *all* aspects of writing. When academic writers deal with issues such as grammar and usage or sentence structure, rules *do* exist that they must comply w ith if they want their writing to be taken seriously. This unit will discuss the parts of speech and their relationships with one another and will address many of the most common grammar, sentence structure, diction, and punctuation errors made by struggling academic writers as they attempt to write in this new language.

Before going into explanations of these rules, a discussion of the two major areas of writing might be helpful: local issues and global output. These terms represent two distinctly different and yet interconnected parts of all writing. **Local issues** deal with the rules that govern matters of grammar, usage, and sentence structure—the basic building blocks such as parts of speech, agreement, clarity, and sentence structure—while **global output** represents the content of the writing. In other words, these following chapters will deal with how *what we want to say* in writing is often affected by *how we say it.* Learning these rules will help you be a more effective and efficient writer.

CHAPTER 1

PARTS OF SPEECH AND SENTENCE STRUCTURE

PARTS OF SPEECH—BACK TO THE BEGINNING

Since sentences are the basic building blocks of paragraphs and essays, knowing what goes into a good, solid sentence is of vital importance to any writer. Sentences can contain such things as nouns, verbs, adjectives, and adverbs, and a writer's use of these building blocks can make the difference between having his writing taken seriously or not. As is the case in many areas of academic writing, we have to make a distinction between how we talk and how we should write; face-to-face conversations allow individuals to communicate without serious consideration of whether the nouns, the verbs, or the adjectives/adverbs they are using are correct or not. However, when we switch from verbal communication to written communication, rules governing nouns, verbs, adjectives, and adverbs come into play—and anyone aspiring to be an academic writer must learn these rules.

Complete sentences, then, must have three things:

PARTS OF A COMPLETE SENTENCE
1. **Subject** (also known as a **predicate**)
2. **Verb**
3. **Complete thought**.

You may be wondering how all of the parts of speech figure into these three aspects. If we investigate these ingredients one at a time, hopefully you will become more aware of how those parts of speech you had to learn long ago figure into the construction of a complete sentence.

NOTE: As you study the parts of speech, what is important to remember is not so much the grammar terms but the functions of each part of speech. For this reason, each part of speech is dissected with the intent of helping you recognize the subject, verb, and complete thought that make a sentence.

SUBJECTS—WHO (OR WHAT) ARE YOU TALKING ABOUT?

Subjects (or predicates) in a sentence, one of the three essential components, give the reader a clear idea of who or what is the focus of that sentence. If this vital aspect of communication is left to the reader, a totally different or even broken message may be conveyed than the one intended by the writer. To avoid this, writers must make sure the reader has all the information needed to get that desired message.

Nouns—People, Places, and Things

When constructing the subject of a sentence, a writer has a few possibilities to choose from, such as nouns (or noun phrases), pronouns, or gerunds (or gerund phrases). **Nouns** are words that represent persons, places, or things. For example, in "*The box is on the table*," the word "box" (a noun) is the focus of the sentence. Nouns can be simple or plural, proper or common, concrete or abstract, collective, or count or non-count, as shown in the following:

TYPES OF NOUNS

Simple noun: Names one person, place, or thing: *book, chair, computer*

Plural noun: Names two or more persons, places, or things: *books, chairs, computers*

Proper noun: Names a <u>specific</u> person, place, or thing: *Oklahoma, Mount Rushmore, John Smith*

Common noun: Names one or more members of a class of things: *state, monument, man*

Concrete noun: Names an object or individual that can be perceived with the senses: *woman, song, cheese*

Abstract noun: Names a quality or idea: *freedom, happiness, ambition, greed*

Collective noun: Names a group of things: *committee, team, herd, army*

Count noun: Names something that can be counted: *car/cars, book/books, chair/chairs*

Non-count: Names something that cannot be counted, including concepts and qualities (*hungry*), emotions (*happy*), activities (*reading*), school subjects (*algebra*)

Pronouns—Playing the Part of a Noun

Pronouns are words such as *he, she, it, they,* or *we* that stand in the place of a noun. For example, in *She put the bowl on the stove,* "she" is a pronoun that is taking the place of a noun as the focus of the sentence. Pronouns are categorized as shown in the following textbox:

TYPES OF PRONOUNS

Personal pronouns – include *I, me, we, us, my, mine, he, she, it, their, they, them,* etc., and take the place of a noun representing a person or thing.

Indefinite pronouns – include such pronouns as *any, every, few, many, some, anyone, everyone, everybody, everything, someone, something, either, neither,* etc., and do not refer to any particular person or thing.

 *NOTE: Indefinite pronouns such as anyone, everyone, everybody, and everything are **always** singular and take the singular form of a verb.*

Reflexive pronouns – include *myself, himself, herself, itself, themselves, ourselves,* etc., and refer to a recipient of an action that is the same as the initiator of that action. (Example: She completed the project by *herself.*)

Intensive pronouns – like reflexive pronouns, these end in *–self/-selves* but emphasize the noun or pronoun that goes directly before it. (Example: The president *himself* took responsibility for the crisis.)

Relative pronouns – include *which, who, whom, that, what, whose, whatever, whoever, whomever, whichever,* etc., and introduce an adjective clause or a noun clause. (Example: The book *that* she borrowed is now lost. – *that* introduces the adjective clause "she borrowed.")

Interrogative pronouns – include pronouns such as *who, which, what, whom, whose, whoever, whatever, whichever,* etc., and introduce a question. (Example: *Which* assignment did you miss?)

Demonstrative pronouns – such as *this, that, these,* and *those* point to a particular thing or group of things. (Example: *That* movie is one of the worst I have ever seen.)

Reciprocal pronouns – such as *each other* and *one another* indicate a mutual relationship; *each other* indicates a relationship between only two individuals or things, while *one another* indicates a relationship among three or more individuals or things. (Example: The fans high-fived *one another* after the touchdown.)

NOTE: Although some of these pronouns look alike, they often have different functions within a sentence, so be careful that you choose the right pronoun for the function you need fulfilled in your sentence. Use a dictionary whenever you are unsure of the meaning of a pronoun.

Gerunds and Phrases—More than a Word, Less than a Sentence

In addition to nouns and pronouns, other types of words and phrases can act as the subject of a sentence. **Gerunds**, the –ing form of a noun or a verb, can function as a noun in the sentence. The following sentence shows the use of a gerund:

Dancing is a great form of exercise.

In this sentence, "dancing" (a gerund) is acting as the subject of the sentence. In other instances, the word "dancing" could be utilized as the verb in a sentence; however, in this case, since the –ing form is acting as the subject of the sentence, it would be classified as a gerund.

In some cases, the subject of a sentence is not just one word but a group of words. **Noun phrases,** groups of related words that are less than a sentence (because they lack a full verb), can also act as the subject of a sentence. A noun phrase contains a noun but must be taken together as the subject of the sentence. The following sentence shows the use of a noun phrase:

The four students dressed in togas arrived late for the party.

The six-word phrase "The four students dressed in togas" does contain a noun ("students"), but the entire phrase is necessary to identify clearly the sentence's subject. Additionally, **gerund phrases**, phrases containing the –ing form of a verb and other related words, can act as the subject of a sentence. The following sentence shows how a gerund phrase can function as the subject of a sentence:

Playing Wii games is his guilty pleasure.

In this instance, the entire gerund phrase "playing Wii games" must be taken together as the subject of the sentence. Just saying "Playing is his guilty pleasure" is too unclear for the reader to get a complete picture of what the writer's focus is. Playing what?

Exercise 1

Identify the subject for each sentence below and what form the subject takes—a noun, pronoun, noun phrase, gerund, or gerund phrase. If it is a noun, specify what kind of noun; if it is a pronoun, list the specific kind of pronoun.

1. We decided to take the interstate to save time.

     a. Subject: _____

     b. Form: _____

2. Steve used to make money moving pianos.

     a. Subject: _____

     b. Form: _____

3. Five sad sophomores sat outside the vice president's office.

     a. Subject: _____

     b. Form: _____

4. Staring blankly into space is a way of clearing one's mind of stress.

     a. Subject: _____

     b. Form: _____

5. They brought nachos to the Super Bowl party.

     a. Subject: _____

     b. Form: _____

6. "Honesty is such a lonely word," wrote Billy Joel.

     a. Subject: _____

     b. Form: _____

7. The senior citizens in wheelchairs got in free.

     a. Subject: _____

     b. Form: _____

8. Women are making great strides in achieving equality in the workplace.

     a. Subject: _____

     b. Form: _____

9. President Obama will address the country tonight regarding the crisis.

    a. Subject: _____

    b. Form: _____

10. Passing the class is my first priority this semester.

    a. Subject: _____

    b. Form: _____

VERBS—WHAT'S GOING ON?

Without verbs, sentences become meaningless collections of words. **Verbs** tell us something about the subject of the sentence—what the subject does or what the subject is. Verbs are the action figures of the sentence; they provide the reader with a clear sense not only of what is happening (action or a state of being) but also *when* the action is happening (past, present, or future). However, for all their importance, verbs can also drive writers to distraction because of the irregular nature of some verbs and the seemingly unending variety of verb forms. For the sake of our discussion, then, we will focus on two basic categories of verbs: **main verbs** (action verbs and linking verbs) and **auxiliary verbs** (helping verbs).

Main Verbs—Action vs. Linking

Main verbs contain most of the meaning in a sentence and usually stand alone. **Action** verbs relate a physical activity and also express a time frame for that action (past, present, future). For example, look at the following sentence:

    He studied for his test all night.

In this sentence, the action verb "studied" tells us not only what this individual did but also when the action happened ("studied" is the past tense form, so the action had to have happened before the writing of the sentence). **Linking** verbs, however, are different in that they do not convey any physical or emotional action; they serve simply to link the sentence's subject to a word or phrase that describes that subject. The following sentence shows the use of a linking verb:

The girl in the pink sweater seems sad.

In this example, the verb serves only to point the reader to the word "sad," an adjective that further describes the subject of the sentence (the girl in the pink sweater).

FREQUENTLY USED LINKING VERBS

appear	believe	look	seem	taste
be	feel	grow	prove	smell
turn	become	remain	sound	

Auxiliary Verbs—Main Verb Helper

Auxiliary verbs combine with main verbs to form verb phrases and help the writer indicate time frame (tense) and mood. Look at the following example:

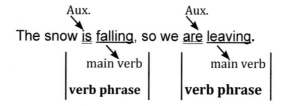

In this example, the two auxiliary verbs ("is" and "are") are both in the present tense, so the reader knows that both actions are taking place in the present. Other auxiliary verbs such as *can, may, could, might, must, need [to], ought [to], will, would,* and *should* indicate necessity, possibility, obligation, willingness, or ability, as shown in the following example:

Your grade <u>must</u> <u>improve</u> on the next text.

Exercise 2

Identify the verb in each of the following sentences as either a main verb or an auxiliary verb. If it is a main verb, tell whether it is an action verb or a linking verb; if it is an auxiliary verb, identify which is the auxiliary verb and which is the main verb in the verb phrase.

1. She brought cookies to the bake sale.

    Main? Yes No   Action?   Linking?

    Auxiliary? Yes No   Auxiliary verb _____ Main verb _____

2. Martin seems happy about his grade in calculus.

    Main? Yes No   Action?   Linking?

    Auxiliary? Yes No   Auxiliary verb _____ Main verb _____

3. My father raids the refrigerator every evening.

    Main? Yes No   Action?   Linking?

    Auxiliary? Yes No   Auxiliary verb _____ Main verb _____

4. The student senate is leaving for the state capital tomorrow.

    Main? Yes No   Action?   Linking?

    Auxiliary? Yes No   Auxiliary verb _____ Main verb _____

5. This course becomes harder at the end of the semester.

    Main? Yes No   Action?   Linking?

    Auxiliary? Yes No   Auxiliary verb _____ Main verb _____

MODIFIERS—ADJECTIVES, ADVERBS, AND SUCH—OH MY!

Sometimes nouns and verbs do not adequately convey a writer's meaning; accordingly, they have to be enhanced by the addition of modifiers. In other words, **modifiers** are any words or phrases that further define the subject or verb of a sentence. Modifiers take two forms: adjectives (or adjective clauses) and adverbs (or adverb clauses). These modifiers act to give a clearer picture to the reader of what is happening and to or by whom. Look at the following example:

The boy read the book.

Here we have a very straightforward complete sentence (with a subject [boy] and verb [read] and a complete thought). However, this statement is very bland and leaves out some potentially insightful information. By adding modifiers, this simple sentence takes on a new, heightened meaning:

The young boy quickly read the book.

The addition of an adjective—"young"—and an adverb—"quickly"—gives the reader more information and makes the statement clearer for the reader. The proper and *discriminate* use of modifiers can make your writing come alive.

Adjectives—Helping Redefine Who, What, When, or Where

Adjectives are those parts of speech that modify nouns or other adjectives. They help give the reader a fuller understanding of who is performing the action, what is involved in the action, when it takes place, or where it takes place. Adjectives can also allow the writer to make comparisons between two or more things or *actions* and can answer the following questions:

QUESTIONS ANSWERED BY ADJECTIVES

1. *Whose*

   That paper was *his* first.

2. *Which one*?

   This trend is alarming.

3. *How many? How much?*

   Her sweater cost *fifty* dollars.

4. *What kind*?

   Ethnic cooking can be traced to *religious* traditions.

As for placement, the above examples show that adjectives are placed before the noun that they are modifying; additionally, adjectives can be found after linking verbs as shown below:

His cooking is *flavorful*.

As shown in the following statement, adjectives can also appear in groups, all modifying the same noun:

The street is lined with *beautiful, leafy* trees.

However, when two or more adjectives function together as an adjective, otherwise known as a **compound adjective**, and come before the noun that it is modifying, those words are always hyphenated as shown below:

The award went to a *fifteen-year-old* girl.

 NOTE: If one of the words in the adjective series is an adverb, the series is not hyphenated. For example, "The problem was a fully exposed electrical wire."

Here are other rules governing adjectives in writing:

MORE RULES ON HOW TO USE ADJECTIVES

When comparing only *two* things, add either an *–er* or the word "more" (but never both at once).

1. Use "-er" ending when the word being modified is short.
   - *The boy is shorter than his brother.*
   - *This class is harder than any other I have taken.*
2. Use "more" when the word being modified is long or hard to pronounce.
   - *His explanation was more intricate than necessary.*
   - *She was more enthused about this semester than last semester.*

When comparing ***three or more*** things, add either an *–est* or the word "most" (but, again, never both at once).

3. Use "-est" ending when the word being modified is short.
   - *He is happiest when he is singing.*
   - *This was the shortest class of all.*
4. Use "most" when the word being modified is long or hard to pronounce.
   - *His essay was the most bizarre.*
   - *She is the most qualified candidate.*

As you can see from these examples, adjectives can appear either before the noun being modified or after the verb. The same can be said of **adjective phrases**, groups of words that, working together, act as a modifier. Take a look at the following example:

My mother's fifty-year-old grandfather clock finally stopped working.

The subject of the sentence is "clock," but the string of modifiers that comes before "clock" constitutes an adjective phrase. Adjective phrases can appear before the noun being modified or as an introductory phrase; however, what can happen when an adjective phrase is misplaced from what it intends to modify will be covered in later sections of this handbook (see *Dangling Modifiers*).

Exercise 3
List the adjectives in each sentence and tell what word or words they are modifying.

Example: A composite frame usually makes a road bicycle more expensive.
      <u>*composite modifies frame; road modifies bicycle*</u>

1. The desk top computer can hold more information but is more prone to problems.

   _____

   _____

2. Van Gogh's paintings became more surreal during his later life.

   _____

   _____

3. During the summer, I often get bored without the structure of a semester.

   _____

   _____

4. Many computer speakers do not have the bass sound that regular stereo speakers have.

   _____

   _____

5. At no restaurant in this town is a jacket and tie required.

_____

_____

Adverbs—Not Just –ly Words

Adverbs describe the action of verbs, modify adjectives or other adverbs, or complete clauses, phrases, or sentences. Adverbs that modify other adverbs or adjectives act as a limiter or qualifier of the words they modify. They answer questions such as are shown in the following text box:

> **QUESTIONS ANSWERED BY ADVERBS**
>
> 1. *How?*
>   He rapidly read the test instructions.
> 2. *Where?*
>   He put the empty pizza box nearby.
> 3. *When?*
>   I met with my academic advisor yesterday.
> 4. *To what extent? To what degree?*
>   She emphasized that she fully understood the consequences of her actions.
> 5. *Under what conditions?*
>   She hurled the softball to her sister hard.
> 6. *How often?*
>   To keep fit, I like to vomit every day.

Just like regular adverbs, **interrogative** adverbs answer questions such as *how, when, why,* and *where*, but these adverbs are used in questions themselves:

When will the package arrive? (Interrogative adverb)

Where you place an adverb determines whether or not it is offset with a comma. When an adverb begins a sentence, it should be set off with a comma, as shown in the following example:

Quickly, the situation deteriorated from bad to worse.

However, if the adverb comes within the sentence or at the end of the sentence, no comma is needed, as you can see in the following:

The situation *quickly* deteriorated from bad to worse.

She leafed through the pamphlet *leisurely*.

 NOTE: To determine whether a modifier is either an adjective or adverb, ask yourself what question it is answering. Remember what questions an adjective answers, and what questions an adverb answers.

Exercise 4

List the adverbs in each sentence and tell what word or words they are modifying.

Example: *The couple leisurely strolled through the tunnels of the New York subway system.*

        leisurely modifies strolled

1. I really want to go outside rather than monotonously complete my exercises.

    _____

    _____

2. Although Best Buy is usually more expensive than Walmart, the customer does not have to deal with as many people.

    _____

    _____

3. Digital watches are much more accurate than analog watches, but I miss the *tick tick* of my old watch.

   _____

   _____

4. I exercise regularly to try to stave off death, but I really wonder sometimes if my efforts are only make the Grim Reaper laugh.

   _____

   _____

5. "I am not usually this morose," he claimed as he sat scowling at the pile of books in front of him.

   _____

   _____

PREPOSITIONS—THE NOT-SO-MISSING LINKS

A **preposition** is any word that is used to introduce a noun or pronoun—or a phrase or clause functioning as a noun—linking it to other words in a sentence. The word or phrase that the preposition introduces then becomes the **object**—the recipient of the action—of that preposition. Together, a preposition and its object are known as a **prepositional phrase.** An example of two prepositional phrases is provided in the sentence below:

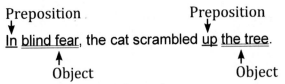

Prepositional phrases can be found at the beginning, in the middle, or at the end of a sentence:

Prepositional phrase beginning the sentence

Throughout the twentieth century, technology advanced at an alarming rate.

Prepositional phrase in the middle of the sentence

She hid her diary under her bed every morning.

Prepositional phrase ending the sentence

The study group met underneath the old oak tree.

Many students, when they think of prepositions, recall words like "as," "at," "in," and such, but many other words can function as prepositions. Notice that most of the prepositions in the list below denote location:

FREQUENTLY USED PREPOSITIONS

about	beneath	inside	since
above	beside	into	through
across	between	like	throughout
after	beyond	near	to
against	by	of	toward
along	concerning	off	under
among	despite	on	underneath
around	down	onto	until
as	during	out	up
at	except	outside	upon
before	for	over	with
behind	from	past	within
below	in	regarding	without

NOTE: Students often have trouble differentiating between the subject of a sentence and the object of a preposition. Recognizing prepositional phrases in a sentence can help you find your subject by eliminating any potential subject that may in fact be the object of a preposition. To find your subject, cross out all prepositional phrases and then determine which of the remaining nouns, pronouns, or noun phrases is performing the action indicated by the verb.

Exercise 5

Cross out the prepositional phrases in each sentence; underline the subject of the sentence once, and underline the verb of the sentence twice.

Example: The rain in Spain fell mainly on the plain.

1. Of all the things I have lost, I miss my mind the most.

2. "Government of the people, by the people, and for the people" is perhaps the best known phrase from the Gettysburg Address.

3. Buehler found the password to the school computer in the slide-out tray of the principal's desk.

4. I am not going to say anything about Jeff not putting his drink on a coaster.

5. The clock on my wall not only tells time but also temperature of the room and the day of the month.

CONJUNCTIONS—VERBAL GLUE

Try to imagine what writing—or speaking, for that matter—would be like if we had no **conjunctions**, those words that function as connectors for words, phrases, clauses, or sentences. Look at the two sentences below and try to figure out what the writer's meaning might be.

> My sister I left on Tuesday for our trip to Disneyland Hollywood San Francisco. She took with her a camera laptop Kindle reader I took only my cell phone suitcase.

Determining the writer's meaning becomes increasingly difficult when the sentences on the page seem only a random collection of disjointed words; we need conjunctions to show relationships and connections of those words and phrases to each other. Conjunctions are usually categorized into three groups: coordinating conjunctions, correlative conjunctions, and subordinating conjunctions.

Coordinating conjunctions connect words, phrases, or clauses of equal weight. For example, look at the following sentence:

I ate a hamburger <u>and</u> fries for lunch.

In this instance, the coordinating conjunction "and" connects the two nouns "hamburger" and "fries." However, coordinating conjunctions can also connect two phrases or independent clauses, as seen in the examples below:

Connecting two phrases

She considered running for office <u>but</u> declined the offer.

Connecting two independent clauses

My left front wheel hit the ice, <u>and</u> my car began to skid.

A list of coordinating conjunctions is shown in the box below:

COORDINATING CONJUNCTIONS
for   and   so   nor   but   yet   or

Another type of connector is the **correlative** conjunction. These conjunctions *always* appear in pairs and serve as a link between grammatically equivalent items. These pairs are shown in the box below and in the examples that follow:

CORRELATIVE CONJUNCTION PAIRS	
both / and	neither / nor
either / or	not only / but also
just as / so	whether / or

<u>Neither</u> he <u>nor</u> his brother confessed to the crime.

<u>Both</u> biology <u>and</u> algebra are required for her degree.

<u>Either</u> he leaves, <u>or</u> I will.

Subordinating conjunctions or **subordinators** introduce a **subordinate** (dependent) clause, link it to an independent clause, and create a **complex sentence**. These subordinators are listed in the box below (for a more complete listing, see the section entitled *Grammar Errors*) and in the examples that follow:

<table>
<tr><td colspan="3">SUBORDINATING CONJUNCTIONS</td></tr>
<tr><td>since</td><td>because</td><td>although</td></tr>
<tr><td>if</td><td>after</td><td>when</td></tr>
<tr><td>while</td><td>before</td><td>unless</td></tr>
</table>

<u>Because</u> I came late to class, I missed the quiz.

I missed the quiz <u>because</u> I came late to class.

NOTE: When the subordinate clause begins the sentence, it should be set off from the independent clause with a comma; when the subordinate clause ends the sentence, however, no comma is used to set off the subordinate clause. For more information regarding subordinators and subordinated clauses, see the upcoming section on punctuation.

SENTENCE STRUCTURE—PUTTING THE PIECES TOGETHER

As mentioned earlier in this chapter, sentences are the basic building blocks of paragraphs and essays, and as such, they are comprised of different pieces all working together—nouns, pronouns, verbs, modifiers—in various roles depending on the particular sentence being written. Knowing *how* these pieces work will do a writer little good if he cannot then put those pieces together in such a way that his message is conveyed as effectively and efficiently as possible to a reader. Just as parts of speech work together in a sentence to make writing smooth and clear, so too do sentences work together in a paragraph; additionally, good writers realize that, in order to enliven their writing, a variety of sentence structures within a paragraph are needed. A writer has three different sentence types to choose from—simple sentences, compound sentences, and complex sentences—and effective academic writers use a variety of all three whenever they write.

Simple Sentences—Nothing Fancy, Everything in its Place

A **simple sentence** consists of an independent clause (containing at least one subject and one verb and conveying a complete thought). These are the types of sentences we learn to read and to write first; they are very effective in conveying information in a straightforward fashion. An example of a simple sentence is given below:

My sister took me to the mall yesterday.

In this sentence, we have a subject ("my sister"), a verb ("took"), a direct object ("me"), a prepositional phrase ("to the mall"), and an adverb ("yesterday"). The writer has given no additional details, nor does the reader necessarily need any. This message is clear, and a simple sentence in this case is the most efficient vehicle to convey that message. What happens when one or more of these important pieces is missing is discussed later (see *Sentence Fragments*).

Compound Sentences—Two Independent Clauses and a Connector

Many college writers begin by writing predominantly in simple sentences, but after a while this style begins to take on a very simplistic, sing-song rhythm that puts the writer in a negative light in the mind of the reader. Academic writing, after all, should go beyond "See Dick run. Run, Dick, run." While a simple sentence contains only one independent clause, a more complex sentence structure is expected by readers of academic writing; therefore, writers of academic prose must be able to produce them. One such complex structure is the compound sentence, as shown below:

Indep. Cl. + comma + connector + Indep. Cl. = Compound Sentence

A **compound** sentence contains *two* independent clauses that are connected by more than just a connector—they must be related to each other in content as well. This is a very important aspect to compound sentences that makes combining any two independent clauses more challenging. The writer—*you*—must make sure that the two simple sentences you are combining have a similar content or topic. Trying to connect two very different independent clauses will only cause confusion for the reader and leave her wondering what piece of this puzzle is missing. Look at the following example of two unrelated yet connected independent clauses:

My dog ran away, and my car is blue.

While these two clauses *are* independent and each conveys a complete thought, together they make no sense.

In order to combine two independent clauses, you must choose a connector—a coordinating conjunction—that will help guide the reader through the connection that these two clauses share. When choosing a coordinating conjunction, the writer must ensure that the one she has chosen conveys the right message for the two clauses she is combining; after all, these conjunctions are not interchangeable, and each carries a very unique connotation:

COORDINATING CONJUNCTIONS DEFINED

For
    "because" or "for the reason that"

And
    "also" or "in addition"

Nor
    "neither" or "and not"

But
    "however" or "on the other hand"

Or
    indicates an alternative

Yet
    "however"

So
    "as a result" or "therefore"

Because these coordinating conjunctions are not interchangeable and has its own function and denotation, the one you choose must conform to the message being sent by the two independent clauses you are joining. Look at the following example and determine which coordinating conjunction you would choose to combine these two sentences:

My best friend is sick. I will take notes in class for him.

As you read these two independent clauses, you will discover that the action of second ("I will take notes in class for him") is directly caused by the first ("My best friend is sick"). Accordingly, some of the coordinating conjunctions will not effectively convey that message. The best choice would be "so":

My best friend is sick, <u>so</u> I will take notes in class for him.

In addition to a coordinating conjunction, you must also have a comma to separate these two independent clauses. If you add the conjunction but not the comma, you will have a fused sentence; if you add just the comma without the conjunction, you will have a comma splice. Both of these will be covered in later sections.

Complex Sentences—One Independent, The Other Not So Much

The third type of sentence structure, a **complex sentence**, is like the compound sentence in that it combines two simple sentences; however, the form that this combination takes is much different from the compound sentence. To construct a complex sentence, you must make one of the simple sentences a dependent clause by adding a subordinating conjunction (or subordinator) at the beginning of it. A **dependent clause** is missing either a subject or a verb or may have both of these but not express a complete thought, and as such this clause can appear either at the beginning or the end of the sentence:

Dep. Cl. + comma + Indep. Cl. = Complex Sentence

Indep. Cl. + Dep. Cl. = Complex Sentence

Notice that, when the dependent clause concludes the sentence, no additional punctuation is needed.

If we look again at the previous two simple sentences we were working with, we can see how complex sentences can be constructed:

My best friend is sick. I will take notes in class for him.

First, you should choose the best subordinating conjunction to combine these two. As mentioned before, the action being performed in the second sentence is caused by the action in the first sentence; as a result, the subordinating conjunction should convey this message to the reader:

Since my best friend is sick, I will take notes in class for him.

Because my best friend is sick, I will take notes in class for him.

While my best friend is sick, I will take notes in class for him.

If you would rather put the subordinated clause at the *end* of the sentence, you may need to do some rewriting or word shuffling so that the message remains intact:

I will take notes in class for my best friend since he is sick.

I will take notes in class for my best friend because he is sick.

I will take notes in class for my best friend while he is sick.

Notice that no comma is needed when the subordinated clause comes at the end of the sentence.

Exercise 6

Combine each of the following pairs of simple sentences into both a compound sentence and a complex sentence.

1. This cold medication is effective. It makes me sleepy.

    Compound Sentence _____

    _____

    _____

    Complex Sentence

    _____

    _____

2. The meal she fixed smelled wonderful. It left us still feeling hungry.

Compound Sentence _____

_____

_____

Complex Sentence

_____

_____

3. He was a great runner in high school. He is not running now.

Compound Sentence _____

_____

_____

Complex Sentence

_____

_____

4. My father got tickets to the Super Bowl. He asked my brother to go with him.

Compound Sentence _____

_____

_____

Complex Sentence

_____

_____

5. I left my book bag in my car. I have nothing to read.

Compound Sentence _____

_____

_____

Complex Sentence

_____

_____

CHAPTER 2

GRAMMAR, DICTION, AND SENTENCE-LEVEL ERRORS

> "There is a satisfactory boniness about grammar which the flesh of sheer vocabulary requires before it can become a vertebrate and walk the earth."
> —*Anthony Burgess*

GRAMMAR ERRORS COMMON TO COMPOSITION STUDENTS

In composition courses, grammar is not considered part of the curriculum and is given little, if any, attention by the instructor, except in grading. The student is expected to enter the subject already competent in this branch of writing. A **composition** course instead focuses on teaching students the rhetorical patterns used in academic writing and applying them in combinations to emphasize meaning and purpose. **Grammar**, on the other hand, is that discipline of academic writing that seeks to clarify the meaning and function of words, or parts of speech, and their relationship to one another in the context of sentences.

Regardless of what level in composition a student is, grammar remains one of the most serious weaknesses in his writing. Moreover, many students have outright disdain for correct grammar usage and punctuation. They believe that it actually interferes with the creative process and writing style. Rather than hinder these areas, however, correct grammar usage helps clarify thought so that it can be effectively communicated to an audience. After all, without it, we would have trouble understanding one another. Other students have argued that the novels, articles, and even the textbooks they read often violate the rules of academic writing and grammar, but these transgressions are most often calculated decisions made by authors who have mastered the rules and break them to suit their own purposes, which is emphasis of meaning. As have all writers before, you must become proficient in grammar and punctuation usage before you have earned the right to break the well-established and logical rules of clear communication.

Teachers and grammar book writers have worked for decades to narrow the most common grammar mistakes down to a handful and, with varying degrees of success, tried to wipe them from the written page. Although teachers label them in different ways, the mistakes are the same throughout composition classrooms. The names and abbreviations that will be used to identify them in your own papers are provided below. Most composition instructors consider the errors marked in bold to be the most serious and exact greater penalties for them.

THE MOST COMMON GRAMMAR ERRORS

- **Subject/verb agreement (v agr)**
- **Run on sentences**
  - **Comma splice (cs)**
  - **Fused Sentence (fs)**
- **Fragments (frag)**
- **Shifts (shift)**
- Dangling/misplaced modifiers (dm/mm)
- **Pronoun agreement (pro agr)**
- **Mixed sentence/faulty predication (mixed)**
- Incomplete Sentences (inc)
- Faulty parallelism (//)
- Stringy

SUBJECT/VERB AGREEMENT (V AGR)—CAN'T WE ALL JUST GET ALONG?

The two key components of a sentence, subjects and verbs, must agree in person and number. Subjects take three forms of **person**, or the manner in which the noun or noun clause representing the subject of the sentence is being addressed. If the author of the sentence is speaking about him or herself, the subject is said to be in **first person.** If the author of the sentence is addressing the reader, the subject is in **second person.** If the author is referring to someone or something else other than himself or the reader, the subject is in **third person.** The lists below provide pronoun examples of these definitions. Do you recognize which types of pronouns are included in the lists?

TYPES OF PERSON		
First Person	**Second Person**	**Third Person**
I, me	you	it, he, she
us, we	you	them, they
my, mine, our	your	his, hers, theirs
myself, ourselves	yourself, yourselves	himself, herself, themselves

Aside from the different pronoun types you might have recognized in the lists, you should also take note that the pronouns come in different **numbers.** Some stand alone, or are **singular,** while others represent groups, or are **plural.** As part of a sentence, the subjects must be complemented with verbs that agree with them in both person and number. This subject/verb agreement is necessary for the clarity of a thought. Take the simple sentences below as examples of subject/verb agreement:

> They run four miles each evening to prepare for the upcoming race.

> I wish I understood the principles of quantum physics more clearly.

> She finally understands the consequences of her actions on the day of the civil trial.

Notice that, although each subject and verb in the sentences agree in both person and number, the verb in the second example seems to have a plural verb. This is because the subject is in first person. First person singular subjects require what look to be plural verbs.

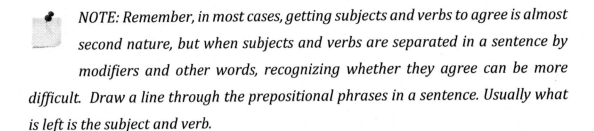

NOTE: Remember, in most cases, getting subjects and verbs to agree is almost second nature, but when subjects and verbs are separated in a sentence by modifiers and other words, recognizing whether they agree can be more difficult. Draw a line through the prepositional phrases in a sentence. Usually what is left is the subject and verb.

Compound Subjects—More Than Their Elements

Compound subjects are nouns or noun clauses connected with the coordinating conjunction "and" or correlative conjunction pairs (either-or, neither-nor, not only-but also). Compound subjects can be either singular or plural depending how they are paired. In the case of compound subjects paired with coordinating conjunction "and," the verb will always be plural. Look at the example below:

> Eating hamburgers *and* drinking beer are two of my father's favorite activities on Saturday afternoons.

When a compound subject is paired with a correlative conjunction pair, the noun closest to the verb determines whether the subject is singular or plural. The examples below demonstrate this rule:

> Not only Keebler but also many mothers across the country make good crackers.

> Neither Brenda nor Scott wants to be working on the first sunny Saturday of the year.

To complicate things a bit further, if the compound subject is preceded by "each" or "every" the verb will always be singular. The sentences below provide examples of these situations:

> Every faculty member and administrator on campus decides for him or herself how to make up for the missed classes due to the heavy snow of the last two weeks.

> Each man and woman determines the future of the English language.

Group Words—Out of Many, One

Group words are nouns acting as subjects that may seem plural because they include collections of people, objects, or ideas, but they are, in fact, singular. In other words, the group or entity represents one thing.

According to *The Godfather*, <u>family</u> <u>is</u> the most important unit of society.

<u>Huckleberry and Associates</u> <u>is</u> not a law firm I would recommend for a divorce settlement.

The <u>U.S. Senate</u> exemplifies what not to do in a private company.

 NOTE: Again, you must clearly identify the subject to be sure it is agreeing with the verb. Sometimes, a group word may be buried in a prepositional phrase and is not, therefore, the subject of the sentence. The noun or noun clause preceding the prepositional phrase is the subject. Consider the following sentence: "The members of the audience alternately cried and laughed while watching the film Old Yeller." The subject of the sentence is "members," not "audience."

GUIDELINES FOR SUBJECT/VERB AGREEMENT

1. When two or more subjects are added together (with "and"), use a plural verb.
   a. *Baseball **is** my favorite sport.*
   b. *Baseball and football **are** my favorite sports.*
2. In cases where there is a choice of subjects (with "either/or" or "neither/nor"), use a verb that agrees with the subject nearest the verb.
   a. *Either Mike or his parents **work** at the restaurant every day.*
   b. *Neither the representatives nor the governor **wants** to address the issue of health care costs.*
3. If word groups come between the subject and the verb, be sure that the verb agrees with the subject, not with the words in between.
   a. *The boy with the pencils **returns** every morning.*
   b. *The pencils sold by the boy **cost** five cents.*
4. Pronouns such as *anyone, anybody, anything, everyone, everybody, everything, nobody, nothing, someone, somebody,* and *something,* (singular indefinite pronouns) when used as subjects, always take singular verbs.
   a. *Everyone in the room **sits** down when he walks in.*
   b. *Nothing in these stores **is** on sale.*
5. Group words (*class, team, family, senate,* etc.) take singular verbs when used as the subject of a sentence.
   a. *The class **is** on probation.*
   b. *The jury **refuses** to be rushed in its deliberation.*
   BUT do not confuse prepositional phrase objects with subjects
   a. *The members of the class **are** on probation.*
   b. *The women on the jury **refuse** to be rushed in their deliberation.*

Exercise 1

Find the subject and the verb in each sentence by drawing a line through the prepositional phrases. Then underline the subject once and the verb twice. Correct the verbs to agree in person and number with the subject. If no error is present, write "C" next to the sentence.

Example: <u>takes</u> *Sometimes when Chet gets nervous, <u>he</u> take long walks off of short piers.*

1. _____ Measles, largely thought to be an annoyance of childhood, are still a potentially deadly disease.

2. _____ Not only Frank but also Susan annoy me.

3. _____ Both my cell phone and my laptop is practically fused to my left hand.

4. _____ The team are ready to take on the Ragin' Magellans in the international ping pong tournament.

5. _____ I often wonders how many times I hit the backspace button when writing an essay.

6. _____ Just as economics determines the mood of the country, so do the production of comfortable chairs.

7. _____ Neither a lender nor a borrower be, but to thine ownself be true.

8. _____ The women of the community eats too much dairy.

9. _____ The subject of the professor's lectures are the regulatory changes in the upcoming legislation.

10. _____ Sometimes two plus two do equal just four.

RUN ON SENTENCES (CS; FUSED)—THEY KEEP GOING AND GOING AND...

A simple **sentence** contains a subject and a verb and expresses a complete thought. **Run on sentences** do not adequately separate these complete thoughts from one another, which can lead to confusion for the reader. Run on sentences come in two forms: comma splices and fused. A **comma splice (cs)** is two independent clauses, or complete thoughts, that are only separated by a comma instead of the proper punctuation. Like two pieces of film, they are merely spliced together. An example of a sentence containing a comma splice is provided below:

> During my freshman year of college, I was surprised to find that the workload was much heavier, I thought the homework would be like it was in high school.

Notice that the first independent clause "I was surprised to find that the workload was much heavier" has only a comma separating it from the other complete thought "I thought the workload would be like it was in high school." The comma is insufficient for indicating to the reader that an independent thought has come to an end. It also may indicate that the author does not have a good idea what a sentence is, even if the reader can understand the text.

Like the spliced sentence, a **fused (fs)** sentence also contains two independent clauses, but the fused sentence has no punctuation whatsoever to separate the two complete thoughts. The thoughts are fused together. Needless to say, this can cause great confusion. Look at the fused sentence below and see if you can tell where one thought ends and another begins.

> I can usually tell when I have studied enough for a test my nerves start to settle.

Without any punctuation to separate the two thoughts, the reader cannot tell where one thought ends and the other begins. Not even a pause between them is allowed the reader. This suggests a lack of clarity of thought for the reader.

The solutions for resolving comma splices and fused sentences are the same. You must end one thought and begin another, coordinate the two clauses, or subordinate one to the other. These methods are accomplished in the following ways:

1. You can, of course, break the thoughts into two parts with a period and add a capital letter to the first word of the next thought. The period ends a thought.

   cs: During my freshman year of college, I was surprised to find that the workload was much heavier. I thought the homework would be like it was in high school.

   fs: I can usually tell when I have studied enough for a test. My nerves start to settle.

2. You can add a semi-colon (;) to separate the two independent clauses. The semi-colon separates the two clauses but still indicates that they are closely related.

   cs: During my freshman year of college, I was surprised to find that the workload was much heavier; I thought the homework would be like it was in high school.

   fs: I can usually tell when I have studied enough for a test; my nerves start to settle.

3. In the case of a spliced sentence, you can place a coordinating conjunction behind the comma. The fused sentence would need both a comma and a coordinating conjunction. A **coordinating conjunction** demonstrates not only the relationship of the thoughts to one another; it also shows that they are equal in importance. As immortalized by *SchoolHouse Rock*, the coordinating conjunctions are again provided below:

LIST OF COORDINATING CONJUNCTIONS		
for	and	nor
but	or	yet
so		

The spliced and fused sentences can be corrected with the following coordinating conjunction:

cs: During my freshman year of college, I was surprised to find that the workload was much heavier, for I thought the homework would be like it was in high school.

fs: I can usually tell when I have studied enough for a test, for my nerves start to settle.

NOTE: You must have some understanding of the meaning of each coordinating conjunction before using it to join two independent thoughts. Each one expresses the relationship between two clauses in unique ways. To be sure you know exactly what each one means and does (see Chapter 1 in the Handbook), try to come up with a synonym for each to help you better understand how it works. For example, the conjunction "but" could be replaced with the synonym "except" or "however."

4. You can also separate the two clauses with a semi-colon, a conjunctive adverb, and a comma. This combination establishes the relationship between the two clauses, as does the comma and the coordinating conjunction; however, the semi-colon establishes a stronger pause and the **conjunctive adverb**, a transition word or phrase that can separate two complete thoughts, puts more emphasis on the relation between the two thoughts. A short list of conjunctive adverbs is below:

SHORT LIST OF CONJUNCTIVE ADVERBS		
however	whereas	moreover
moreover	nevertheless	therefore
consequently	nonetheless	subsequently
namely	accordingly	comparatively

Choices of conjunctive adverbs were made to emphasize the relationship between the thoughts of the spliced and fused sentences. What conjunctive adverbs would you have used? Which other conjunctive adverbs can you think of that are not listed? Can a conjunctive adverb consist of more than word?

cs: During my freshman year of college, I was surprised to find that the workload was much heavier; moreover, I thought the homework would be like it was in high school.

fs: I can usually tell when I have studied enough for a test; namely, my nerves start to settle.

NOTE: As with the coordinating conjunctions, you must fully understand the meaning of the conjunctive adverbs you are using in a sentence to get your intended meaning across to your reader.

5. You can also subordinate one of the independent clauses to the other with a subordinator. In this way, you are turning an independent clause into a subordinate clause. Remember, a **subordinate clause** supports the independent clause but is not a complete thought in itself. Below is an abbreviated list of subordinators. Again, you must understand the meaning of any word you choose to subordinate a clause to be sure your intended meaning gets to your reader.

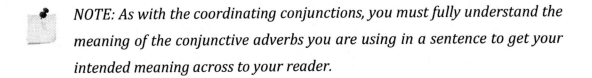

ABBREVIATED LIST OF SUBORDINATORS		
after	before	until
because	although	since
as soon as	whether	whomever/whoever
which	that	unless
why	whatever	whenever
while	as	if
then	as long as	who/whom

NOTE: When a subordinate clause precedes the independent clause, you must separate the two clauses with a comma. If the subordinate clause follows the independent clause in the sentence then no comma should be used.

The examples of the spliced and fused sentences both contain subordinate clauses. Notice how not only the subordinator itself but also its place in the sentence alters the emphasis and meaning of the thought. What other ways could you alter the meaning of the sentences with subordinator choice and placement?

cs: During my freshman ~~year~~ of college, I was surprised to find that the workload was much heavier because I thought the homework would be like it was in high school.

cs: Because I thought the homework would be like it was in high school, I was surprised to find the workload was much heavier during my freshman year of college.

fs: I can usually tell ~~when~~ I have studied enough for a test whenever my nerves start to settle.

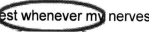

fs: Whenever my nerves start to settle, I can usually tell ~~when~~ I have studied enough for a test.

NOTE: Sometimes you must alter the structure of a sentence when you add a subordinate clause in order to preserve clarity.

Exercise 2

Identify each of the sentences below as containing a splice (cs), is fused (fs), or has no issues. Correct the each of the sentences that do contain errors with all of the methods previously discussed in the text.

Example: __cs__ I could not stop for death, he kindly stopped for me.

   a. *period: I could not stop for death. He kindly stopped for me.*

   b. *semi-colon: I could not stop for death; he kindly stopped for me.*

   c. *comma and coordinating conjunction: I could not stop for death, so he kindly stopped for me.*

   d. *semi-colon, conjunctive adverb, and comma: I could not stop for death; therefore, he kindly stopped for me.*

e. *Subordinate clause: <u>Because I could not stop for death, he kindly stopped for me.</u>*

1. ____Technology is making our lives more complicated, it should be making it easier.

   a. period: _____

   _____

   _____

   b. semi-colon

   _____

   _____

   _____

   c. comma and coordinating conjunction:

   _____

   _____

   _____

   d. semi-colon, conjunctive adverb, and comma:

   _____

   _____

   _____

   e. subordinate clause:

   _____

   _____

   _____

2. ____Most businesses today do not allow smoking in the offices, instead, remote areas are designated for those with the habit.

    a. period: _____

       _____

       _____

    b. semi-colon

       _____

       _____

       _____

    c. comma and coordinating conjunction:

       _____

       _____

       _____

    d. semi-colon, conjunctive adverb, and comma:

       _____

       _____

       _____

    e. subordinate clause:

       _____

       _____

       _____

3. ____Many educators believe the role of the university is to train students for the professional world others believe the university's role is to create critical thinkers.

a. period: _____

_____

_____

b. semi-colon

_____

_____

_____

c. comma and coordinating conjunction:

_____

_____

_____

d. semi-colon, conjunctive adverb, and comma:

_____

_____

_____

e. subordinate clause:

_____

_____

_____

4. ____Professors have learned to allow only one student at a time in their offices this prevents any damage to the furniture.

a. period: _____

_____

_____

     b. semi-colon

_____

_____

_____

     c. comma and coordinating conjunction:

_____

_____

_____

     d. semi-colon, conjunctive adverb, and comma:

_____

_____

_____

     e. subordinate clause:

_____

_____

_____

5.   ____Millions of Americans and their cats watched the president's speech last week the cats liked batting at the screen.

     a. period: _____

_____

_____

     b. semi-colon

_____

_____

_____

c. comma and coordinating conjunction:

_____

_____

_____

d. semi-colon, conjunctive adverb, and comma:

_____

_____

_____

e. subordinate clause:

_____

_____

_____

FRAGMENTS (FRAG)—BROKEN THOUGHTS, BROKEN DREAMS

A **fragment** has a capital letter at the beginning and a period or other ending punctuation at its close but is not a complete sentence. If a sentence contains a subject, verb, and a complete thought, then a fragment is missing one or more of these elements. Many students fail to recognize fragments in their own writing because they are used to writing and speaking informally. Three tests of your "sentences" can reveal whether they are in fact complete or fragments.

HOW TO TEST FOR FRAGMENTS

1. Look for a verb, the action being performed by the subject, or noun, in the clause.
2. Look for the subject of the clause, the noun or noun clause that is performing the action.
3. Look for any subordinators in the clause that may make the thought incomplete or dependent, even if it does contain a potential subject and verb.

Missing a Verb or a Complete Verb—All Talk, No Action

The clause below begins with a capital letter and ends with a period, but it is **missing a verb**. No action is being performed; therefore, the clause is not an independent thought, or complete sentence. Look at the example below and determine what would be necessary to complete the thought.

Dozens of people in line for the new chipotle sandwich at Chili's.

This clause needs an active verb to complete the thought. The inclusion of the verb allows the subject "people" to perform an action, thereby completing the thought.

Dozens of people *stood* in line for the new chipotle sandwich at Chili's.

A clause may have what looks like a subject and part of a verb, but the helping verb is missing. It does not have a **complete verb**. What helping or auxiliary verb(s) is needed to complete this thought?

Rebecca going to class.

Without an auxiliary verb, the audience has no clue just exactly when the subject will perform the action "going." The helping verb will determine the tense of the action thereby letting the reader know whether the action is happening in the past, present, or future.

Past
Rebecca **was** going to class.

Present
Rebecca **is** going to class.

Future
Rebecca **will be** going to class.

 NOTE: For more information on verb tenses and helping verbs, refer to the section on parts of speech earlier in Chapter 1 of the Handbook.

Missing a Subject—What Are You Talking About?

To determine whether a clause has a subject or simply a noun or noun clause, you should see what is performing the action described by the verb in the clause. If you cannot find a noun that would be logically performing the action, the clause is missing its subject. Which, if any, of the nouns in the sentence below could be said to be logically performing the action described by the verb?

Threw the squirrel in the tub with my sister.

This clause has three nouns in it. Are any of them performing the action of throwing? Obviously, the perpetrator of this action is only indirectly mentioned in the clause, but the pronoun "my" cannot logically perform the action. An antecedent for the pronoun will provide the missing subject, which could be almost anyone. In this case, the writer's so-called friend performed the act:

Harold threw the squirrel in the tub with my sister.

Subject and Verb Preceded by a Subordinator or Preposition—Huh?

A clause may contain a verb, a word describing action, and a noun, something performing the action, but the thought is fragmented because it is a dependent clause whose function is to modify a complete thought. It is not a complete thought in itself. When a subordinator or preposition precedes the subject and verb, the thought cannot be completely expressed.

By the time I get to Phoenix.

After he completed the driver's exam.

Notice that even though one fragment is begun with a preposition and the other with a subordinator, they are both behaving as subordinate, or dependent, clauses. More information is needed by the reader to know what the actual subject is and what action is being enacted. In other words, the author of both fragments has no point. The examples below complete the thought:

By the time I get to Phoenix, half my vacation will be over.

After he completed the driver's exam, he waited the required thirty days to take it again.

Exercise 3

Identify the clauses below as fragments (frag) or complete sentences (S). Correct any fragments to complete the thought.

Example: _frag_ *When the new semester begins.*

> _When the new semester begins, I will be prepared for each class._

1. ____He will work on the assignment as soon as he gets home.

_____

_____

2. ____ Ran with scissors, a razor blade, and a blow-torch.

_____

_____

3. ____If we make it to Tulsa.

_____

_____

4. ____Veronica sliding down the stair rail.

_____

_____

5. ____Dozens of people at the bookstore.

_____

_____

6. ____ The well of my inspiration has gone dry.

_____

_____

7. ____Careful analysis of the situation.

_____

_____

8. ____When the Chinese take over as the world's leading economy.

_____

_____

9. ____Melissa reading alone on the upper floor of the library.

_____

_____

10. ____Quoth the raven, "nevermore."

_____

_____

SHIFTS (SHIFT)—DISAGREEMENT BETWEEN PARTS OF SPEECH

A **shift** is any abrupt change that results in inconsistencies in the grammatical elements, parts of speech, of a sentence. A shift is a break from one of the most important rules in writing—_be consistent._ The first sentence of a paragraph usually dictates who the speaker is and in what time frame he will be speaking. More than a grammar error, a break or shift from these decisions indicates the author has lost sight of his topic, voice, audience, or purpose. Shifts are one of the most common errors committed by beginning writers because the term encompasses such a large number of issues. Shifts are errors in grammar that are not limited to a single sentence but can, and usually do, spread throughout several sentences, an entire paragraph, or even an essay. To detect them, you must look at your writing as a whole, or globally.

Shift in Tense—Getting Angrier

A shift in **verb tense** is any change from past to present or vice versa. Whatever verb tense the first sentence of a paragraph or essay begins with is the tense that should be adhered to consistently throughout the writing unless logic dictates otherwise.

Exercise 4

Rewrite the following paragraph with consistent and correct verb tense based on the verb tense of the first sentence

Jamie's writing process is a mystery to behold. First, he sits staring at the computer monitor, and then he decided to go for a walk around the dorm. When he returned to his room, he tries to find anything else to do but write; he dusted the furniture, straightened the book shelves, and did a load of laundry before he sits back down at his desk. Finally, when he exhausts all other possibilities, he started writing his essay.

_____

_____

_____

_____

_____

_____

_____

_____

_____

Shift in Person—Who's on First?

A shift in **person** indicates a change from first to second or third or any combination thereof. For example, a writer who begins speaking in first person should consistently speak in the same voice to avoid confusion. The same holds true for third person. Bear in mind, however, that although speaking in second person consistently is not a shift, it is considered a serious error in diction. Avoid speaking in second person unless dictated to do so explicitly by your instructor.

Exercise 5

In the paragraph below, you will notice that the option of adopting whatever person the first sentence introduces has been removed. Rewrite the following paragraph in consistent first or third person.

Each student who attends this university is expected to do everything in your power to do well in your classes. I know that if you do not do everything the instructor tells me then I will not pass the course. Students must take more responsibility in performing well in my classes.

Further, students must get help from your instructors when they do not understand an assignment or something. Your success is up to you.

_____

_____

_____

_____

_____

_____

_____

_____

_____

_____

Shift in Number—Three is the Magic Number

A shift in **number** indicates a break from singular to plural or the other way around. This is one of the most prevalent forms of the shift in student writing. Just as subjects and verbs must agree in number so too must any nouns and pronouns referring back to the subject, or in this case the antecedent, agree in number.

Some pronouns look plural but are actually singular; some pronouns may be singular or plural depending on the prepositional phrase following them; and some pronouns are always plural. These pronouns are known as **indefinite pronouns**. A list of pronouns that are always singular is provided in the list below:

SINGULAR INDEFINITE PRONOUNS		
everybody	anybody	nobody
everything	everyone	anyone
someone	something	somebody
another	much	nothing
no one	either	

As mentioned, some pronouns are singular or plural depending on the prepositional phrase that follows. The examples below illustrate this point:

Half of the pie is gone.

Half of us need to work on our quadriceps.

A list of pronouns that may be either singular or plural is provided below:

SINGULAR OR PLURAL INDEFINITE PRONOUNS			
half	some	any	all
most	none	more	

Indefinite pronouns that are always plural are provided below:

PLURAL INDEFINITE PRONOUNS			
both	few	many	several
others			

Exercise 6

Rewrite the sentences below to ensure that the nouns or pronouns agree in number with the antecedent. You may need to change other words in the sentence to maintain grammatical integrity.

Example: Each student must bring their own beverage to the party

Each student must bring his own beverage to the party.

1. Whether or not the community agrees with the ordinance, they must abide by it.

   _____

   _____

2. Thom Yorke of Radiohead released their solo album called *The Eraser* in 2006.

   _____

   _____

3. Apple revolutionized technology when they released the iPhone.

   _____

   _____

4. Every book on the shelf was in their rightful place.

_____

_____

5. Kleenex should realize they could market their tissue boxes as shoes.

_____

_____

Shift in Mood—Sad but True

A shift in **mood** means the writer has moved from imperative to subjunctive, or indicative. An **imperative** sentence is a command, in which the subject is understood "you." A **subjunctive** sentence expresses a wish, a suggestion, or possibility and is usually begun with the word "if." An **indicative** sentence denotes an action and is usually the form your writing will take. See if you can distinguish between the three moods in the sentences below.

To his credit, he washes the dishes every night.

If I were writing an essay, I would avoid using second person.

Put the mayonnaise on the sandwich first, and then put on the Cap'n Crunch.

NOTE: The subordinate clause in a subjunctive sentence has a plural verb even when the noun preceding it is singular. This is an exception to the subject/ verb agreement rules. The plural verb indicates a wish or hypothetical situation.

Exercise 7

Rewrite the following paragraph to be consistent in mood with the first sentence of the paragraph.

Set your header, that portion of the document in which you show your last name and the page number for that particular page. Each page (except the first) is required to have your last name and the page number in the upper right hand corner **one-half (½) inch** down from the paper's margin. Never try to insert these manually. Make sure you are inside the header to insert this information. If you need help with this, see the instructions for your word processing program.

_____

_____

_____

_____

_____

_____

_____

_____

_____

Shift in Voice—Growth Spurts

A shift in **voice** signals a move from active to passive voice. **Active voice** in a sentence means the subject is performing the action. **Passive voice** indicates the subject is having the action performed upon it. Whenever possible, active voice is the preferred method of writing because it usually is more descriptive, requiring stronger, more vivid verbs. Look at the examples below and see if you can tell the difference between active and passive voice and understand why active voice is preferred.

My lunch order was taken by the surly waitress with questionable hygiene.

The surly waitress with questionable hygiene took my order.

The key to keeping your writing in active voice is to keep the focus of your sentences on the individual or thing that is either performing the action of the verb in the sentence or is being described by the verb in the sentence.

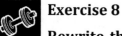 **Exercise 8**

Rewrite the following paragraph so that each sentence is in active voice.

When I bought my car, I was given a very different impression of the vehicle than what reality was later to reveal to me. I was told by the overly friendly salesman that this particular model was very efficient in gas mileage and that any time I had any problems at all he could be reached by phone. As I was driving home, a disturbing rattle reached my ears, so I called the dealership. My comments were recorded by a voice mail machine that promised me that Friendly Salesman would be returning my call within the hour. Four days later, I realized that I had been given a run-around and that no return call would be forthcoming.

_____

_____

_____

_____

_____

_____

_____

_____

DANGLING (DM) AND MISPLACED MODIFIERS (MM)—NO CONNECTION, MAN

As discussed in Chapter 1 of the Handbook, **modifiers** are any words or phrases that describe a noun, verb, or any other word or phrase in a sentence. Modifiers can even describe other modifiers. If a modifier has nothing in the sentence to describe, it is a **dangling modifier**. A dangling modifier leads to confusion because the reader has no idea what is being described. If the modifier is too far away to make it clear what word or phrase is being described, it is a **misplaced modifier**. A misplaced modifier confuses the reader because he is uncertain exactly what is being described, and this can sometimes alter the meaning of the sentence, occasionally to humorous effect. *As a general rule, a modifier should immediately precede or follow the word it is describing.* The sentence below provides an example of a dangling modifier:

The electric plant lit up the night strolling along the river side.

Going by the logic of the sentence, the electric plant seems to have magically grown legs and begun walking. Of course, this makes no sense. The problem is that the modifier "strolling along the river" has nothing in the sentence to describe. What is missing is the person or couple who are most likely to be the ones taking the leisurely walk. Correcting the sentence for clarity requires you to rewrite it. Look at the example below to see if the sentence is clearer:

Strolling along the river side, Carl and Esther noticed the electric plant lit up the night.

The modifier in the sentence above is now clearly stating exactly who is strolling along the river side. Notice also that the modifier immediately precedes the noun phrase it is describing. Also, since it is introducing the independent clause, the modifier is set off with a comma.

Misplaced modifiers, again, have words or phrases in the sentence to modify, but they are too far away in the sentence to make it clear what is being described. Look at the example below and decide what the meaning of the sentence is when the modifier is misplaced:

The dedicated students excel in their classwork only.

Judging the meaning of the sentence by the placement of the modifier "only," the reader can only determine that students will do well on classwork but perhaps fail at all other aspects of life. Hopefully this is not the intended meaning of the sentence. Look at the example below and determine if this rewording is closer to the author's intent:

Only the dedicated students excel in their classwork.

Notice that once more the modifier is as close as possible to the word or phrase it is modifying. This time the sentence makes more sense, indicating the level of determination a student must have to do well in school.

HOW TO IDENTIFY MISPLACED OR DANGLING MODIFIERS

1. Look for all modifiers, words or phrase that describe other words or phrases, and circle them.

2. Draw an arrow from a circled modifier to the word or phrase it is describing.

3. Ask yourself whether the modifier is immediately preceding or following the word or phrase it is describing. If it is not, move it closer. If the arrow has no word or phrase to land on, the modifier is dangling.

Exercise 9

Identify the following sentences as having a dangling modifier (dm), a misplaced modifier (mm), or no modifier errors (C). If the modifier is misplaced, circle it, draw an arrow to the word or phrase it is modifying and rewrite the sentence to correct the issue. If the modifier is dangling, circle it and rewrite the sentence to correct the error.

Example: ___dm *Broken down by the side of the road, Boris knew he was going to miss his interview.*

> *When his car broke down by the side of the road, Boris knew he was going to miss his interview.*

1. ____ Stalin nearly killed thirty million of his own people in attempt to consolidate his power.

   _____

   _____

2. ____ Styrofoam containers in hand, the concert seemed to be more enjoyable.

   _____

   _____

3. ____ The dinner was good except for the service, complete with New York strip and a baked potato.

   _____

   _____

4. ____ The fire engine, already emanating smoke from its windows, pulled up to the burning house.

   _____

   _____

5. ____Running through the forest in desperation, the sounds of a nearby highway could be finally heard.

_____

_____

6. ____ Due to lack of business, Mr. Martin warned his employees that a layoff was imminent.

_____

_____

7. ____When the weather does warm up, shedding the winter pounds finally will be necessary.

_____

_____

8. ____Leaking from under the bathroom door, Xavier saw the rug darken with water.

_____

_____

9. ____The chairs belong out on the porch in the kitchen.

_____

_____

10. ____After the nine hour car ride, I need to stretch my legs.

_____

_____

PRONOUNS (PRO)—NOUNS WITH JOBS

As previously discussed, **pronouns** are words that are used to substitute for other nouns. For example, "he" could replace "boy"; "she" could replace "woman"; or "it" could replace "building." Pronouns help the writer avoid needless repetition, enhancing the coherence of his or her sentence structure. However, in addition to unwanted shifts of which incorrect usage of pronouns is often the culprit, pronouns can also take the wrong form or **case**. Pronouns come in three cases as the examples below (broken down by first, second, and third person) illustrate:

PRONOUN CASES		
Subjective Case Pronouns	**Objective Case Pronouns**	**Possessive Pronouns**
I	me	my or mine
you	you	yours
he or she or it	him or her or it	his or hers or its

Subjective Case Pronouns—It Depends on Your Point of View

Pronouns in the **subjective case** are often acting as the subject of a sentence. These pronouns can also serve as a **complement** to the subject, a word or phrase that helps to complete a thought. Subjective pronouns can also function as all or part of an **appositive**, a noun or noun phrase that is used to define the subject or its complement. Examples of subjective case pronouns performing the aforementioned functions are provided below:

Subject
They welcomed the New Year by displaying a banner with subversive messages on the side of the federal building.

Complement
When the police men arrived, they knew that at least one member of the guilty party would be *he*.

Part of an Appositive
The miscreants, the two who escaped and *he*, were held responsible for inciting mayhem.

Objective Case Pronouns—Be Reasonable

Pronouns in the **objective case** take the place of nouns that serve as the direct object or indirect object of a predicate (a verb or verb phrase). A **direct or indirect object** is the noun or noun phrase that is the recipient of the action or state of being identified by the verb. As discussed in the previous chapter, prepositional phrases also contain objects; when the object of a preposition is a pronoun, it is also in the objective case. A third instance that requires a pronoun in the objective form is when an appositive, or part of one, is replacing an object. Finally, the subject of an infinitive is in the objective case. An **infinitive** is a verb phrase that includes the word "to" and a verb (to +verb). Below are more concrete examples of these definitions:

> *Direct Object*
> I talked *her* off the ledge after the midterm exam.

> *Indirect Object*
> The policeman in the small town through which the highway cut was kind enough to give *me* a speeding ticket.

> *Object of a Preposition*
> Behind *her* is the safe that holds my prized album collection.

> *Inside an Appositive*
> The class of two elected members for the student senate, Delvin and *me*.

> *Subject of an Infinitive*
> I wrote *him* to ask a question about your mother.

NOTE: If any word comes between the word "to" and its verb in an infinitive, the write has committed the split infinitive error. For example the sentence "I want to really ask the instructor about his personal hygiene" has split the infinitive with the word "really."

Subjective versus Objective Case Pronouns—Death Match

The case of some pronouns can be confusing to composition students. Here are some tips to help you distinguish subjective pronouns from objective ones:

1. When determining whether to replace a noun with either of the pronouns "we" or "us," you must decide whether the noun to be replaced is acting as the subject or the object of the sentence or phrase. If the noun is in the subjective case, then you should use "we"; on the other hand, when the noun is in the objective case, then you should use "us." Examples of these subjective and objective forms are provided below:

   Subjective Case Using "We"
   On the first of April, *we* will be on alert for any pranks.

   Objective Case Using "Us"
   The Swingline stapler helps to identify *us* as cubicle slaves.

   Do not be confused about a subject being placed at the end of a sentence. Notice the pronoun case used in the following sentence is still subjective: *The only people who care about the Queen's English seem to be we teachers.*

2. These same lessons of recognizing subjective and objective cases apply to pronouns such as "I," "she," and "me, and "her." "I" and "she/he" always act in subjective case while "me" and "him/her" are objective. See if you can recognize the difference between the two cases in the sentences below:

   Subjective Case Using "I" or "She/He"
   The person responsible for the vandalism was *I*.

   Objective Case Using "Me" or "Him/Her"
   The teacher extended an invitation to Rueben, Klaus, and *her*.

3. To dispel any confusion about the use of "who/whoever" and "whom/whomever," understand them in the same way as the use of other pronouns in the subjective and objective cases. "Who/whoever" is subjective, and "whom/whomever" is objective. The sentences below help to clarify the difference between the two cases:

   Subjective Use of "Who/Whoever"
   The man oddly dressed in the plaid polo shirt is the one *who* ate all of the sharp cheddar from the sample tray.

Objective Use of "Whom/Whomever"
You can date *whomever* you like; I never want to see you again.

To recognize whether "who" or "whom" should be used in a sentence, substitute the pronoun with "them" or "him." If the sentence makes sense, then you are using the correct pronoun case; in other words, the pronoun is objective and should be "whom." If it does not make sense to make this substitution, then the pronoun is in the subjective case and should be "who." The sentence below provides an example of this trick:

him

These tickets are for ~~whoever arrives at the arena first~~.

Notice that him is an acceptable substitution in the context of the sentence, letting the writer know that the pronoun "whoever" is in the wrong case; it should be "whomever," the objective rather than subjective case.

NOTE: The same lessons of subjective and objective usage apply to interrogative pronouns. Simply reword the question in the form of a statement to determine which case should be used. "To whom are you writing the letter, mother?" could be rephrased "You are writing the letter to whom, mother." This makes the subject and object more recognizable since they are in the places in the sentence you would normally expect them.

Possessive Case Pronouns—That Isn't Yours, Brother

Adjective forms of **possessive case** pronouns, such as "mine," "his," "your," and "theirs," indicate ownership. Unlike most nouns that take the possessive form, possessive pronouns do not include an apostrophe. Possessive case pronouns come directly before a noun, replace that noun, or appear before a gerund. Examples of possessive case pronouns used in sentences are provided below:

In Front of a Noun
His books seem to be in *his* car more than in the classroom with him where they belong.

Replacing a Possessive Noun
The responsibility for coming to class prepared, including printing PowerPoints of the day's lecture, is *theirs*.

Before a Gerund
She fell to the ground in giddy delirium upon hearing *his* speaking.

Knowing When to Use "That," "Which," or "Who"

One of the most common sources of confusion for beginning writers is determining whether to use "that," "which," or "who" when substituting a pronoun for a noun. The pronoun "that" is used, rather than "which," when the noun phrase, known as a **restrictive clause** (otherwise known as an appositive), is essential to the meaning of the sentence. Much like an afterthought, a **non-restrictive clause** uses the pronoun "which" and provides further clarification of the sentence's meaning, but its absence does not damage the integrity of the sentence. The restrictive clause is not essential to the sentence.

Another common error is the use of "that" or "which" when referring to a human being; to be clear, the only pronouns acceptable for replacing nouns that represent a person or people is "who," "whom," or "whoever/whomever." Examples of each of these pronoun cases are provided in the following sentences:

That (as part of a restrictive clause)
The car *that* Gustav bought was, in fact, stolen property.

Which (as part of a non-restrictive clause)
The movie, *which* starts on Friday, has gotten bad reviews.

NOTE: Notice in the sentences above that the restrictive clause using the pronoun "that" is not set off by commas while the non-restrictive clause using "which" is set off by commas. This rule should be applied to all restrictive and non-restrictive clauses.

Who (rather than that)
Elmer is the man *who* is confounded by a simple hindgut digester on a daily basis.

That (rather than who)
In Elmer's defense, the mere hindgut digester *that* confounds the hunter is actually quite articulate and crafty.

Exercise 10

Underline the pronouns in the sentences below and determine whether they are in the correct case. If the pronoun is in the wrong case, replace it with the pronoun in the correct case. If the sentence is without errors, write "C."

who

Example: Reginald is the student ~~that~~ missed the final exam and has to retake the course.

1. The trip to Mexico was exhausting, but it was him who never ran out of energy.

2. Who are you going to include in the study group for biology?

3. The invitations were mailed yesterday by him and me.

4. My ex-girlfriend is now referred to by we group of three as her who shall not be named.

5. Colombia is the South American country which has been made infamous by *Scarface.*

6. I thought the iPad was her's, but it actually belongs to he.

7. I was distracted from my studies by him singing.

8. "Hey teacher, leave us kids alone!" has become the anthem for many of we students in high school.

9. The student's file which was confidential was lost somewhere on the campus grounds.

10. You're shirt is untucked, slick.

MIXED SENTENCES (MIXED)—AN UNSAVORY BLEND OF CLAUSES

Complex sentences, of course, are a combination of dependent and independent clauses. As such, these clauses must make sense together, or *coordinate*. When the parts of speech contained in the dependent clause are incompatible with those of the independent clause, the sentence is **mixed.** This is most often caused through the misuse of subordinators, prepositions, or noun phrases in the dependent clause or the lack of necessary words for clarity. Another error, technically known as **faulty predication**, occurs when the subject or object of the sentence is performing an action or is in a state of being that is illogical. This is also said to be mixed. Like run on sentences and fragments, mixed sentences are considered to be serious errors and are penalized more heavily because they indicate the student does not have a firm grasp of what constitutes the basic element of the new language of academic writing—the sentence. Examples of mixed errors are provided below:

> *Mixed*
> By learning the basic parts of speech, ensures you will be able to recognize grammar errors more easily.

Notice that the dependent clause also contains what would logically also be part of the subject while what should be the independent clause is lacking a subject. The sentence can be corrected in two ways. One way to fix the sentence is to remove the preposition acting as a subordinator at the beginning of the sentence:

> *Correct*
> Learning the basic parts of speech ensures you will be able to recognize grammar errors more easily.

Another way to fix the sentence is to supply the subject missing from the independent clause as shown below:

> *Correct*
> By learning the parts of speech, you will be able to recognize grammar errors more easily.

Below is a sentence that is mixed due to faulty predication:

> *Mixed or Faulty Predication*
> Freedom is where the citizens of a country can speak and behave as they choose so long as their actions do not infringe on the rights of others.

In conversation, we use indicators such as "where" and "when" all of the time, but logically freedom is an abstract concept that cannot physically inhabit a time or place. Acts of freedom only can do this; therefore, the sentence must be rephrased as follows:

> *Correct*
> Freedom is a basic right that allows the citizens of this country to speak and behave as they choose so long as their actions do not infringe on the rights of others.

Notice that the sentence cannot be revised without significant restructuring. The meaning of the sentence must be understood and rewritten almost completely to correct the error.

In the sentence below, a poor choice of preposition has created a mixed sentence:

> In Tuesday, Fred takes his Foot Locker salesman exam.

Prepositions have been so ingrained into the English language that the logic behind them has succumbed to tradition. We do not say "in Tuesday"; we say "on Tuesday." Conversely we are said to look forward to an event within a month rather than on it. These old, seemingly random, rules tend to confuse many students whose second language is English. The only way to avoid these errors is through memorization and practice.

Exercise 11

Determine whether the sentences below are mixed or correctly structured. If the sentence is mixed, rewrite it to maintain its original intent and correct the error. If the sentence contains no errors, write "C" next to it.

Example: In striving to do our best is when we often fail.

> *We often fail when striving to do our best.*

1. A good grade in Basic Writing would be the ideal situation.

   _____

   _____

2. To be all that you can be is the Army's slogan.

   _____

   _____

3. On March, I will celebrate the death of poor Julius.

   _____

   _____

4. By running for my life from the zombie horde, kept me alive for another day.

   _____

   _____

5. Vladimir's phone is always calling me at inappropriate times.

   _____

   _____

INCOMPLETE SENTENCE (INC)—FUZZY THOUGHTS

An **incomplete sentence** has all of the ingredients (subject + verb + complete thought) that keep it from being a fragment, but words or phrases are still missing that could make its meaning more obvious. In short, the sentence is usually missing modifiers or details that would otherwise make clear what exactly is being said. The sentence below is incomplete. What modifiers could eliminate the errors?

Incomplete

His interpretation of teen angst in Salinger's *Catcher in the Rye* is much better developed than his interpretation of Cheever's "The Swimmer."

At first glance, nothing seems to be wrong with this sentence, but a closer look reveals that the writer neglected to define the type of analysis being applied to Cheever's work. The sentence is clearer in the example below:

> *Corrected*
> His interpretation of teen angst in Salinger's *Catcher in the Rye* is much better developed than his interpretation of suburban dystopia in Cheever's "The Swimmer."

Aside from elaborate comparisons, words or phrases can be missing from simple sentences, confusing the reader as shown below:

> *Incomplete*
> His apartment is closer to campus than the bus stop.

This sentence is unclear because the reader is uncertain whether the bus stop or the campus is closer to his apartment. When corrected, the geography of both the sentence and the student's environment become clearer:

> *Corrected*
> His apartment is closer to campus than it is to the bus stop.

Exercise 12

Revise the sentences below to correct any confusion caused by missing words or phrases. If the sentence is clear, write "C."

Example: One example is the lack of motivation many students have when returning from Spring Break.

> *One example of the issues many teachers face is the lack of motivation many students have when returning from Spring Break.*

1. Starshine's attitude is better than Moonbeam's.

   _____

   _____

WRITING IN A NEW LANGUAGE: AN INTRODUCTION TO ACADEMIC WRITING

2. The Wichita State Shockers has the best team in the division.

   _____

   _____

3. The forests of North America are much more extensive than Europe.

   _____

   _____

4. Four p.m., I get out of class and run like a savage to my car to leave campus.

   _____

   _____

5. My car has better gas mileage.

   _____

   _____

PARALLELISM (//)—WALKING A FINE LINE

Parallelism is already discussed in relation to thesis statements in Chapter 3 of Unit I, but the concept sometimes escapes beginning writers. Not only do thesis statements utilize parallelism to emphasize separate but equal points but topic and supporting sentences do as well. For these reasons, taking a second look at parallelism is worthwhile. In mathematics, parallelism describes two or more lines that are equidistant. The same principle applies to the concept in grammar: whenever two or more distinct but equal points are being expressed in a simple, compound, or complex sentence, they must match grammatically to be **parallel**. Usually parallel issues arise when a sentence contains three or more items in a series, but similar problems can occur in sentences that contain coordinating conjunctions or correlative conjunction pairs. The following tips should help you maintain parallelism when necessary:

1. *Item in a Series*

   When a sentence contains two or more items in a series, all of the items must be noun phrases, verb phrases, gerund phrases, or prepositional phrases. The examples below illustrate this rule:

   > *Parallel Noun Phrases*
   > The extensive road construction affects *commuters who have no alternative route*, *businesses that have blocked entrances*, and *emergency services that must navigate the streets in a quick, safe manner.*

   > *Verb Phrases*
   > When preparing for a college exam, a student must *eat healthy food*, *get plenty of sleep*, and *study over a period of several days.*

   > *Gerund Phrases*
   > Most people are unaware that bicycle maintenance regularly involves *truing the wheels*, *adjusting the derailleur*, and *tightening the bottom bracket.*

   > *Prepositional Phrases*
   > The championship curling match will be held *in four days*, *at Miller's Pond*, *by the dead squirrel.*

2. *Coordinating Conjunctions*

   You have probably noticed that coordinating conjunctions are often used to connect two or more items in a series, but these linking words also connect two independent clauses to form a compound sentence. In a compound sentence, the two independent clauses should also grammatically and structurally match as closely as possible to maintain parallelism. See if you can detect how the example below helps demonstrate this principle:

   > *Compound Sentences*
   > Nicolas Cage is famous for choosing a wide range of movie roles, but he is also famous for punching the end of his lines for dramatic effect.

3. *Correlative Conjunction Pairs*

   Whenever a correlative conjunction, such as "neither" or "not only," is introduced into a sentence, the reader naturally searches for its partner, "nor" or "but also," to express fully the thought. When one set of the pair is missing, the sentence will not be parallel, and the thought is incomplete. The sentences below correctly demonstrate how to maintain parallelism using correlative conjunction pairs:

> *Correlative Conjunction Pairs*
> *Just as* Keebler makes a good cracker *so* too does Hickory Farms make a tasty sharp cheddar.
>
> Thankfully, *both* the House of Representatives *and* the Senate must pass a bill for it to become law.

Exercise 13

Identify the sentences below as being either parallel (P) or non-parallel (NP). Correct any sentence that is not parallel.

Example: NP Sometimes neither Frank or his dog can find the way back to the cabin.

> *Sometimes neither Frank nor his dog can find the way back to the cabin.*

1. ____The road to happiness is often fraught with pain, struggle, and leaves the traveler frustrated.

   _____

   _____

2. ____I have to go to the grocery store, to campus, and the bank before I can go home.

   _____

   _____

3. ____Eating ice cream, watching movies and to cry were how I used to spend my Saturday nights before I read Nietzsche.

   _____

   _____

4. ____Regardless of whether he knows them, a student is responsible for the rules set by the syllabus.

_____

_____

5. ____I would have gotten away with it if it were not for those meddling teenagers and running into their amazingly articulate dog.

_____

_____

STRINGY (STRINGY)—CAN'T...BREATHE

Fairly well established by this point in the textbook is the fact that a compound sentence consists of *only* two independent clauses linked together by a coordinating conjunction. Whenever a sentence consists of more than two independent clauses linked by two or more coordinating conjunctions, the sentence is **stringy**. In other words, the writer is stringing together independent clause after independent clause without proper ending punctuation such as a period or question mark. A stringy sentence disrupts the rhythm of speaking and writing, not allowing the reader to pause. The sentence below demonstrates the confusion caused by this error:

Stringy
The band Explosions in the Sky became famous for creating the soundtrack to the film *Friday Night Lights,* but many of the albums produced by the group before and since have gone largely unnoticed, and this has led to them being neglected by many fans who idolize Radiohead for the same musical style, yet the members of Explosions continue to enter the studio to create more surreal rhythms, almost if they were doing it for themselves alone.

Exercise 14

Revise the sentence above to eliminate any stringy errors; separate independent clauses and replace coordinating conjunctions with transitions where necessary.

_____

_____

_____

_____

_____

Writing is like putting a puzzle together – until all the pieces are in the right places, the whole picture is not going to be visible; and once they are in the right places, the picture becomes more than just a collection of pieces but a coherent whole.

CHAPTER 3

CHOOSING THE BEST WORDS TO COMMUNICATE YOUR MEANING EFFECTIVELY

DEFINING DICTION AND ITS PLACE IN AMERICA

The elements of writing in the new language of academia certainly include organizing and developing paragraphs, using the best rhetorical patterns to fit your purpose, understanding the parts of speech, and recognizing their relationships to eliminate errors in grammar and punctuation; however, one vital element remains to elevate your language to that of the academe. That missing piece is the proper and best use of language to communicate your meaning effectively—**diction**. Without proper diction, or choice of words, the writer risks alienating his readers or dismissing them. As compromising as grammar errors are, diction errors betray the writer as someone who is not worthy of the reader's attention, and also like grammar, instructors expect their students to enter composition classes already able to practice proper diction. Along with the abbreviations used to label them in a student's graded writing, the most common diction errors, to be discussed in this section, are listed in the table below:

COMMON DICTION ERRORS		
Person (1st or 2nd)	Contractions (cont)	Empty phrases (weak)
Jargon (jar)	Slang (slang)	Colloquial Language (coll)
Cliches (cliché)	Euphemisms (euph)	Pretentious (pre)

PERSON (1ST OR 2ND)—MAKE UP YOUR MIND

Unless you are writing about your own experiences in a narrative or anecdote, most of your academic level writing should be in *third person, present tense*. Any writing not in third person will not only show as a grammar error but also as a diction error. If the writing shifts from third to *first person*, the error will, therefore, be two-fold as "shift/1st." In other words, you will be committing not only a grammar error but also a diction error. In almost no situation in academic writing will you address the reader directly—you will not use *second person*. This is considered a serious grammar and diction error and will be marked "shift/2nd." Examples of these errors appear in the sentences below:

> *Person (1st)*
> Many of *us* are addicted to technology at the sacrifice of interpersonal skills.

> *Person (2nd)*
> Almost hourly during *your* waking day, *you* log on to a computer or check *your* messages on a cell phone.

 NOTE: If the examples above were written without an antecedent for the pronouns, three errors would have been committed: 1st/dm/shift.

CONTRACTIONS (CONT)—GROWING PAINS

Contractions are two words abbreviated into one with the remaining portions of the two words separated by an apostrophe. In most cases, contractions are used to combine a verb with the word "not" (shouldn't, didn't, can't) or to combine a noun with auxiliary verbs such as "is" or " has" or "are" or "will" or "am"(he's, they're, she'll, I'm). While most of us commonly speak with contractions, their use in writing is considered too informal for an academic audience and should be avoided. Consider how seriously you would be taken when writing on the following subject using contractions:

> *Contractions*
> When evaluating the practical value of stem cell research to mankind, the *politician's* got to set aside her sense of morality. She *shouldn't* let her personal beliefs interfere with the will of the majority. Instead, *she'd* be better served leaving religion out of the discussion altogether.

EMPTY PHRASES (WEAK)—AVOIDING THE POINT

Empty phrases are any words or groups of words in a sentence that distract the reader, contribute nothing of value, or call unnecessary attention to the writer. This weak writing comes in three forms:

1. *Distractions*

   Phrases such as "in my opinion" or "I think" in a sentence add nothing of value to a sentence; instead, such phrasing, known as a **distraction**, indicates the writer's lack of confidence in his own opinions and is redundant. The reader already knows whose opinions are being expressed because the author's name is at the top of each page. Look at the example below and decide how apt you would be to adopt the author's point of view:

   Distraction

   In my opinion, students should be allowed to carry guns on campus for their own safety.

2. *Announcements*

   As discussed in Chapter 3, **announcements** of the writer's intentions, such as "in this paper, I will discuss," do nothing to contribute to the direction a piece of writing will take. Instead, an announcement calls unwelcomed attention to the author himself and reveals to the reader that he is stalling rather than getting to the point of the discussion. In the sentence below, you can see that no clear direction is apparent to the reader:

   Announcement

   This essay will evaluate the quality of motion pictures of the twenty-first century to the quality of those made in the silent era.

3. *Expletives*

   Expletives are phrases such as "it is," "there are," or "here is" that rearrange the usual order of a sentence; when done properly, this can emphasize meaning. In most cases, however, the use of expletives weakens a sentence by adding more words than are necessary or substituting for stronger, more vivid verbs. The sentences below illustrate this point:

   Expletives

It was a dark and stormy night.

There are 206 bones in the human body.

Here are four reasons I will not go out with you.

NOTE: Expletives, you will notice, contain pronouns, but unlike most pronouns when properly used, expletives refer back to no direct antecedent. Do not confuse an expletive with a phrase containing a pronoun that has a direct antecedent, which is not considered weak.

Exercise 1

Rewrite the paragraph below to eliminate any diction errors involving person, contractions, or empty phrases.

This paragraph will discuss my obsession with time. I can't help but be sure to measure it out no matter what I'm doing or where I'm at. In addition to my planner, I've got two calendars in the bedroom of my apartment and three calendars in my office. This does not count the two clocks in my office, even though one doesn't work anymore. One of the clocks in my office, as does my watch, also gives the date and day of the month, not to mention the temperature. I don't need to tell you I might have a problem. I should probably seek psychiatric aid because, in my humble opinion, I may be obsessive-compulsive. You should also probably know that there are two alarm clocks in my bedroom, in addition to the three wall clocks I mentioned earlier, as long as it is confession time. As you can see, I like to keep track of the time, but it's getting to be a problem.

_____

_____

_____

_____

_____

_____

_____

_____

_____

_____

JARGON (JAR)—WHERE DID IT GO?

Jargon is the use of specialized terms specific to a field of study or a profession that those outside of the discipline would not necessarily be familiar with. Jargon is considered a diction error only when a specific term is not properly defined for the reader. This indicates a lack of familiarity with or concern for the reader. Examples of jargon that are not adequately defined are provided in the sentences below:

Jargon
Many students criticize the instructor's *PowerPoints* for their *motif* of various cheeses.

The prominent use of *isobars* indicated that the city could soon expect rain.

My *mp3* player holds *eighty gigs*.

My turntable can play an infinite number of *LPs* and *45s*.

SLANG (SLANG)—YOU FEELIN' ME?

Slang, otherwise known as a neologism, is phrases that have come into the language so recently that that they are not accepted as standard English. Another issue with slang is that it is usually trendy and not likely to be adopted by those outside of a specific group. Neologisms are often adopted from motion pictures, current musical hits, or social fads, and pass out of favor soon after they are brought in, dating the writer's language. Writers also run the risk of alienating readers who may not be familiar with the terms used; moreover, writers jeopardize their own credibility. Some familiar and unfamiliar slang is used in the sentences below to demonstrate their ephemeral and sometimes ridiculous nature:

> *Slang*
> I have so many friends *texting* me that they are *blowing me up*.
>
> His *butt-comb* is *groovy*, *man*.
>
> Your new friend doesn't have the *juice* to *hang* with us.

COLLOQUIALISMS (COLL)—Y'ALL MET MY MEEMAW?

Colloquialisms are phrases and terms specific to a region or expressions of familiarity with family members or friends. As with slang, colloquial language will not necessarily be understood beyond the group it is used within most commonly and should be avoided to prevent alienating the readers. One specific kind of this diction error is the improper use of idioms. **Idioms**, culturally specific phrases whose literal meaning is removed from the expression, are usually used in a specific way due more to tradition than logic. Except for their region-specific nature, they are similar to clichés in that they are overused expressions. For example, idioms such as "That dog won't hunt," "If the shoe fits, wear it," and "Put on your thinking cap" are poor substitutes for the writer's own thinking and not likely to be understood by the reader. As with prepositions, students whose second language is English often misuse idioms because of the apparent lack of logic attached to them. Again, idioms, as with all colloquialisms, are language and culture-specific and do not translate well to those outside of the culture. To be sure your intended meaning is getting across, avoid them.

> *Colloquialisms*
> My *mom* keeps *dogging* me about taking out the trash.
>
> Let's go get a *pop* after class, or as you say, a *tonic*.
>
> My cousin asked me to *carry her* to the Piggly Wiggly.
>
> We had to stand *on line* for four hours to get tickets to the Eminem concert.
>
> The completion of the essay was a *watershed moment* for Jinksie.

Exercise 2

Underline the phrases containing jargon, slang, or colloquialisms in the paragraph below.

Now that I am a major in English, I am starting to pick up what my professors are laying down. I am getting hip to enthymemes and logical fallacies. I can tear down my girlfriend's arguments in a heartbeat. For example, we were fighting about where to eat the other night, and out of the blue she called me a neo-maxi zoon dweebie. I calmly replied that she did not need to degrade the discussion through the use of ad hominems. She was nonplussed by my retort and hopped out of my ride. I gratefully laid rubber to go to my "BFF" Jolene's, hoping she and I could hook up. Ditching my ex was the best move I ever made, but don't tell my nanny.

CLICHÉS (CLICHES)—A NO BRAINER

Clichés are words and phrases that have been used so often that they have lost their intrinsic meaning. Unlike idioms, they are not regionally specific, but like idioms, they are a substitute for the writer's own thinking, indicating a lack of true imagination and consideration of the subject. Look at the sentences below to see if you agree with this assessment and can recognize any of the clichés:

Clichés
I had not studied for the test, but I had an *ace up my sleeve*.

Rain fell during most of the vacation, but *as luck would have it*, Maurine and I could see *as far as the crow flies* on the last day of the trip.

One of the main reasons I am able to succeed in college is because my parents have always *been there* for me.

EUPHEMISMS (EUPH)—YOU CAN'T HANDLE THE TRUTH

Euphemisms are supposedly inoffensive words or phrases that substitute for any potentially offensive language. Euphemisms are examples of poor diction because they patronize the reader, assuming he or she will be offended by the reality of the message being conveyed. The examples below reveal the often silly nature of euphemisms:

Euphemisms
I nearly *kicked the bucket* when I heard that my best friend had *bought the farm*.

I was anxious to see my sister and her new *bundle of joy*.

I want Gerard to have my extensive collection of *magazines of questionable repute* when I *pass away*.

PRETENTIOUS (PRE)—HARUMPH

Pretentious language includes any language that is unnecessarily boastful or of an unneeded high diction level. Language that is too braggart replaces hard evidence with dubious self-praise. Do not tell your reader how great you and your writing are; let the work speak for itself. Moreover, language that is too complicated or makes use of big words for their own sake diffuses the writer's point and, contrary to the view of many basic writers, does not sound academic. Good writing makes use of the simplest language possible to get a point across to the reader. Economy of language shows precision of thought and is, therefore, the best use of diction. The sentences below demonstrate how pretentious language clouds the writer's intent:

Pretentious
My extensive analysis of *The Adventures of Huckleberry Finn* reveals that Twain did not, as most accuse him, lose interest in writing the novel after the first epiphany of the protagonist.

I despise the rules of grammar and punctuation because they only interfere with my creative genius.

Exercise 3
Underline the phrases containing clichés, euphemisms, and pretentious language in the paragraph below.

As far as the English faculty of my high school is concerned, my fecal matter definitely does not offend the refined olfactory nerves. On the contrary, my former teachers tell me that my first drafts of essays are better than most students' third revisions. My adept use of narrative arc and subtle denouement bring many to tears of infinite joy and sorrow, so powerful is my command of the Queen's English. I do not have to tell you, my current evaluators of my worthiness to be accepted into this great world of academia, that my writing is armed to the teeth with flowing prose and allusions to the great authors and orators who have come before me. When I graduate and eventually go to my reward, I have no doubt that you will want to preserve this humble yet inspiring illustration of my capabilities in perpetuity. Please let me know your decision of my fate as soon as possible so that at the eleventh hour I and you may celebrate the works to come that will stand against the sands of time.

CHAPTER 4

PUNCTUATION AND CAPITALIZATION

PUNCTUATION—THE TRAFFIC SIGNS OF COMPOSITION

As you travel, you probably have found that your trip is a lot easier (and less stressful) if you notice and obey traffic signs—stop, yield, caution—that can help you navigate more successfully. Writing in the academic world is very similar; it has "traffic signs," or punctuation marks, that allow you to send signals to your reader: "pay attention to this," "this is different from that," or "take a break here." Knowing how to use commas, apostrophes, semi-colons, dashes and hyphens, quotation marks, and parentheses can help you get your point across more clearly and more successfully.

THE COMMA—"IT LIFTS, IT SEPARATES"

Until now, we have mentioned commas mostly in the context of sentence structure—its use in compound and complex sentences in order to separate dependent and independent clauses—but commas have more uses than just that. You also can utilize commas to do the following:

1. *Separate things in a series*

   When you have a series of three or more items (be it things or phrases), you should use a comma to separate them.

   The chef prepared a dinner of *roasted pork, grilled endive salad, and parslied potatoes.*

   We *ate all the food, enjoyed the atmosphere, paid the bill, and left.*

2. *Draw attention to important words or phrases, such as introductory words or phrases or important words or phrases within a sentence.*

> *After a night of partying*, I was not in the mood for an exam.
> She worried that her legacy, *that portion of the family estate that was coming to her*, was lost.

3. *Separate dates and addresses*

> He is scheduled on *March 30, 2011*, to take his entrance exam.
> Her family moved here from *Missoula, Montana*.

Notice that all state names get spelled out in full; do not use postal abbreviations.

4. *Prevent confusion (if a word or phrase has been omitted or if two words in a row echo one another)*

> As the old saying goes, "to err is human; *to forgive, divine*."
> In the case of Japan, what we feared might *happen, happened*.

APOSTROPHES—NOT JUST FOR CONTRACTIONS

As (hopefully) you know by this point, contractions are not considered good writing in the academic world; unfortunately, many students take this to mean that apostrophes cannot be used at all. This is not the case. Apostrophes *do* serve a useful purpose besides denoting a contraction:

1. *To denote missing letters in familiar phrases*

> He was a *rock 'n' roll* devotee.

Notice that the "a" and "d" are missing from the word "and." Whenever letters are omitted from a word, an apostrophe is used.

2. *To denote a quotation within a quotation*

> "The mayor used President Kennedy's *'Ask not'* phrase to get the community to stand behind him."

3. *To denote possession (for nouns). With singular nouns, the apostrophe comes before the "s"; with plural nouns, the apostrophe comes after the "s."*

> He cleaned the *cat's* litter box but complained bitterly about it.
> The *senators' aides* were treated to dinner at the Governor's Mansion.
> We left the package by the *Jones's* front door.

NOTES: Add the apostrophe and "s" onto the last word of a hyphenated compound adjective, as in "We went to the concert in my brother-in-law's car."

Add the apostrophe and "s" to the last noun when the object in question is shared, as in "The study group met in Tina and Jackie's dorm room"; however, when dealing with two separate, unshared objects, add the apostrophe and "s" to both nouns, as in "Tina's and Jackie's textbooks were lost in the fire."

4. *To form plurals of letters that appear in lowercase*

> Mississippi has *four s's and two p's.*

NOTE: No apostrophe is needed when forming the plural of capitalized letters, numbers, and symbols, as in "That instructor must be difficult; she only gave two As last semester."

SEMI-COLONS—MORE POWERFUL THAN A LOCAL COMMA

Up to this point we have talked about semi-colons only in relation to their use in sentence structure—using them with a subordinating adverb in a compound sentence. Like the lowly comma, semi-colons can do much more, such as separate things in a series in which one or more items contain a comma, as shown in the following example:

> The committee voted *to table the motion, made by the city attorney; to consult a public relations firm about the new city logo; and to conduct a survey of the citizens' reactions to the proposed tax hike, which is scheduled to go into effect next year.*

Here we have three things that the committee acted on, so normally only a comma would be needed to separate these things in a series. However, two of these items have phrases set off with commas in them; for clarity, then, you should set off the series items with semi-colons instead of commas.

COLONS—HERE COMES THE BIG REVEAL

Think of colons as a kind of punctuation that introduces something, be it a clause, a list, or something that you want to draw the reader's attention to. The rules below give you some guidance on when to use them effectively:

1. *To join two independent clauses when you want to emphasize the second.*

   His pleading fell on deaf ears: he was going to flunk the class.

2. To set off an independent clause when it is followed by a list, an appositive, a quotation, or an idea directly related to the independent clause:

   List
   Our travel itinerary includes the following cities: *Cleveland, Ohio; Lynchburg, Virginia; and Louisville, Kentucky.*

   Appositive
   She said motherhood had trained her for a second career: *traffic cop.*

   Quotation
   Before the police descended on the concert hall, the band's lead singer cried: "The man is here to bring us down; get him!"

   Related idea
   His chief duty is clearly defined by the job description: *do anything he is asked to do by anyone asking him to do it.*

DASHES/HYPHENS—ONE IS NOT FOR ALL

Dashes and hyphens may *look* alike, but actually they are quite different and perform very different tasks. The **hyphen** is for joining words, and the **dash** is for emphasizing a point.

Hyphens—Bringing It All Together

While the hyphen may look like its cousin the dash, it is a much quieter functionary in the punctuation arsenal. The following rules show how to use this symbol:

1. *To join two or more words serving as a single adjective before a noun*
   a one-way street

   chocolate-covered peanuts

 NOTE: When compound modifiers come after a noun, they are not hyphenated ("The peanuts were chocolate covered." "The author was well known.")

2. *To form compound numbers*
   forty-six
   sixty-three
   Our much-loved teacher was sixty-three years old.

3. *To avoid confusion or an awkward combination of letters*
   re-sign a contract (vs. resign from a job)
   semi-independent (but semiconscious)
   shell-like (but childlike)

4. *To add prefixes such as ex- (meaning former), self-, all-; with the suffix -elect;*

   between a prefix and a capitalized word; and with figures or letters
   ex-husband
   self-assured
   mid-September
   all-inclusive
   president-elect

Dashes—More than Just a Cooking Measurement

As the writing in this book clearly indicates, dashes can be quite useful for emphasizing a point. However, this book is designed to get you, the writer, to pay attention to key ideas and rules; you should use dashes more sparingly in your own writing. Most students are familiar with the dash but do not seem to know how to make one correctly. To set off a word or a phrase for emphasis, use a dash (made with **two** hyphens with no space on either side [--]). The following examples demonstrate how a dash can emphasize a point. Notice how the dash *should look* in your own work:

> Students *writers—especially* beginning student *writers—have* a difficult time learning the rules that govern composition in an academic setting.

> The *Beatles—John*, Paul, George, and *Ringo—made* an indelible mark on the history of popular music.

PARENTHESES—SUPPLEMENTS AND AFTERTHOUGHTS

Using parentheses in writing gives a writer the chance to add supplemental (or additional) information or minor digressions for the sake of the point being made. You can think of the parentheses as a whisper. The rules and examples below show the correct use of the parenthetical statement:

1. *To add supplemental (additional) information*

> Once the nurse has taken a patient's vital signs *(blood pressure, pulse, and temperature)*, he must then record these accurately on the patient's chart before handing it over to the doctor.

2. *To add a minor digression*

> Once I picked out the dog *(more the size of a small pony than a regular dog)* at the kennel, I spent a fortune buying supplies for it.

3. *To give the reader an acronym or abbreviation to be used again in the essay*

> My father once worked for the National Aeronautics and Space Administration *(NASA)*.

> My friends and I are going to attend a benefit for the World Wildlife Foundation (WWF) tomorrow night.

NOTE: Once you have given the acronym or abbreviation in parentheses, you can then use only the abbreviation from that point forward.

QUOTATION MARKS—WHAT WAS THAT YOU SAID?

Saying that quotation marks go around direct quotations may seem common-sensical, but many writers struggle with the exact placement of these marks in conjunction with other punctuation. The following will guide you in the correct placement of quotation marks:

1. *At the beginning of the quotation and after the sentence-ending punctuation if the quotation ends there*

   John Lennon once wrote, *"Life* is what happens when you're making other *plans."*

1. At the beginning of the quotation and after the comma if more of the sentence follows

   "Life is what happens when you're making other *plans,"* wrote John Lennon.

2. *To signify the titles of shorter works such as essays or articles*

   In class we discussed *"How* to Say Nothing in 500 *Words"* by Paul McHenry Roberts.

QUESTION MARKS—WHY DO YOU ASK?

As their name implies, question marks are punctuation marks that denote direct questions or interrogative statements; however, many students put question marks where they are not needed. The rules and examples below demonstrate the correct use of question marks:

1. *At the end of a direct question*
   Who let the dogs *out?*

2. *At the end of each question if they appear in a series, even if the series is not in complete sentences*
   We all wondered how late the professor would be today. Fifteen *minutes?* Thirty *minutes?* An *hour?*

NOTE: In your readings you will see fragments, but in Basic Writing and composition courses, these will be considered errors and should be avoided. Not until you have mastered the rules can you break them to emphasize your points.

3. *A question mark is **not** needed if the statement is a polite request in the form of a question*
   Would you please bring me the stapler from the lab next *door.*

Notice in this instance what would normally be a question is actually a polite command and does not require an answer. Only in this type of instance can the writer omit a question mark for an interrogative statement.

You will become familiar with other punctuation marks as your academic writing journey continues. However, for our immediate purposes, these are the ones that you should concentrate on since, as history has proven, many student writers struggle with these punctuation marks more than any others.

Exercise 1

For each of the following sentences, choose one of the following to indicate how the comma is used in each (you may have more than one answer per question).

    a. To set off appositives

    b. To set off introductory or transitional words/phrases

    c. To separate things in a series

    d. To separate parts of dates or addresses

    e. To separate independent clauses with a coordinating conjunction

1. __D__ Early registration started on March 26, 2011, but few people attended because of the weather.

2. __A__ The comma, that smallest of punctuation marks, often causes the most problems for student writers.

3. __b__ Regretfully, I cannot accept your invitation for lunch tomorrow.

4. __E__ My friend and I searched the entire parking lot, but her car was not there.

5. __C__ His typical daily schedule consists of sleeping, eating, and playing World of Warcraft.

6. __b__ During spring break, my family participated in a Habitat for Humanity build in a nearby town.

7. __b__ Many students, unfortunately, forget about homework until the due date passes.

8. _B_ In the 21st century, technological advances give us plenty of opportunities to communicate, but many people use them to isolate themselves from society.

9. _C_ He claimed his favorite meal would consist of meatloaf, mashed potatoes, and braised green beans.

10. _A_ Love, that most elusive of emotions, still baffles most of us.

Exercise 2

The following sentences contain errors in semi-colon use – either using it where it is not needed or leaving it out where it is needed. Rewrite the sentence to correct any errors you find. If the sentence is correct, write "C" in the space provided.

1. _____ Unfortunately; his idea of "world travel" is driving to the casino in a neighboring county twice a month.

   _____

   _____

2. _____ Her art sells well outstanding orders keep her busy most of the year.

   _____

   _____

3. _____ To err is human; to forgive, divine.

   _____

   _____

4. _____ The shopping list for our upcoming hiking trip includes heavy socks; a sturdy tent, preferably one big enough to accommodate all six of us; lots of bottled water; and energy snacks.

   _____

   _____

5. _____ Each semester begins with an abundance of hope and optimism however, by spring break, many students and faculty alike are ready for the semester to be over.

_____

_____

Exercise 3

Each of the following is missing dashes, quotation marks, parentheses, or a colon. Rewrite the sentence providing the missing punctuation where it is needed.

1. Engineers with the National Aeronautics and Space Administration NASA recently released the latest pictures from the Hubble telescope.

_____

_____

2. Former President John Kennedy challenged a nation with his statement Ask not what your country can do for you.

_____

_____

3. Felicity's resume consists of only one occupation homemaker.

_____

_____

4. Testing that necessary evil of education has come under increasing scrutiny by education professionals.

_____

_____

5. Speeding defined by the state of Oklahoma as driving in excess of posted limits is the law most transgressed by far.

_____

_____

CAPITALIZATION—MAKING A BIG DEAL OF THINGS

Sometimes in writing we must draw attention to certain things—like the first word in a sentence, the first word in a direct quotation, certain titles, names, or proper nouns—in order for our meaning to remain clear. These rules may seem arbitrary at times, but to be considered a good writer (especially in academic writing), you must become familiar with these rules in order to make your writing more effective. The following major rules and their subsets should help you eliminate any capitalization errors:

Rule #1—Capitalize First Words

Obviously, you capitalize the first words of sentences, but sometimes the first words of a sentence can be buried within another sentence. In other instances, proper format for outlines requires capitalization. The rules below make these points more clear:

1. *First words of sentences (including quoted sentences)*
   The professor stated quite emphatically, "*All* students who arrived late to class will be penalized ten points."

2. *Do not capitalize the first words in these instances*

   a. An indirect quotation or paraphrase
      The professor stated quite emphatically that all students arriving late would be penalized.

   b. A fragment of a quotation
      The professor stated quite emphatically that all students arriving late would be *"penalized."*

3. *First words of a formal question or statement that follows a colon:*

Today's debate brought up an interesting question: **W**here *have* all the flowers gone?

NOTE: Use lowercase for ordinary statements after colons. For example, the sentence "He said he had a reason for his tardiness: his sister was making his life miserable" should not put strong emphasis on the second clause.

4. *First words of each item in a formal outline*

   I. Qualities of a good student

      A. Maturity in a crisis situation

      B. Time management skills

5. *Most words in the title of a book, a short story, a film, a play, an essay title, song titles, or other works of art, film, music, and literature*

Spoiled Rotten America by Larry Miller

"The Yellow Wallpaper" by Charlotte Perkins Gilman

6. *Do not capitalize the following words in titles unless the word begins the title*

a. Articles (a, an, the)

The Great Gatsby

Letters from the Earth

b. Prepositions and "to" in an infinitive

From Here to Eternity

"To Infinity and Beyond"

Of Mice and Men

"The Sounds of Silence"

c. Coordinating conjunctions

The Sound and the Fury

"And the Angels Sang"

NOTE: Major works of art, literature, film and music are italicized. For example, you would italicize the title of a novel, an album or a movie.

Rule #2—Capitalize Proper Nouns

Proper nouns are the names of a *specific* persons, places, or things. Recognizing a proper noun is not always easy. The rules below should help make detecting them clearer:

1. *Specific persons, ethnic groups, tribes, nationalities, religions, and languages, and specific places*
   Tulsa, Oklahoma
   Lincoln Memorial
   Czechoslovakia
   Mississippi River
   Ballroom C

2. *Specific organizations, companies, or brand names*
   Xerox
   League of Women Voters
   American Society for the Prevention of Cruelty to Animals
   Snickers candy bar

3. *Days of the week, months, holidays, holy days*
   Wednesday
   August
   Arbor Day
   Passover

4. *Historical events, periods, and documents*
   Cuban Missile Crisis
   Iron Age
   Americans with Disabilities Act

Note: when referring to centuries, movements, or beliefs not culturally recognized as a religion, do not capitalize: eighteenth century, feminist movement, or mysticism for example.

5. *Educational institutions, including specific departments, specific courses, specific classes of students, and specific academic degrees*

    Rutgers University

    Department of Math and Science

    History 2487

    Junior Class

    M. A. in Fine Arts

6. *Titles preceding names*

    Chief Justice John Roberts

    Governor Arnold Schwarzenegger of California

*NOTES: If the title comes after the name, it is not capitalized **unless** the title is of high national or international distinction. The following examples demonstrate : Elizabeth II, Queen of Great Britain; John Roberts, chief justice of the United States Supreme Court; and Arnold Schwarzenegger, governor of California.*

If the title appears instead of a name, you can capitalize it: The President met with the Queen yesterday in London.

Rule #3—What You Should Not Capitalize

Some words look as if they should be capitalized, and, in certain instances, they may be. The rules below should help you understand when not to capitalize certain words:

1. *Points on the compass*

    The ship's course was set for *south by southeast.*

NOTE: Do capitalize directional names when they refer to specific and recognizable sections of the nation or the world. The sentence "The summit was about tensions in the Middle East" names a specific region as does this next sentence: "States throughout the Midwest had a particularly bad winter."

2. *Names of seasons*

    Nothing is more bipolar than an Oklahoma *winter*.

    The *summers* on the beach are my favorite childhood memory.

3. *Words reflecting family relationships*

    He is Richard's *uncle* and Michael's *brother-in-law*.

    My *mother* and *father* went on a cruise to the Yucatan for their anniversary.

NOTE: Do capitalize when the word is used as a title before a name. The following two sentences include a title as part of the persons' names and, therefore, should be capitalized: "He introduced me to Uncle Richard." AND "Aunt Fern taught me how to sew, but I do it badly."

4. *Names of academic disciplines (unless they are specific course titles or proper nouns)*

    She is majoring in *finance* and *fine arts* and minoring in Spanish.

Exercise 4

Correct the following instances of improper capitalization; if the sentence is correct, mark it with a "C."

1. The suspect left the scene in a dark blue Prius and headed South on Main Street.

    _____

    _____

2. He plans to major in architecture and spanish so he can expand his employment possibilities.

_____

_____

3. Arnold Schwarzenegger was, until recently, Governor of California.

_____

_____

4. Six delegates from the Study Abroad program met with the President last week to discuss international tension.

_____

_____

5. Her appointment today is with the chair of the health and sciences department at Oklahoma State University's Tulsa campus.

_____

_____

SLASH—TAKE THAT!

In writing, the forward slash (also known as a **virgule**) is used to separate or to show relationships. The rules and examples below show how to use the virgule properly:

1. *To separate lines of poetry quoted in your text, with a space before **and** after the slash*
   Shakespeare wrote, *"Let me not to the marriage of true minds / Admit impediments. Love is not love / Which alters when it alteration finds, / Or bends with the remover to remove."*

NOTE: Make sure that you show the lines as they appear in the poem; do not put in line breaks where one does not exist.

2. *To demonstrate alternative names or designations*

    To get to my house, you must take the *Pearl Harbor Expressway/State Highway 169.*

    His flight lands tomorrow afternoon at the *Dallas/Fort Worth International Airport.*

3. *To mean "per"*

    The pork chops, which were *$3.50/lb.* yesterday, had doubled in price by today.

4. *To denote fractions in math when the fraction is preceded by a whole number*

    The recipe called for *1 2/3* cups of milk, but I wondered if that was too much for such a small cake.

*NOTE: When the fraction is **not** preceded by a whole number, spell out (and hyphenate) fractions: "Less than one-third of the county's registered voters participated in the last general election."*

Exercise 5

If the punctuation mark is used correctly in the following sentences, identify it as correct by putting a "C" in the space provided; if the punctuation mark is used incorrectly, rewrite the sentence to show the proper punctuation for the sentence.

___ 1.   My sister and her husband had a flat tire on Interstate 44-Will Rogers Turnpike.

_____

_____

___   2.   The mushrooms cost $6.50/lb., so we did not buy them.

_____

_____

___   3.   The directions for the experiment called for 1 3-4 grams of sulphur, but when I added 13.4 grams, the beaker exploded.

_____

_____

___   4.   When Shakespeare wrote, "But if the while I think on thee, dear Friend,/All losses are restored and sorrows end," he was referring to Christopher Marlowe.

_____

_____

___   5.   More than one-quarter of the student body participated in the rally.

_____

_____

CHAPTER 5

MLA FORMAT AND GRADING

FORMATTING YOUR PAPER FOR MLA GUIDELINES

The Modern Language Association (MLA) is a formatting and documentation system developed by humanities scholars for use in academic writing. This system complements the common language of academic writing through a standard format and citation style that all English students use on a regular basis and all humanities scholars recognize. Just as you are asked to write in a common language in order to communicate effectively, you are required to format and document your paper in such a way that identifies your writing as scholarly and worthy of note. Additionally, other courses in the liberal arts such as political science, history, communications, or art may also encourage the use of this style, so the sooner you become familiar with the formatting required for MLA style, the more productive and successful your writing experiences will be.

Since this particular course requires no research and, subsequently, no documentation, we will be focusing strictly on the **format** used in MLA style: the guidelines governing margins, spacing, and header/heading placement. Below are the steps you should take the first time you set up a document for this class. Once you have the document formatted, you should be able to use it as a template for all of your other writing assignments for this class; save it as "Basic Writing template" or "MLA format template."

Steps to Formatting Your Document—Doing It Right the First Time

Certain guidelines for how a formal academic writing assignment should look have been established since the nineteenth century. These guidelines set a precedent for humanities scholars that are internationally recognized and make your paper, be it a reading response, paragraph, or essay, easy to read and recognize. The guidelines below and example essay on the following pages should help you format your papers for this and other humanities courses:

1. *Set your margins*
   The top and bottom and left and right margins of your paper should be set at one inch (1").

2. *Set your font, the style in which the text will appear*
   According to MLA, both Arial and Times New Roman fonts are acceptable; however, in this class you will choose *only* Times New Roman font; the size of the font should be 12 point.

3. *Set alignment*
   Alignments determine whether your text will be flush left, centered, flush right, or fully justified with the margins set for your document. MLA format dictates that you *align left.*

4. *Set your heading*
   Heading includes all information about yourself and the class that you are writing for and appears on the *first page only* of your document. Headings for this class should include the following information in *this* order:
   a. Your Name (for example, John Littlesmith)

   b. Your Instructor's Name, shown with his or her preferred prefix (Ms., Mrs., Mr., or Dr.) and last name (for example, Mr. Jones)
   c. The Section Information for your particular class (for example, ENGL 0003.005)
   d. The Date in European format (for example, 12 March 2011).

5. *Set your header, that portion of the document in which you show your last name and the page number for that particular page*
   Each page (except the first) is required to have your last name and the page number in the upper right hand corner *one-half (½) inch* down from the paper's margin. Never try to insert these manually. Make sure you are inside the header to insert this information. If you need help with this, see the instructions for your word processing program.

6. *Set your spacing*

   According to MLA, you *must double-space.* Holding down the space bar until the end of the line of text or hitting the Enter key twice at the end of each line is going to create errors in your format. Use the line spacing option on your processor. *Be sure* that the spacing you have chosen for your document does *not* include extra spaces added between paragraphs that are the default setting for the most recent Microsoft Word versions. For example, when you set up your heading, you will often find what looks like your lines of text have more space between them than they should for the double-space option. Go back into your paragraph settings and remove those extra spaces.

7. *Format your title*

   The title is aligned center on the next line after the heading. Be sure to type your title in regular sized and style font. *Do not* bold, underline, italicize, or put quotation marks around it.

NOTE: Students often put little, if any, thought into the titles of their works. Many times they will simply put "Writing Assignment 1" or "Essay 4." The title is the first glimpse that a reader has into the content of anyone's writing and should be given due attention. A good title should capture both the topic and direction of the work in as few words as possible. For example, if you were writing a paragraph about your first impression of college, you should be sure the title captures your narrower topic and attitude you have about it such as the following title does— "Braving the Lecture Hall." This title at least encompasses the student's concerns and focuses on exactly what part of college will be discussed. Take the time and effort to give your paper a good first impression.

8. *After entering your title, align left again to start writing your paragraph or essay.*

   The first line of each paragraph you write should be indented one-half (1/2) inch. Again, you can set this one-half inch margin through your tab key. If the tab key default is not already one-half inch, go back into your paragraph settings and reset this default.

9. *Save and close this document as a template for all future writing endeavors that require MLA format.*

Heading: 1" from top and left

Clyde Fuster

Ms. Rhonda Doorstop

ENGL 0003.005

14 August 2011

Title centered

First line of each paragraph: indented ½" inch

Why I Decided to Become a Cop

The phone call came at 1:46 AM on a bleak, wintry Wednesday morning when I was seventeen years old. The voice on the other end of the line was female and obviously distraught: "Mr. Fuster, this is Meghan with the Collinsville Police Department. Your brother has been involved in a hit-and-run accident and is being air-flighted to Regional Hospital." I vaguely remember mumbling some sort of response, and the voice continued. "When you get there, ask to speak to Sergeant Hopkins; he'll have all the details." The drive to Regional Hospital passed in a blur, and the next thing I recall is being pointed to the end of a hallway where a uniformed policeman stood, talking with two men in white lab coats. When he saw me approach, he came toward me with his hand extended. "Mr. Fuster, I'm Bill Hopkins of Collinsville PD, and I'm here to help you. Let's go somewhere where we can talk privately." He ushered me into a nearby room where he sat with me and explained what had happened to my brother, assuring me that he would see to it that the individual responsible for hitting my brother and then leaving the scene would be found and arrested. His calm and respectful demeanor and his willingness to answer all of my questions had a life-changing impact on me. I knew from that moment that I wanted to be a policeman, just like Sergeant Hopkins, because I, too, wanted to help people in need, to see that those who break the law are brought to justice, and to respond calmly and efficiently in crisis situations.

Sergeant Hopkins inspired me to become a policeman so I can help others in need. On that awful night at Regional Hospital, he stayed with me even though he was

Header: ½" from top   Fuster 2

probably needed elsewhere. That is what good policemen do; they sacrifice themselves and their time to be of assistance to those who might need it. The sergeant's willingness to sit with me and patiently answer all of my questions was deeply appreciated by not only me but also by my entire family. Days later, Sergeant Hopkins came by the hospital to see if I or my family needed anything. He even offered to get a crew together to shovel the snow that had fallen on our home driveway while my brother was in the hospital. A good policeman does things like that, and that makes me want to be one.

In addition to helping others in need, Sergeant Hopkins' dedication to finding the person responsible for my brother's injuries made me want to be a policeman, too. I could tell that this was not just another case to him; he made it his personal goal to see that this individual would be punished for breaking the law. Some policemen often get a fatalistic attitude toward their jobs, as though they can do nothing about crime or criminals, and their fatalism can extend to how they interact with victims' families. Good policemen, however, never lose sight of the fact that bringing a criminal to justice is something they can do for a victim that neither the victim nor the victim's family can do for themselves. I want to know that what I do as a policeman will help not only society as a whole but also individuals who have suffered because of these crimes.

Finally, Sergeant Hopkins' ability to react calmly and efficiently in this time of crisis for my family inspired me to become a policeman. During that horrific night, I was impressed by Sergeant Hopkins' patience and his ability to communicate effectively and efficiently not only with fellow policemen but also with the medical staff at the hospital and with my family. Dealing with members of the medical community can be frustrating, but if Sergeant Hopkins was frustrated, he never let it show. From the hospital waiting room where we were all assembled, he coordinated with two other police crews to start a search for the individual who caused this accident and coordinated with the doctors assigned to my brother's case so that my family could get regular updates on my brother's condition and what was being done for him. A good policeman must be level-headed and calm, especially when the people around him are emotionally distraught, and Sergeant Hopkins' calm and efficient handling of this crisis made me want to be a policeman just like him.

A willingness to help those in need, a dedication to the law, and a calm demeanor in the face of crisis are all hallmarks of a great policeman. These are traits that I saw in Sergeant Hopkins that awful night long ago, and they are traits that I still see in him today. I can attribute my fourteen years on the police force—and my constant source of inspiration—to that man who, on a painful, dreary night, shook my hand and said, "I'm Bill Hopkins of Collinsville PD, and I'm here to help you."

HOW YOUR WORK IS GRADED—DISPELLING THE MYSTERY

By this point, you have read the book and are ideally building the habits and learning the rules that can help you improve as a writer. Hopefully, you have now learned to devote hours and even days on an assignment, constantly refining it for that ultimate submission to a grade. You may be surprised to find that, despite your best efforts, you do not receive the grade you hoped for. Understandably, this can be very frustrating. Students sometimes wonder why a grade does not reflect the effort that went into the work. Unfortunately, grades are not based on effort in college level writing. The task of this course is to prepare you for success in your composition courses and beyond—to build a foundation that will carry you through your academic and professional lives.

In a more perfect world, we could write what we wanted without fear of misunderstanding or error; unfortunately, academic writing is *not* that world. As a college student, everything you write for a class, in one form or another, will be assessed and graded for its clarity and its adherence to the rules of academic writing. What, then, you may ask, explains the variations of grading that occur across the academic spectrum?

Students often complain that grades for writing are too subjective or even random. Despite its seeming focus on quantifiable measures of performance (i.e., spelling, sentence structure, diction, grammar, and so on), grading is, admittedly, a somewhat subjective enterprise: an individual always lurks at the other end of that pencil or ink pen, an individual whose feelings and emotions may come into play during the grading process. Indeed, you may find that each instructor has slightly different criteria or standards for assessment of your work. Teachers within disciplines often grade differently as do teachers across disciplines; quite often, students shake their heads in disbelief, wondering how an essay that literally got torn to shreds by one professor got a good grade from another. Here again, subjectivity rears its head.

Rubrics—Solving the Puzzle

In an effort to make grading as objective as possible, the instructor of your Basic Writing course has instituted **rubrics**—a guide listing specific criteria for grading or scoring academic papers—to give you a better understanding of how your grade, piece by piece, on a specific paper was determined and to show you where your particular strengths and weaknesses lie as a writer. These rubrics are not meant to be punitive (strictly punishment); on the contrary, they are meant be a guide for you as you revise that particular assignment or approach a new assignment. Scores on a rubric can act as a benchmark, a signpost to mark your progress as an academic writer. These rubrics contain not only numerical grading but also comments from your instructor that often speak to specific areas where attention should be paid or growth is needed. To get the most out of the rubric attached to your writing assignment, you should read these comments carefully, comparing them to annotations made on the paper itself, and should determine how best to address the problem areas noted.

That being said, the rubrics sheets attached to your writing may not always fully clarify your strengths and weaknesses for you, or you may not completely understand what the comments mean and the exact criteria are. In most cases, your instructor will do whatever he or she can to help you improve your work, but the burden for understanding the material ultimately lies with you. As a college student, your success or failure is your responsibility. The amount of effort you put into your work and the help you seek when you do not understand something is your responsibility.

As your graded work is returned to you, notice that the rubrics will change depending on the type of assignment being graded. For example, the rubric for a paragraph assignment will be markedly different than the rubric for a full essay.

In the remaining pages of the text, you will find examples of a graded paragraph and essay and the rubrics that accompany them:

Example of Graded Paragraph with Rubric

Marie Drexelman

Basic Writing   — *MLA*

Mr. Simpson

31 March 2011

Texting While Driving

Texting while driving is illegal in many states. This is because of the fatalities and injuries that have been caused by it. Driving safely on highways, cars require a driver's full attention. And you can not give your car your full attention if you're texting. I've never had a problem with it myself, I can text and drive at the same time. One time, my mom was in the car with me and she nearly had a cow when I started texting a friend of mine to tell her where we were going. But my mom freaks out about the least little thing anyway, so I didn't pay much attention to it. I guess I showed her, huh? Anyway, some people get into trouble when they text and drive, like getting a ticket or speeding or you can get into an accident, that's why people should be careful if they're texting while driving.

Formal Writing Assignment Evaluation

Format / Set-up (5 points)

_0_ Essay format is adequate and complies with formatting guidelines in assignment _Font Header/Heading_

Introduction (5 points)

_2_ Introduction with strong hook and smooth transition

Thesis Statement (15 points)

_4_ Thesis statement with clear topic, direction, and preview of main points

Paragraph Elements (45 points)

_9_ Topic sentences with specific, clearly stated topic and direction _some statements of fact_

_8_ Logically ordered, coherent, and unified paragraphs

_8_ Topic sentences are well supported

Conclusion (5 points)

_2_ Conclusion restates thesis and echoes hook and transition _very weak_

Grammar and Usage Errors (15 points)

spelling, clarity

_10_ Grammar and usage errors

Diction Errors (10 points)

- 2nd person, contractions, slang, clichés

_5_ Formality and word choice

Comments:
- Watch spelling-- "aliterate" is not the same as "alliterate" or "illiterate."
- Focus -- your paragraph support tends to wander off topic

GRADE: _53_ /100

Example of Graded Essay with Rubric

Claude Schustermeier

Basic Writing I

March 4, 2011

What does it mean to be alliterate? Allitercy means you can read but choose not to. Many Americans are aliterate, they do not know how to read and have trouble with the simplest things in life like reading traffic signs or picking out the right foods at the grocery store. I am not alliterate because I have been reading since I was a kid, I read facebook and texts every day, plus I skim my text books for class.

Ever since I was very little , my mother would read books to me like The Cat in the Hat and other Seuss books. Since then I have fell in love with the Harry Potter Books. I also like to read magazines like Maxim and People. I am not sure how important being aliterate is any more with technology like computetrs and cell phones. The world is so fast paced that you don't have time to sit and read a big book like the Great Gatsby like people could in the 70s. I still try to read when I can but get distracted by my playstation or I just would rather hang out with my friends. Reading can be a waste of time to tell you the truth.

Even though I don't read books like I used to, I still read facebook and texts from my friends this allows me to keep in touch with them and be there for them. Sometimes we can go to Dennys or Chilis and still text while we're at the same table. Stupid, I know but we like too. We can talk about other people in the room and they don't even know it. I bet you do too if you admit it. One time I was texting while working on a paper for this class that's how I got the idea for this paper.

I am slo not illiterate because I skim my textbooks for class. You have to read your books to be successful in college. Sometimes I read when I am at work. I am a security guard at a storage place. There I can go over my math problems and history. Sometimes I don't read enough and am not ready for a quiz or something, but generally I am ready for classes. One day I forgot my textbook for basic riting and Dr. T kicked me out of class I wont do that again. You have to read to be good in school, expecially colleges.

announcement?

a question?

To sum it all up, I am not illiterate because I read as a kid, I text and keep up on face book, and I do my homework at work. What does it mean to gbe aliterate. I t means that you can read but choose not to. I don't always want to read but I do and you should to.

drop

CONT

fused

drop

to/too ?

Formal Writing Assignment Evaluation

Format / Set-up (5 points)

2   Essay format is adequate and complies with formatting guidelines in assignment

heading

Topic Sentence (15 points)

10   Topic sentence with clear topic and direction

too broad

Linking Sentence (5 points)

4   Linking sentence narrows topic sentence and introduces support

Support (45 points)

14   Paragraph contains 3-5 short, interrelated examples with major and minor support or contains vivid extended example

10   Logically ordered, coherent, and unified paragraph

Concluding Sentence (5 points)

2   Concluding sentence restate topic sentence in new way and provides paragraph closure

Grammar and Usage Errors (15 points)

5   Grammar and usage errors   — *splices & shifts*

Diction Errors (10 points)

5   Formality and word choice   — *2d person, coll. language & contractions*

Comments: *Narrow your topic to one that can be adequately covered in a paragraph. For each major support sentence, provide minor support. Stay on topic. Diction and grammar must be improved for coherence.*

Grade: 52 /100